A Guide to
Living
Abroad

The Daily Telegraph

A Guide to Living Abroad

SEVENTH EDITION

Michael Furnell and Philip Jones

With a contribution from BLACKSTONE FRANKS

KOGAN PAGE

First published in 1986 entitled *Living and Retiring Abroad*
Sixth edition 1992
© Michael Furnell 1986, 1988, 1989, 1990, 1991, 1992

Seventh edition 1994 entitled *Living Abroad*
© Michael Furnell and contributors

Kogan Page Limited
120 Pentonville Road
London N1 9JN

British Cataloguing in Publication Data

A CIP record for this book is available from the British Library.

ISBN 0-7494-1218-6

Typeset by DP Photosetting, Aylesbury, Bucks
Printed and bound in Great Britain by
Clays Ltd, St Ives plc

——— TRIDENT INTERNATIONAL PORTFOLIO ———

SAFE

Britannia (Isle of Man) Limited offers the perfect combination for expatriate investors.

Not only will you receive a high rate of interest paid gross (i.e. with no U.K. income tax deductions), but you will also have peace of mind knowing that your money is completely secure.

In our safe haven you will find a sound investment opportunity in the shape of the Britannia Offshore Deposit Account. Part of our Trident International Portfolio, this account allows you to make the most of your savings while overseas. It offers both high interest and monthly income options, so you can either let your investment build up until your return to the U.K., or benefit from the interest straightaway.

And because the rate of interest will be automatically increased as your balance grows, the account requires little maintenance.

BRITANNIA
BUILDING SOCIETY
(ISLE OF MAN) LTD.
DOUGLAS OFFICE

&SOUND.

You can also have access to your money whenever you want, provided you maintain a minimum balance of £10,000 after each withdrawal.

We also have the full backing of Britannia Building Society, one of the U.K.'s leading building societies, so you can rest assured that your investment will be in the best possible hands.

The Britannia Offshore Deposit Account. With high interest and no risks, your money will be sound as a pound. For further information, fill in the coupon below.

Please send me full details of the Britannia Offshore Deposit Account.

Name _____

Address _____

_____ Post Code _____

Britannia
(Isle of Man) Limited

Post to: Britannia (Isle of Man) Ltd., 8 Victoria Street, Douglas, Isle of Man. Telephone: 44 624 628512. Fax: 44 624 661015

Deposits made with an Isle of Man office of Britannia (Isle of Man) Limited are covered by the Depositors Compensation Scheme contained in the Banking Business (Compensation of Depositors) Regulations 1991.

Contents

Introduction

Considering the traumas that the European residential property market has suffered over the past three years, it is pleasing to find the demand for my book is still sufficient to encourage my publisher to invite me to prepare the seventh edition of this book.

For the new edition it has been decided to make certain alterations to the contents and to shorten the title to *Daily Telegraph Guide to Living Abroad*. This does not mean, however, that the needs of those planning to retire overseas are being completely ignored. Data on some of the most popular countries has been expanded and certain localities of limited general interest, such as Tunisia and the Caribbean islands, have been omitted.

Currently the two most popular regions are France and the state of Florida, USA, and with great pleasure I disclose that I now have a co-author, namely Philip Jones, who has contributed the chapters on these two locations.

Philip has edited four editions of the *Daily Telegraph* handbook, *Buying a Property in France*, and was the producer of DBC television documentaries, *A Fistful of Francs*, *For a Few Francs More* and *Francs a Million*. He also produced a video guide on Provence. Thus he has a profound knowledge of the land of Marianne and has undertaken a detailed study of buying homes in the USA's Sunshine State.

Once again it has been necessary to rewrite many sections of the information about the other countries which have appeared regularly in this series, to update the facts and figures contained therein. I am constantly amazed at the changes that take place in matters concerned with residential property and living arrangements, year after year.

The recession has certainly caused an upheaval in demand for all categories of homes throughout Europe over the past half decade but some encouraging reports are now reaching me of a gradual improvement in demand after the market hit rock bottom during 1992 and the early part of 1993.

Some international removal firms tell me that they are now being approached more frequently for quotations to carry household furniture and effects from addresses in England and Wales to Spain and Portugal, which is heartening, as these two countries in the Iberian peninsular were the most severely affected by the recent downturn in demand. At the time of writing there are many excellent bargains among new and resale villas and flats in these two countries, so obviously now is a very good time to buy a permanent or holiday home in these locations.

There are some signs of new life in the Italian and Greek property markets. Countries with good ski facilities such as Switzerland and Austria are enjoying a modest revival, although it should be remembered that both these centres have imposed strict limitations on the purchase of homes by foreigners, in order to protect their own nationals from exploitation.

Andorra, high in the Pyrenees, continues to attract modest numbers of new residents who enjoy living in a peaceful small country away from the coast.

The Mediterranean islands of Malta and Cyprus are enjoying good support from tourism, which will undoubtedly improve the demand for house purchase by foreigners in due course. Meanwhile prices are remaining fairly stable.

My correspondent in Turkey tells me that in the Bodrum area the property market is still bobbing along with limited numbers of retiree buyers and expatriates currently working abroad, but seeking a more relaxed environment for eventual retirement. There are also some holiday-home seekers.

Australia continues to welcome substantial numbers of new settlers from Europe and the Far East, provided they are skilled in occupations which are in demand.

When I wrote the original book, *Daily Telegraph Guide to Living and Retiring Abroad*, in 1986, I was editor of the monthly magazine, *Home Overseas*, and property correspondent to *The Sunday Telegraph*. At that time I was travelling abroad at least once a month to visit some of the numerous housing developments being offered to British people and others in many southern European countries. These journeys proved invaluable for my work as a specialist residential-property journalist, as they enabled me to make personal contact with a wide cross-section of people involved in the sale and purchase of villa and apartment developments and also with experts on the legal side and international property conveyancing.

Now that I am semi-retired I travel overseas less frequently than in the past, but I still have a vital nucleus of friends active in property spread throughout Europe and I am deeply indebted to them for their help and patience in answering my questions and keeping me

up to date about the property market in the spheres that are their speciality.

Finally, I think readers may be interested to know that I gained personal experience in purchasing and owning a home overseas in the 1970s. When my family was young we owned an apartment in one of the popular resorts on Spain's Costa del Sol. Not surprisingly, in those early days, we did experience some problems in the purchase procedure, but with the help of expert and qualified advisers, we resolved the difficulties and for a decade we enjoyed having a holiday home in the sun. Our experience was certainly worth while and I know many other families who have derived much pleasure from owning a home across the seas.

Michael Furnell

United Kingdom telephone numbers are due to change on 16 April 1995. After that date, please check any numbers in this book that you plan to use.

Part 1
Before You Go

Chapter 1
Retirement overseas

Many of those approaching retirement age, who are in reasonably good health or could benefit from living in a warmer climate, may consider the possibilities of cutting ties with their homeland and starting a new life overseas, in one of the southern European countries or elsewhere. How do they select the location for their retirement home? Well, many older couples will have enjoyed family holidays on the Continent or may have journeyed further afield to the north American continent over a period of years. Others will have enjoyed business travel to places on the other side of the world. These experiences may have assisted them to form opinions about their most favoured location for a life of leisure, without boredom.

The choice

The first essential should be to narrow down the choice to perhaps one or two countries, where they would feel happy to establish a new home. Depending on family commitments, it may be necessary to take into account accessibility to the UK if a crisis occurs back home, but with the ease and speed of modern air transport, this factor may not be of major importance.

Having chosen likely locations, the next step should be to undertake a really detailed examination of the day-to-day facilities and attractions of the selected area(s). This process should undoubtedly entail a number of visits to likely locations for preliminary impressions, followed by a stay of at least a month in the most promising area. This visit should be in the off-peak season, when holiday-makers have gone home and some of the amenities are closed until the next season. Popular resorts full of lively families in summer can look very different in the cooler months of January and February and the climate may not be so attractive. If you are going to live there permanently you will have to experience all the seasons, and the winter climate may not suit you. Do not be afraid to make two or three forays before making your final decision (see also Chapter 12) and, if you can stay in a rented villa or apartment rather than a hotel, you will gain some experience of catering for yourself in a foreign land.

Having found your 'ideal' spot, the next step will be to decide if you want to live all year round in an apartment block or a villa. Apartments are often built close to the sea and may be a little exposed to cool winds in the winter, yet you may feel more secure in a building surrounded by other inhabitants. Remember, however, that there could be a noise problem, or the majority of owners may only use their accommodation for summer holidays with perhaps an occasional visit in the off-peak season, say in December over Christmas. Thus the building might be almost empty for half the year.

Detached villas generally appeal to retirees because they have more private, spacious accommodation, and a garden for relaxation and exercise. But pueblo-style developments and town houses are becoming more popular, particularly in Spain where land costs are increasingly expensive. This style of living is more neighbourly than residing in isolation and attracts the more gregarious.

Remote country cottages are not suitable for the most frail or those suffering from medical disabilities, because they may be too far from shopping facilities, doctors or public transport.

In regions which attract tourism, living costs may be more expensive, but social activities should be easier to enjoy and access to international airports could be much more satisfactory.

Having completed this vital research and selected your chosen destination, you may experience some opposition from your family at home, for they may be concerned about your plans to live hundreds or thousands of miles away from them. They may want to know how you will cope on your own and if you will really like living in a foreign land.

On the other hand, they may welcome your wise decision to live in a less severe and varied climate where you should enjoy improved health and the challenge of starting a new life, instead of gradually vegetating in your old family home which has grown too large for normal needs, too expensive to maintain and requires an excessive amount of work to keep it clean.

With parents living abroad permanently the family has the opportunity of spending part or all of the summer holidays with them in their new home or renting a nearby property. Furthermore, with ever-improving international communications, parents can return to Britain occasionally for short holidays with the family at, say, Christmas or Easter. So the problem of family ties may not be such a difficult one to solve as originally envisaged.

In larger countries popular with expatriates there are often bridge clubs, garden societies and regular gatherings for English-speaking nationals. In some places there are British churches of various denominations which help new residents to meet each other.

If you are a TV addict it is now possible to receive BSkyB and your favourite British programmes via satellite TV in some European countries. It is also easy to keep in touch with life in the UK via the excellent news and cultural programmes broadcast by the BBC World Service.

Chapter 2

Tax and Financial Planning

Bill Blevins, David Franks and Robert Maas
Investment and tax specialists of Blackstone Franks, Chartered Accountants

UK residence

The emigrant and expatriate are usually hoping to cease to be both
'resident' and 'ordinarily resident' in the UK, to avoid UK income
tax and capital gains tax on their world-wide income and capital
gains. To succeed, one has to understand the meaning of the terms
'resident' and 'ordinarily resident'. Ordinary residence is explained
on page 24, and residence is explained below.

Resident in the UK has a very wide meaning. A tax year starts on
6 April and ends on the following 5 April. As a general rule, an
individual will be resident in the UK in a particular tax year if:

1. he lives in the UK for more than 182 days in any one tax year; or
2. he lives in the UK for more than three months on average over
    four consecutive tax years; or
3. he normally lives in the UK and is there for some time during the
    tax year.

In applying the three-month average test, the Revenue will ignore
days spent in the UK for reason of 'exceptional circumstances
beyond the individual's control', such as being taken ill shortly
before returning abroad after a visit to the UK. This concession,
which is wholly at the discretion of the Revenue, does not, however,
apply to the 182-day test.

The above rules may be overridden by double taxation agreements where the individual is resident both in the UK and in another
country.

If an individual who normally lives in the UK spends most of a tax
year abroad, eg he goes on a working holiday travelling around the
world for a year or two, the fact that he is present in the UK for less
than 91 days in the tax year will not make him non-UK resident. If,
however, he is working overseas full time in an office or employment
under a contract that spans a complete tax year he will, by
concession, be regarded as non-UK resident for that year. It does
not matter if the employment involves some UK duties provided
that these are *merely incidental* to the overseas duties.

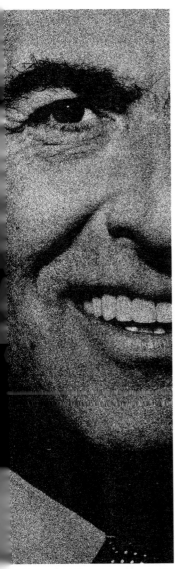

I'm working abroad. How far do I have to go for financial advice?

If you're working abroad, or about to return home, you need go no further than the nearest telephone and call Barclays Expatriate Services Centre. Whether your needs are simple or complex, we can give specialist advice on the most tax efficient investment of income or capital. We also have a range of deposit accounts paying interest gross on sterling currency. Or if you haven't yet taken up your overseas posting you might find one of our Country Reports useful. They are available for thirty different countries and contain information covering everything from economic conditions to local customs and etiquette. For financial advice, who better to ask than the bank with more offices in more countries than any other UK clearing bank? Send off the coupon for more information about our range of expatriate banking services.

- -

11/TG/D/0105

Please send me details of the Expatriate Advisory Service

Name Mr/Mrs/Miss/Ms _____

Address _____

Country _____ Postcode _____

Occupation _____

Employer _____

Nationality _____

Date of departure from/return to UK if applicable _____

Please return the coupon to either of the offices below.
You may choose the island location to suit your personal preference.

- -

Lucie Aimy, Expatriate Advisory Officer, Barclays Bank PLC, Expatriate Services Centre, PO Box 435, St. Helier, Jersey, Channel Islands. Tel: 0534 78511.
Colin Freeman, Expatriate Services Manager, Barclays Bank PLC, Expatriate Services Centre, PO Box 9, Barclays House, Victoria Street, Douglas, Isle of Man. Tel: 0624 682244.

BARCLAYS
OFFSHORE
BANKING

The Inland Revenue will take a harsh line on the definition of 'merely incidental' duties. The more senior the employee the harder it is likely to be to establish that UK duties are merely incidental. Visiting the UK to report to your boss is usually regarded as incidental. Attending a board meeting may well be such if you are a manager but will not be if you are a director as it is regarded as an integral part of your job.

The Revenue will look at the quality of duties undertaken in the UK rather than the time spent on them, to determine whether or not they are merely incidental.

A husband and wife are looked at separately. Thus it is possible for the husband to be non-resident while his wife is a UK resident. For example, if the husband is in genuine full-time employment overseas he will be regarded as non-resident even though he may visit the UK for short periods during the year. On the other hand, his wife, if she is not employed overseas, may remain a UK resident and therefore liable to tax on her income world-wide (even though she is living with him).

The diagram on page 21 will help you through the maze of rules on residence. However, it must be stressed that the residence rules are not defined precisely and your individual circumstances always need to be considered. In particular, if you plan your life so as to keep marginally within (1) and (2) above, or so as to remain outside the UK for a single tax year and a day or two on either side, there is a significant risk that the Revenue could successfully challenge your anticipated non-resident status.

It is important to keep a detailed record of all your time spent in each country, showing dates of arrival and departure and places stayed at. This could be important evidence in the event of a dispute – but also read 'How do they know where I am resident?', on page 25.

The residence maze

To help you to work out whether or not you are likely to be resident in the UK in a tax year, follow the maze below:

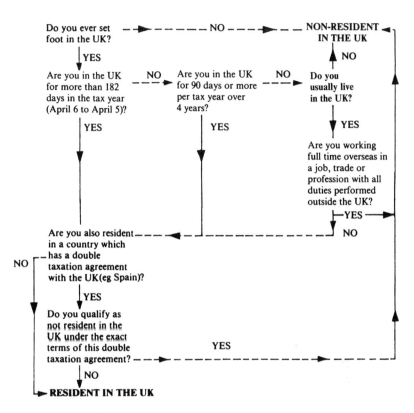

For tax years ended before 6 April 1993 an individual was also regarded as UK resident if he had accommodation in the UK 'available' for his use and visited the UK during the tax year even, in theory at least, for just a few minutes. A person did not have to own residential accommodation or have a legal right of occupation for a property to be 'available' to him. Merely having a place set aside for his use (eg, a bedroom in someone's home) could be sufficient.

The date of non-residence

Technically your UK residence extends for the entire tax year ending 5 April after you leave the UK. However, by concession, if you leave

PRIVATE BANKING IN GUERNSEY

You are certainly spoilt for choice when establishing a Private Banking relationship with a bank in Guernsey. There are seventy-four banking institutions on the Island, holding total deposits of some £37.6 billion. The banks, whilst being predominantly British, include representation from sixteen other countries, with eleven banks from Switzerland. Many of the banks have been established on the Island for over twenty-five years and a few for more than a century.

The principal Private Banking services provided are the acceptance of deposits in all major currencies, provision of interest bearing current accounts, in sterling or US dollars, investment management on an advisory or discretionary basis, trustee services, company management and credit facilities.

Individuals who use the services of an off-shore bank are mostly living outside of their "home" country and due to the laws of their "host" country are able to enjoy significant savings in tax by locating their assets in a low or nil tax jurisdiction such as Guernsey. Additionally, individuals who would wish to invest on an international basis may find that the banking and investment services they require are not available from their domestic bank.

The main-stay of Private Banking is the use of the bank's deposit services. The flexibility of retaining cash on call deposit at fluctuating interest rates or placing funds for a term of between seven days and one year at a fixed interest rate, linked with the ability to switch monies from one currency to another, facilitates the successful management of liquid assets. In addition the Bank can provide access to those assets through international money transfers, cheque books, bank drafts, traveller's cheques, credit and debit cards.

Many banks now recognise that it is difficult for them to advise on all investment mediums and thus will offer clients core investment products such as international bond and equity funds and utilise the investment services of outside fund managers for specialist equity or emerging market funds. With the volatility of international markets and world currencies a key objective for clients is the preservation of capital and thus Private Banking has an important role to play in respect of asset and currency allocation.

Guernsey continues to be favoured as a jurisdiction to establish off-shore trusts and these can form an important element of a Private Banking relationship. Creating a trust remains a primary way of protecting assets and ensuring that heirs will enjoy the benefit of those assets. There are many reasons why an individual might consider establishing a trust as they can fulfill a variety of planning objectives. A trust can, for example, assist in preserving the continuity of a family business or home. A trust can also be used to make gifts to charities and friends as well as for relatives. Whilst tax saving may be a motive, a desire to safeguard assets for family members is often a primary requirement.

The aim of Private Banking is to provide a highly personalised service which will contrast significantly from the service received from a large retail organization. Interestingly many of the larger banks have now established Private Banking departments with a view to improving the level of service provided to their more substantial clients. The key to successful Private Banking, from both the perspective of the client and the bank, is the relationship between the client and the bank's representative. Private Banking recognizes that the requirements of each customer do differ and that they can only successfully be met by personal attention from experienced staff.

Robin A. Barnes
Manager of Private Banking at Bank of Bermuda (Guernsey) Limited.

YOUR PARTNER...
WHEN MOVING ABROAD

At the Bank of Bermuda, we have built our business by developing relationships and creating working partnerships with each client. As our clients' needs expanded, we expanded – strategically placing offices in jurisdictions best suited to their financial needs.

As a self-governing island with its own legislation and laws, Guernsey has developed favourable policies and responsible regulatory controls making the island a leading sterling based jurisdiction.

We believe the Bank's range of banking, trust and investment services gives us solid credentials as an international financial partner. We invite you to contact **Robin A. Barnes**, Manager-Private Banking to discuss how the Bank can be of help to you when moving abroad.

Bermuda
IN ✦ GUERNSEY

Bank of Bermuda (Guernsey) Limited
P.O. Box 208, Bermuda House, St Julian's Avenue,
St Peter Port, Guernsey, GY1 3NF.
Telephone: (0481) 726268   Facsimile: (0481) 726987

*Deposits made with Bank of Bermuda (Guernsey) Limited in Guernsey
are not covered by the Deposits Protection Scheme under Banking Act 1987.*

*Rules and regulations made for the protection of investors by the United Kingdom
regulatory system may not apply and investors may not be entitled to benefit from the
investors compensation scheme. The contents of this advertisement have been approved
for the purposes of Section 57 of the Financial Services Act 1986 by Bermuda
International Securities (UK) Limited, a member of IMRO.*

*Registered under the provision of the Protection of Depositors (Bailiwick of Guernsey)
Ordinances 1971 as amended.*

Copies of the most recent audited accounts available on request.

Bermuda • Hong Kong • Singapore • London • New York • Luxembourg • Cayman Islands • Guernsey • Isle of Man the UK to take up permanent residence abroad you are normally regarded as becoming non-resident the day after you leave the UK, even though this may be in the middle of a tax year. As explained earlier, a tax year starts on 6 April and ends on the following 5 April. This concession applies for both income tax and capital gains tax. If you leave to take up full-time employment abroad for a period which will exceed a complete tax year you are regarded as leaving to take up permanent residence abroad for this purpose. By concession, so is your spouse if she goes with you and establishes that she is non-UK resident while she is living overseas.

The Inland Revenue can refuse to apply the concession if they consider that you have timed your departure, or entered into a transaction, specifically to avoid capital gains tax.

It is less clear if they could seek to refuse it merely because you realise a large capital gain while you are overseas on the basis that the concession was introduced for income tax purposes. Professional advice should be sought if there is a large UK capital gains tax liability at stake.

Ordinary residence

Unlike most other countries, the UK recognises two forms of residence: residence and ordinary residence. *Ordinarily resident* is not defined by the Taxes Act, but is generally understood to denote the status of someone who is usually resident as opposed to extraordinarily or casually resident for one tax year only.

You will normally be ordinarily resident in the UK if you spend more than three months in the UK on average over four tax years. This concept is crucial for capital gains tax as you have to be *both* not resident and not ordinarily resident in the UK to be free from UK capital gains tax. You have only to be not resident to avoid UK income tax on income other than UK income.

Because other countries do not have a concept of ordinary residence, double tax agreements do not deem a person not to be ordinarily resident in the UK.

You are also likely to be ordinarily resident if you leave the UK for a year or two only and maintain your base in the UK while you are away. This particularly applies if you have accommodation available for your use and visit the UK for a short period each year. If you retain a house in the UK which is let out, it will not normally be available for your use during the period for which it is let.

'How do they know where I am resident?'

We are often asked how the tax men of the world can find out whether or not you are resident in their country, and how they can then tax you. There are many points to be aware of.

In most countries it is your responsibility to make yourself known to the tax authorities if you are tax resident. If you are caught not declaring your tax residence you can be fined, or even gaoled. In Spain, for example, the fine can be six times the tax, plus interest, plus a gaol sentence.

There is usually a huge amount of information which is automatically passed to your new country's tax authority. This may include yacht registration, becoming a company director, buying a property or receiving bank interest. Often you need a tax reference number just to open a bank account. Most double tax treaties enable information to be passed to the other country.

Many non-residents totally confuse tax residence with two other kinds of residence – immigration and exchange control. The definitions of tax residence, immigration residence and exchange control residence are normally completely different.

Being non-resident for exchange control or immigration purposes has nothing to do with your tax residence. Your tax residence is determined by completely different rules; therefore you must make no assumptions, but take good professional advice in order to understand your position.

It is no good saying to the tax man in country A that you are resident in country B unless it is true. He might well immediately ask for your tax identification number in country B, so that he can make contact to check out your story.

As you wonder how they can tell where you have been for the last 183 days (or whatever) as your passport is never stamped, think about the massive trail of paperwork which you leave behind you – telephone bills, electricity bills, bank statements, credit cards, parking fines, correspondence with professional advisers or files with doctors/dentists etc. All stand by to give evidence of your whereabouts on a daily basis. Airline manifests are not sacrosanct. In Spain a few years ago, American Express were forced to disclose to the tax authorities the names of all holders of their Gold Card. Most tax men have power to obtain this kind of information direct from third parties. Computers are phenomenal at storing and retrieving information easily.

Try firing your gardener, divorcing your wife, upsetting a neighbour or falling out with a business partner. These people are well known for shopping 'ghosts' (individuals who are tax resident in a country but never declare themselves). In many countries, such as Spain, there is a system of 'denunciation' where individuals may be rewarded for passing on information to the tax or rating authorities.

Most reasonably sophisticated tax authorities have the right to interview you, and possibly your spouse. Quite often the onus of proof can be placed on the taxpayer rather than the tax inspector.

Moreover, if they have not asked the right questions during your lifetime, you may find that when your death certificate is filed an inspector of taxes becomes interested in how you managed to die in his country when you do not have a tax file number! You, of course, are not too interested at this point. But your wife may find that your estate disappears into paying large back-taxes, penalties and interest.

Finally, your assets can be frozen in your country if you are caught, making you bankrupt, and your debts may be chased into other countries.

Take good professional advice to avoid tax legally – there is no need to go the illegal route.

Avoiding capital gains tax – non-residence: the general rules

This section sets out the UK capital gains tax position for someone going to live *anywhere* outside the UK.

The definitions of 'resident' and 'ordinarily resident' are to be found on pages 18–24.

For UK domiciled	*Capital gains tax liability*
Resident	UK capital gains tax due on all assets throughout the world.
Not resident and not ordinarily resident	*Not liable* even if the assets are located in the UK (unless assets used for a trade in the UK; see pages 28–9).

By concession, an individual leaving the UK is treated as not resident the day after he has left the UK. This concession can be refused if the Revenue think tax has been deliberately avoided. It is therefore safer to realise capital gains in the tax year *after* you have left the UK (ie the year starting 6 April after you have left).

Note that the effective date a capital gain is realised is on the making of a contract, which in some cases can be even before a

A FULL RANGE OF OFFSHORE BANKING SERVICES FOR THE EXPATRIATE.

At Bank of Scotland (Isle of Man) Ltd you'll find a whole range of banking services under the one roof – all designed to help you make the most of your expatriate status.

Not only do we offer you the most competitive rates on all kinds of current and deposit accounts, our insurance and investment management

—— please call us on ——
0624-623074

specialists are always on hand to give you the very best advice. (After all, being a wholly owned subsidiary of the oldest UK clearing bank we're placed to give you the right answers to all your personal finance questions.)

For full details on any of these services please call us on 0624-623074 or complete the coupon below.

Bank of Scotland (Isle of Man) Ltd was incorporated and is situated in the Isle of Man. The paid up capital and reserves of Bank of Scotland (Isle of Man) Ltd as at 28th February 1993 were £5.975 million. Registered with the Isle of Man Financial Supervision Commission for Banking and Investment Business.
Deposits made with offices of Bank of Scotland (Isle of Man) Ltd in the Isle of Man are not covered by the Deposit Protection Scheme under the Banking Act 1987.
This advertisement is issued by Bank of Scotland (Isle of Man) Ltd and its contents have been approved by Bank of Scotland, a member of IMRO. Bank of Scotland is an Appointed Representative of Standard Life, a member of Lautro for life assurance, pensions and unit trust business only.

Please send me a FREE Information Pack on Bank of Scotland (Isle of Man) Ltd Expatriate Services.
Send to: Bank of Scotland (Isle of Man) Ltd, Bank of Scotland House, PO Box 19, Douglas, Isle of Man.

Name _____ Address _____

_____ Postcode _____

BANK OF SCOTLAND (ISLE OF MAN) LTD

DT LA 8-93

formal unconditional exchange of contracts, not on completion. A verbal agreement has been held to constitute an enforceable contract. Remember also that the Inland Revenue have the right to see all correspondence, file notes, memos etc, leading up to a contract, and often request such documents from you, your accountant, your solicitor, the purchaser and even from the purchaser's solicitor to check if a contract might have come into existence prior to the signing of the formal sale agreement.

If you realise a capital gain in the tax year during which you leave the UK and before the date you leave, the gain is obviously liable to UK capital gains tax, subject to the annual exemption and the other exemptions mentioned below.

To avoid UK capital gains tax, you have to be not resident and not ordinarily resident. It is safest to be not resident for three complete consecutive tax years.

There is a possible exception: if you have a full-time job overseas, and you are absent for a complete tax year, the Revenue's normal practice is to treat you as both not resident and not ordinarily resident in that year. However, you must have a genuine job full time overseas, and this is a concession which can be withdrawn by the Inland Revenue if they believe the employment has been created mainly to save tax. Furthermore, it was introduced for income tax purposes and you should be wary of relying on it if you intend to realise a large capital gain.

Some people feel that it is not necessary to work full time during the year overseas provided that you live in one place throughout the year and do not set foot in the UK during that year. This is based on the decision in a court case, Reed *v* Clark, where the judge felt that a distinct break in the pattern of Dave Clark's life of just over a year was sufficient to say that he had not left the UK for the purpose only of occasional residence abroad. The judge also indicated that he thought that occasional residence is the converse of ordinary residence. Accordingly, it can be inferred that an absence from the UK of just over a year spanning a complete tax year is sufficient for a taxpayer to be not ordinarily resident in the UK. However, as the case was concerned with a different aspect of the tax legislation it may be dangerous to rely on this. The Dave Clark case was decided six years ago and the Inland Revenue have not amended their standard test of ordinary residence in the light of it.

Assets used in a trade: the general rule

If you own an asset used in a UK trade and the asset is situated in the UK, even if you become not resident and not ordinarily resident, you will remain liable for capital gains tax.

Example
Mr and Mrs Lowes owned a successful freehold nursing home which they operated as a partnership. They left the UK in February 1994, leaving a manager in charge of the home. In May 1994, the manager agreed to buy the nursing home, giving the Lowes a capital gain of £430,000. Unfortunately, Mr and Mrs Lowes remain liable for UK capital gains tax, even though they are both not resident and not ordinarily resident.

The reason why they are liable is that section 10 of the Taxation of Chargeable Gains Act 1992 continues to tax a gain made on:

● assets situated in the UK; and
● where those assets are used in a trade – this includes business premises, work in progress, or goodwill.

Thus a partner disposing of an interest in assets used in the UK partnership would remain liable to UK capital gains tax.

It is also worth pointing out that letting a UK property, held as an investment, is *not* a trade, and therefore not liable to be taxed by this trap. Even disposals of short-term holiday lettings, regarded as a trade for some sections of the Taxes Act, are not caught by section 12 of the Capital Gains Tax Act.

If you cannot avoid the tax based on any of the above points, there are some other tax planning hints set out below.

Tax planning
Mr and Mrs Lowes could have avoided UK capital gains tax by one of two methods.

(a) *Incorporation.* If the business had been incorporated, the property could have been transferred to the new company or left in their own names and let (at a market rent) to the company. In either case, the sale of the shares and/or the nursing home freehold would have been free of UK capital gains tax if sold in the tax year after leaving the UK, provided that the Lowes remained both not resident and not ordinarily resident. However, it is very important that the incorporation occurs *before* Mr and Mrs Lowes leave the UK, as otherwise it would trigger a chargeable gain under the provisions introduced by the Finance Act 1989.

(b) *Renting the freehold.* An alternative way would have been for the Lowes to let the nursing home to the manager. He would sign a lease, paying a market rent. Later, having left the UK, established non-residence and non-ordinary residence, they could have sold the rental property to him free of UK capital gains tax. Because of the 1989 Finance Act, the lease must be granted *before* leaving the UK.

There is one word of caution about such tax planning. There have been several tax cases (and one in particular called Furniss *v* Dawson) which enable the Revenue to ignore a series of transactions which have no real commercial purpose other than the avoidance of tax. They can impose tax as if the transactions have not occurred.

Avoiding both UK capital gains tax and the overseas tax

We have explained some methods of avoiding UK capital gains tax, but clever avoidance of UK tax could end up becoming a case of 'out of the frying pan and into the fire'. You also have to avoid paying tax on your gain in your new country.

There are several ways of achieving this: for example, by being a fiscal nomad for a few months. Alternatively, you can make your capital gains disposal during a period when you are living in the new country *but* neither resident there nor in the UK. Another plan makes use of the fact that some countries treat the individual as making notional disposal and reacquisition at market value of all assets at the time when he becomes, or ceases to be, resident there. Better still, some countries do not tax capital gains.

Professional advice should be sought to ensure that all taxes are properly avoided.

Letting your home – tax-deductible costs

If you decide to continue to own your UK house but to let it, you will continue to be liable to UK tax on the rental income even if you are not resident and not ordinarily resident in the UK. The UK includes England, Northern Ireland, Scotland and Wales.

The following costs can usually be deducted against the income:

water rates where paid by the landlord;
council tax for which the landlord rather than the occupier is
    liable;
agent's fees;
legal fees relating to the letting (including VAT);
repairs and redecorations;
postage and telephone costs directly relating to the letting;

wear and tear;
other services (electricity, gas, TV paid by the landlord);
insurance;
inventory fees;
ground rent;
valuation fees for insurance purposes;
gardening costs or window cleaner, if imposed on the landlord
by the lease;
accountancy fees;
interest costs (provided the lender is UK resident);
VAT charged.

Rent receivable

The income is *not* the rent paid; it is the rent due under the terms of the lease in any tax year (6 April to 5 April). No adjustment is to be made for pre-paid rent. The accounts need to be drawn up for the year to 5 April (although, in practice, the Inland Revenue do not always insist on this). Only if it can be shown that unpaid rent due is irrecoverable, after all reasonable steps have been taken to recover it, can the income be reduced to take account of unpaid rent.

Deducting interest on a UK property

Interest on a loan is deductible against the rental income if:

- the loan was used only to purchase or improve the property;
- the property is let at a commercial rent, not at a low rent to a friend or relative;
- the property is let for at least 26 weeks in a 52-week period which includes the interest payment date and is either available for letting or under repair for the remainder of the period;
- in most cases the interest is paid to a UK bank, not an overseas one; and
- the interest is payable on a loan, not an overdraft.

If these conditions are met, there is *no limit* on the loan, unlike the £30,000 limit applied to your home mortgage when you live there. However, relief for the interest can be given only against UK rental income. It cannot be claimed against any other UK income.

UK capital gains tax – your own home

If you sell the property in a tax year in which you are both not resident and not ordinarily resident, there is no UK capital gains tax due. If you are planning to return to the UK and have a potential

UK capital gains tax liability on your house, you may be better off selling it in the tax year *before* you return when you are not resident and not ordinarily resident. That way, you will avoid UK capital gains tax.

Provided that a house has been your only or main residence at some time, the last three years of ownership are always exempt from capital gains tax.

There are many other rules about avoiding capital gains tax on a principal private residence (your own home) which are rather complex, but worth setting out in detail as this is often a key point for the working expatriate. Note that the rules for interest relief (MIRAS etc) and capital gains tax exemption are entirely separate.

More than one residence

It must be borne in mind that you can have two residences available to you without owning them both. A home which you rent counts as a residence. An overseas flat or house, whether owned or rented, is also a residence.

It is not wholly clear whether the house you live in overseas constitutes a second residence for the purpose of the exemption. As a person who is not resident and not ordinarily resident in the UK is outside the scope of capital gains tax it is arguable that a house owned while the person is living overseas is not one which is eligible for the private residence relief, and that therefore it can be ignored in applying the restriction on the relief. However, it is probably safer to assume that an election needs to be made for the UK house to be treated as the principal residence.

If you own (or have available) more than one residence, you can elect which property should be regarded as the principal private residence for the capital gains tax exemption. Such an election, which must be in writing, must be made within two years of the acquisition of the second house. The election can be varied at any time by giving a fresh notice, but the variation cannot apply to any period over two years before the date of the new election. If no election is made, the Inspector of Taxes will choose, on the basis of what appears to him on his examination of the facts to be the main residence at the time. A second property which you let to bona fide tenants (or keep available for letting) is not treated as being your residence.

Time limit for election

It has been held by the High Court that the time limit for making the election is two years from the date the second residence first becomes available. Most people doubt this interpretation of the legislation and the case in question may well go to appeal. In the past elections were sometimes accepted outside this limit (but not to operate more than two years retrospectively). For the time being it must be assumed that the election needs to be made within two years of the second residence becoming available. The Revenue have stated that where the taxpayer's interest in one of the properties has 'no more than a negligible capital value in the open market' and the taxpayer was unaware that an election could be made, they will extend the time limit to a reasonable time after the individual first becomes aware that he is entitled to make an election. They will then treat it as having effect from the date on which he acquired the second residence (Inland Revenue Extra-Statutory Concession D21). This concession is intended to cover the position where one of the properties is rented and the taxpayer did not realise that it constitutes a residence.

Husband and wife
A husband and wife can have only one main residence between them while they are living together. Where a private residence election affects both (eg joint ownership) it must be given by both.

The capital gains computation
If you let your house (or leave it unoccupied) and sell it in a tax year when you are resident (or ordinarily resident) in the UK, you may have a capital gains tax liability for the period the property was let (or unoccupied). The amount of the gain which remains free of capital gains tax is:

$$\text{Total gain} \times \frac{\text{Number of weeks owned as principal private residence}}{\text{Number of weeks owned}}$$

Remember that:

- the number of weeks which count as your owning it as a principal private residence always includes the last 36 months, even if let;
- weeks prior to 1 April 1982 are ignored for both the numerator and the denominator of the above calculation.

Where part or all of your home has been let, up to £40,000 of the gain attributable to the let period is tax free. The amount of relief depends on various factors, including how long it has been let.

Periods of absence
In the above calculation, certain periods of absence can also count

as being periods when the house is your principal private residence, even though factually it was not (eg it can even be let). These periods of absence are as follows.

1. Any period (or periods) not exceeding three years; *plus*
2. Any period where you worked overseas as an employee and all the duties were performed overseas. There is no time limit. Note that if the husband works but the wife does not, she would still be eligible for relief for her part ownership as long as she is living with the husband. Note that this exemption does not apply if you are self-employed, nor does it apply if any of the duties were performed in the UK, however incidental they might be; *plus*
3. Up to four years where your job in the UK requires you to live elsewhere (this usually means more than 100 miles away).

There are several major traps in obtaining any of the above three periods of relief. You must meet each of the following three conditions.

1. The house must be your main residence *before* the start of the period of absence; *and*
2. It must be your main residence at some time *subsequent* to the period of absence. This means that you must re-occupy the house before you sell it. There is no legal limit on the minimum time the house must be occupied, and some say that even one week is sufficient, so long as you have no other residence available. The Inland Revenue have stated that they believe the minimum period is three months, but their view has not been tested in the courts. There is one exception to having to re-occupy before you sell. The Inland Revenue have granted a concession where you are forced by your job to live elsewhere in the UK on your return; *and*
3. You must have no other residence eligible for relief during the periods of absence. Of course, while overseas you are bound to have your overseas house available for your use as a residence. In practice, the Inland Revenue tend to ignore this. You might consider submitting a written election to the Inland Revenue within two years of going overseas that your UK home is to be treated as your principal private residence. If you do not make the election, the Inland Revenue might claim that your overseas home is your main residence, and hence you will fail to meet this condition. In practice, an election is not needed.

Separation or divorce
Where a married couple separate or are divorced and one partner (usually the husband) moves out and subsequently, as part of a financial settlement, disposes of the home (or his interest in it) to the

other, it can be regarded as continuing to be the husband's main residence during the period up to the date of the transfer, provided that it continues to be the wife's main residence throughout that period and the husband does not have another property which he is claiming as his main residence (Inland Revenue Extra-Statutory Concession D6). It should be noted particularly that this applies only where the house is ultimately transferred to the wife. If it is sold and all or part of the proceeds paid to her, the concession will not operate. In such a case it may be preferable to transfer the property to the wife and allow her to sell it.

Buying a UK home while overseas

An expatriate who buys a UK house while he is overseas would not have met the rule of using the house both *before* and after a period of absence as his principal private residence. While there may be relief for interest purposes, there is no relief for capital gains tax purposes. Instead, the expatriate should consider selling the house in the tax year *before* he returns, while he is both not resident and not ordinarily resident, when he is exempt from all capital gains tax. By concession, if you work full time overseas, the Revenue will regard you as both not resident and not ordinarily resident until the day you return to the UK, in which case it appears unnecessary to sell the house in the tax year before you return; selling before you return, even in the same tax year, would be sufficient. However, if possible you should not rely too heavily on this concession as it can always be withdrawn.

Avoiding capital gains tax and keeping the house

As an alternative to selling to a third party in the tax year before return, you could transfer the property to a trust for yourself and your wife's benefit. The transfer into the trust will be tax free if the requirements of not resident and not ordinarily resident are met, and any subsequent disposal by the trust will also be tax free if the property is occupied by you under the terms of the trust.

Working abroad and MIRAS

Keeping a house in the UK will not in itself affect your UK tax residence status. You may still even be able to continue with your MIRAS relief (Mortgage Interest Relief At Source).

Since 6 April 1983 (or in some cases even earlier) mortgage interest on house loans may be paid after deduction of tax at the basic rate, for the income tax year in which the payment becomes due, if the interest is 'relevant loan interest' paid by you as a 'qualifying borrower' to a 'qualifying lender'.

1. 'Relevant loan interest' is interest paid and payable in the UK to a 'qualifying lender' and it is interest on loans for the purchase of a residence, including a residential caravan or houseboat in the UK, which when the interest is paid is used wholly, or to a substantial extent, as the only or main residence of the borrower. Before 5 April 1988 relief was also available for the purchase of a residence for a dependent relative or separated or former spouse and for home improvements. Interest relief will continue for such loans until they are repaid *or* replaced.

2. 'Qualifying borrower' is any individual who pays 'relevant loan interest'. There is an exception to this. If you or your husband or wife receive(s) earnings that are exempt from UK tax, eg certain Crown and Foreign Office appointments, neither of you can qualify for MIRAS. There are very few tax exempt occupations.

3. A 'qualifying lender' includes a building society, a local authority, the Bank of England, an insurance company authorised to carry on long-term business (eg life assurance) in the UK, a trustee savings bank, an existing lender under the mortgage option scheme, and any recognised bank or licensed deposit-taking institution authorised by the Treasury.

MIRAS enables you to reduce your mortgage interest payments by the tax relief due, which is at a reduced rate of 20 per cent for the year to 5 April 1995 and 15 per cent for the following year. It is limited to interest on the first £30,000 of a loan to buy your principal private residence. Even though you, as an expatriate, are no longer living in the UK and may have no UK income, you can still obtain MIRAS relief because of an Inland Revenue concession.

Where you are required by reason of your employment to move from your home to another place either in the UK or abroad for a period not expected to exceed four years, any property being bought with the aid of a mortgage, which was being used as your only or main residence *before* you went away, will still be treated as such, provided that it can reasonably be expected to be so again on your return. It is *not* sufficient to claim the first four years of an expected five-year absence. The maximum period is four years, but if there is a further temporary absence after the property has been reoccupied for a minimum period of three months, the four-year test will apply to the year of absence without regard to the previous absence.

If you are already working abroad and buy a property in the UK in the course of a leave period and use that property as an only or main residence for a period of not less than three months *before* your return to the place of your overseas employment, you will be regarded as satisfying the condition that the property was used as your only or main residence before you went away.

If you let your property at a commercial rent while you are away, the benefit of the concession may be claimed where appropriate if this is more favourable than a claim for relief against letting income. You cannot, however, claim MIRAS relief and then claim further relief against letting income to bring the total relief back to 40 per cent.

If you go abroad but leave your family in your UK house, MIRAS relief will not be subject to the above-mentioned four-year time limit.

Council tax

Council tax started on 1 April 1993. It is loosely based on property values by allocating properties to one of five tax rate bands. The tax is normally imposed on the occupier. In some cases, such as where the property is in multiple occupation or it has been unoccupied for more than six months, it is payable by the property owner.

UK rates of tax

For 1994–95, the rates are:

Income	Rate
First £3000 of taxable income	20%
Next £20,700	25%
Excess over £23,700	40%

UK personal allowances

The main personal allowances are:

	1993–94	1994–95
Married couple	£1720 plus single allowances	£1720 plus single allowances
Single person	£3445	£3445

Age allowance	1991–92 Single	1991–92 Married	1992–93 Single	1992–93 Married
65–74	£4200	+£2465	£4200	+£2665
75 or over	£4370	+£2505	£4370	+£2705

Age allowance is reduced by one half for income over £14,200 for 1994–95.

From 6 April 1989, expatriates can obtain a much larger tax allowance than before.

- There is no restriction on claiming personal allowances, and thus no need to declare your world-wide income.
- Both husband and wife will be eligible for the allowance, and can each make a separate claim.

If an expatriate has a UK bank deposit account or 'non-resident' UK building society account, the interest is tax free by virtue of an extra-statutory concession known as B3. However, such interest is taken into account when personal allowances are claimed in the UK against UK income. It is advisable to keep such deposit accounts outside the UK (eg in the Channel Islands) to avoid UK tax.

UK pensions

UK pensions paid to a non-resident are liable to UK tax unless the pensioner is exempted by a double tax agreement or the pension is paid out under one of the following schemes:

1. India, Pakistan, Burma and colonial schemes;
2. pension funds for former public service employees of overseas territories;
3. the Central African Pension Fund;
4. the Overseas Service Pension Fund;
5. pension funds set up for overseas employees of UK employers.

Most double taxation agreements tax pensions only in the country in which the individual is resident, with the exception of pensions paid out of public funds in the UK, which remain taxable in the UK. Public funds include pensions paid to former servants of the Crown, and pensions paid for services rendered to a local authority in the UK. Such public fund pensions may be free of UK tax under the double taxation agreement if the pensioner is a national of the other country.

If your pension is going to be liable to UK income tax or foreign tax, it is normally better to elect to take a tax-free lump sum and to reduce the level of pension liable to tax.

If you are moving to an EC country, there are flexible agreements over pension and many other social security benefits. UK social security pensions are payable in your new EC country, including cost of living increases, though these will be related to the British cost of living index. There is a leaflet (SA29) produced by the DSS which discusses some of these points (for address, see pages 302–3).

In addition, the UK has agreements with non-EC countries, primarily covering retirement pensions.

UK dividends

Dividends from UK companies constitute taxable income. However, they carry with them a tax credit which covers the first 20 per cent of the shareholder's liability – and effectively, the whole of that liability where the shareholder is liable to basic rate tax. For example, a £100 dividend can be expressed as follows:

Dividend	Tax Credit
£100	£25

The £25 tax credit is 20 per cent of the aggregate sum. A basic rate taxpayer who receives the dividend has no further tax to pay. A higher rate taxpayer must pay a further £25 tax, to bring his total tax to £50 or 40 per cent of £125. A non-taxpayer may be entitled to reclaim the £25 tax credit. In general non-UK residents are not entitled to reclaim the tax credit. However, a British citizen who is entitled to claim personal allowances will also be entitled to reclaim the tax credit against such allowances.

In addition it is possible to reclaim part of the tax credit under many of the UK's double taxation agreements. The refund normally effectively leaves the UK taxing the non-resident at 15 per cent of the total of the dividend plus the tax credit. For example, on a dividend of £100 the UK can charge 15 per cent of £125 or £18.75. The balance of the tax credit, £6.25, will be reclaimable by the non-resident.

If an overseas company, but not normally an individual, controls 10 per cent or more of the company (whether directly or indirectly) the tax refund is generally higher. The agreement will normally only allow the UK to keep 5 per cent of the £125 aggregate figure, thus creating a refund of £18.75 of the tax credit on £100 of dividend.

It is possible for a UK company to enter into an arrangement with the UK Inspector of Foreign Dividends to pay in effect the tax refund to non-resident shareholders covered by a double tax agreement without their needing to make a formal claim. Many companies are unwilling to take on the increased administration and the liability to pay the Revenue any tax refunded to which it has subsequently been discovered the shareholder was not entitled.

UK interest (banks and building societies)

Normal 'onshore' building society and bank accounts are not

advisable for UK expatriates. Many societies and banks advertise 'international accounts', suggesting that interest payments may be made gross without risk of UK income tax. At first sight these appear highly attractive when compared to the returns available on high interest money market bank accounts. In fact, such income is liable to UK tax, but by concession the Inland Revenue do not normally charge such tax if you are non-resident for the entire tax year and do not claim a tax repayment in respect of any other UK income that has suffered tax by deduction at source. Where other UK income arises in the UK, the tax may be easier to collect. For example, where a non-resident is in receipt of a government pension, there may be less reluctance on the part of the Inland Revenue to apply the concession. Many building society depositors who are living outside the UK have found that an assessment has been raised in these circumstances.

In addition, if the non-resident is not domiciled in the UK he would be putting his capital at risk unnecessarily to a charge to UK inheritance tax.

UK gilts

Gilts are publicly quoted stocks backed fully by the British government. (The name 'gilt' comes from the original certificates which were issued with gilded edges.) At no time has a British government failed to meet any of its funded debt obligations whether in the nature of capital or income. But do not be fooled into thinking that gilts are always safe. If you have to sell before maturity, you can lose a lot of money. How much you lose or gain depends on what has happened to interest rates since you purchased your stock.

When you buy a gilt, you are lending the government money at a guaranteed interest rate (called the 'coupon'). Repayment is normally due at a specified date, so you can work out exactly how much you will receive and when, although the government has the right to repay some stocks at any time over a three- to five-year period. Rates of return are often higher than from a bank or building society, and the guarantee is stronger – the government is less likely to go bankrupt than Barclays Bank or the Halifax.

UK tax position
Interest on gilts is liable to UK income tax and the majority have tax deducted at source. However, there are a number of gilts on which there is no tax due either on income or capital gain if you are not

resident in the UK, although it will be up to you to prove your non-resident status. It is not enough simply to provide a foreign address; you may have to give details of your tax reference number and district in the overseas country. In order to obtain approval, you should obtain Form A1 from the Inspector of Foreign Dividends, Lynwood Road, Thames Ditton, Surrey KT7 0DP. Unless you have already been cleared as not resident, expect some searching questions about your long-term plans, duration of visits, location of home and so on.

The list of gilt stocks which are free of tax to residents abroad may be obtained from the Bank of England, Threadneedle Street, London EC2R 8AH.

Seventeen ways to avoid UK inheritance tax

UK inheritance tax is payable after death by:

(a) UK domiciled individuals on their world-wide assets, wherever they may be resident;

(b) non-UK domiciles on any assets situated in the UK.

It is very difficult to shed your UK domicile. Thus you may live outside the UK for many years, but *remain liable for UK inheritance tax on your death on your world-wide assets*. Here are some ways to avoid tax.

1. Giving it away tax free

If you give away no more than £150,000, there is no inheritance tax (IHT) to pay. After seven years, you can give a further £150,000 (and so on every seven years and one day). Both husband and wife each have their own £150,000 limit. In addition, each year you (and your wife) can give away £3000. Thus over a period of seven years and one day you can give away:

	Husband	*Wife*	*Total*
2 × £150,000	£300,000	£300,000	£600,000
8 × £3000	£24,000	£24,000	£48,000
	£324,000	£324,000	£648,000

2. Giving away 'in consideration of marriage'

Each parent can give away an additional £5000 to a child or £2500 to a grandchild and £1000 to anyone else on the recipient's marriage. The rules are very strict and professional advice on how to do it should be taken, in advance of the marriage.

3. Normal income expenditure

Regular amounts can be gifted as 'normal expenditure out of income' representing perhaps as much as 10–50 per cent of annual income *free of IHT*. Careful use of this exemption can significantly reduce, or even eliminate, your IHT problem.

4. Unlimited lifetime transfers to individuals or trusts

You can give *unlimited* amounts to any other individual during your lifetime or to most trusts (but not discretionary trusts). The gift could be money, or shares in a company, or any other asset. If the gift is of unquoted shares or assets used in a business (or is of a controlling interest in a listed or USM company) and the recipient is a UK resident, capital gains tax can be avoided by signing a holdover relief election, though there may be none to pay if the donor is both not UK resident and not ordinarily resident. In the event of the donor dying within seven years, there will be IHT to pay but at reduced rates. If he dies within three years of the gift, there is no tax reduction. Trusts can be very useful for giving wealth to grandchildren under the age of 25.

5. Avoid 'reservation'

Gifts 'with reservation' will not be exempt from tax under 4. above. The gift must be given absolutely. A gift where the donor enjoys any interest or rights is not acceptable. Thus the gift of a house, with rights for the donor to reside in it, is not an absolute gift, nor is the gift of shares with the right to an exceptional salary from the company. So avoid giving anything which has reservation of interest. This is a very technical area. It may be possible to carve out for oneself a right to reside in the house prior to making the gift. Professional advice should be sought before attempting such a gift.

6. Fifty per cent discount

Even if you are going to pay the tax, if you give away *before* your death the tax rates are halved (maximum 20 per cent instead of 40 per cent). If you die within three years of the gift, the saving will not be so great.

7. Keep the back door open

You could give away any amounts into a discretionary trust, where you are *not* a beneficiary but other relatives, including your wife, are the named beneficiaries. You could remain as the controller of the assets in trust (called the trustee). A series of trusts is recommended for technical reasons. As long as your gifts are within the limits set out in 1. above, there will be no IHT due. Careful draughtsmanship and planning are required in this area. Your wife can also establish a similar series of trusts.

8. *Life insurance*

Life insurance can be a surprisingly cheap way of covering any eventual IHT bill. For example, if your estate was worth £330,000, you and your wife were aged 50, and you left all your assets to her on your death, the IHT payable at the second death would be £72,000. For an annual outlay of about £900 per annum, a tax-free benefit under trust of over £90,000 can be obtained, and indeed is projected to be worth over £220,000 on the death at age 85 of the survivor.

Alternatively, at 65 you could invest £25,000 in a last survivor investment bond (under trust) with life cover of a sum assured at the second death of just under £100,000.

These costs can be reduced considerably by purchasing term life insurance which provides cover for a fixed number of years only. You choose how long. During the time you pay regular premiums, if you die, the policy pays out a fixed amount. If you survive to the end of the term, you receive nothing back and premiums cease.

9. *Equalising estates*

If the husband's estate is worth £500,000, the IHT payable is £140,000, leaving £360,000 as the net estate. If estates are equalised between husband and wife and each wills the estate to children/grandchildren/relatives, the IHT payable is reduced to approximately £80,000, saving £60,000. The estates do not actually need to be equal. The key thing is for each spouse to have at least £150,000 of the joint assets.

10. *Residential property*

If a donor gifts a property and continues to stay in it, or even visit it for other than short periods, the gift is treated under the 'reservation' rules, unless a commercial rent is paid.

Various solutions are possible. If a leasehold can be created on a freehold property, it is likely (but not certain) that the gift of freehold will be outside the donor's estate. Once the leasehold has expired, the donor would have to vacate the property or pay a commercial rent.

If a property can be sold and the proceeds gifted, the beneficiary could purchase a new property and allow the donor to live there rent free. Capital gains tax could be avoided subsequently if the beneficiary is not ordinarily resident.

11. *Company shares, business assets and woodlands*

Private company (ie close company) shares are eligible for a special 100 per cent business relief, for IHT purposes, for a controlling interest (which is defined as a shareholding of over 25 per cent for this purpose). The effect is to take such assets out of the scope of inheritance tax completely. If you hold a little under 25 per cent of a close company, consideration ought to be given to increasing your holding to over 25 per cent to qualify for this exemption. A lesser interest than 25 per cent attracts a 50 per cent reduction.

Another way to reduce the value is to form another company (owned by the ultimate beneficiaries) and build up this new company in preference to the existing one. Assets used in Lloyd's underwriting or in any other business you carry on are also eligible for 100 per cent reduction.

Certain other property used by a private company or a partnership is also eligible for business relief at the reduced rate of 100 per cent. Similar rules apply to agricultural property but the rate is increased to 100 per cent if there is vacant possession. Woodlands can also qualify for the 100 per cent relief.

12. *Single premium bonds*

An investment bond can be a useful way to reduce your estate yet retain an income. The beneficiary of the bond is a child or grandchild instead of the investor. Inheritance tax may be payable at the time of buying the bond, but inheritance tax is avoided on any growth in value of the bond.

Alternatively, a trust can be established and an interest-free loan made to the trustees, who then use the loan to purchase an investment bond. 'Income' can be taken in the form of loan repayments. No IHT is payable on the loan and, with the exception of any outstanding loan, the trust fund remains outside the settlor's estate.

13. *Giving away shares in newly formed companies*

Making gifts of assets likely to appreciate is an effective way of reducing your estate. The gift is valued at the date it is gifted, not the subsequent value. Giving away shares in a newly-formed company to trusts for your children's benefit can make sense.

14. *Giving away when cheap*

The best time to make gifts is when the value of an asset is depressed. Watch out for opportunities. For example, for about a year following the October 1987 crash, values of equities were low. In 1991 and 1992 property values were low.

15. *Generation skipping*

If your own children are already wealthy, pass your estate on to your grandchildren instead. This skips a generation and reduces the likely IHT on your children's death.

16. *Writing in trust*

Life insurances and death benefits from pension schemes may form part of your estate for IHT purposes. You can set up the policy to pay the benefits direct to your children, in which case they do not attract IHT. If you are concerned that your wife, should she survive you, should receive the benefit, it is advisable that you write the policy benefits in trust for your children, unless your wife survives you by 30 days in which case she receives the benefit.

17. *Interest free loans*

An interest free loan is *not* a gift as long as:

- the loan is documented; and
- the loan is repayable on demand or at very short notice.

Such loans can be used to purchase assets from the donor. Professional advice should be sought before granting such loans.

Working abroad – UK tax

If you work abroad and live abroad for a period of less than one year, you will normally remain liable in full to UK tax.

If you work abroad for a period of at least 365 days (whether or not this covers a complete tax year), you will be exempt from UK tax on those earnings. This is regardless of your residence status in the UK. The performance of some duties in the UK will not cause this relief to be lost.

This relief is not given to the self-employed but only to the employed; some tax planning points for the self-employed are set out below.

There is a trap, however. To achieve your 365 days of continuous employment abroad, you cannot during that period:

- spend more than 62 days continuously in the UK for any reason;
- spend days in the UK which in aggregate exceed one-sixth of the length of the total period from the start of the 365 days up to each time you visit the UK.

Note in particular that just avoiding spending more than 62 days in the UK is not sufficient. You must also avoid breaching the 'one-sixth' rule each time you visit the UK.

A day will be considered to be a day of absence if you are outside the UK at midnight. If your flight leaves the UK at 11 pm in the evening, that is normally regarded as an entire day spent abroad, although there is no legislative basis for this and it is accordingly unwise to rely on it. If you return from abroad at 11 pm, even after a hard day's work, the legislation provides that this must nevertheless be taken as a day in the UK.

The legislation looks at days of absence from the UK, not days spent working overseas. It does not matter what the taxpayer is doing while he is overseas.

The one-sixth limit is applied very rigidly. An unplanned or unexpected visit to the UK can spell disaster in trying to establish the 365-day minimum period. Careful planning is required, as shown in the following example:

	Date	Days abroad	Days in UK	Total days
Leaves UK for Spain	12.8.93			
Returns to UK for Christmas	15.12.93	125		125
Leaves UK for Spain	20.01.94		36	161
Returns to UK for grandfather's funeral	07.02.94	18		179
Leaves UK for Spain	10.02.94		3	182
Returns to UK	09.12.94	304		485

The number of days spent in the UK between two periods of absence cannot exceed one-sixth of the total number of days in the period under consideration. In the above example, the individual spends 485 days from the time he leaves to work in Spain to the end of his assignment. On returning to the UK on 7 February 1994, there is a total period of 179 days. One-sixth of 179 is 30, but he has spent more than this in the UK as he was here for 36 days. Thus, the period from 12 August 1993 to 20 January 1994 is *not* a qualifying one. The calculation now starts again on 20 January 1994. He spends 18 days abroad, then three days in the UK, and finally 304 days abroad before returning permanently. Since this is a total of 325 days and is less than the required 365, no part of the 485-day period will count as exempt from UK tax. Instead, UK tax is payable in full, even though this taxpayer has been on an overseas assignment which lasted about 16 months. Thus, going abroad for a short period and then returning to the UK can be very dangerous.

The relief under the 365-day rule is given by a deduction of 100 per cent of the employment earnings. This is better than exempting the earnings from tax, as they remain relevant earnings for pension purposes. Thus, on your return to the UK you could use your earlier overseas earnings as a means of increasing your UK pension contributions in order to save even more tax.

National Insurance contributions

Social security and pension schemes

The system of UK social security, known as National Insurance, is administered by the Contributions Agency, an executive agency of the Department of Social Security (DSS) through a network of local offices around the country and specialist offices.

Wherever you or your employer have any overseas involvement your National Insurance contribution position can become very complicated. All such matters are the responsibility of the DSS Overseas Branch, whose address is given on page 302.

Travelling expenses, and board and lodging

If you work in a job the duties of which are performed *wholly* outside the UK, the following expenses are not taxable:

(a) travel from any place to take up the employment;
(b) travel to any place in the UK at the end of the employment;
(c) board and lodging provided by or reimbursed by the employer.

If only *part* of the duties are performed outside the UK, the following expenses are not taxable:

(a) travel from any place in the UK to the place of performance of any of the duties outside the UK; or
(b) travel from the overseas place of performance of any of the duties to any place in the UK

provided that the duties concerned can only be performed outside the UK and the journey is made *wholly and exclusively* for the purpose of performing the duties or returning after performing the duties.

Family travel

No tax is payable on travel costs provided or reimbursed by the employer for the taxpayer's spouse or children under 18 to visit overseas. To qualify for this relief, the taxpayer must be working overseas for a continuous period 60 days or more.

'Continuous' means that even a single day back in the UK, for whatever reason, will debar the relief (or start a fresh 60-day period after the employee returns overseas).

This relief is only given for travel between a place in the UK and the place (or places) of performance of duties. It applies to not more than two outward and two return journeys by the same person in a UK tax year. A child must be under 18 at the beginning of the outward journey, and can include a stepchild and an illegitimate child.

Chapter 3

Letting and Insuring Your Home*

Many home owners going to live abroad will be looking for a tenant to live in their house or flat while they are away.

The case for letting, as opposed to leaving your home empty or selling, hardly needs to be put today when squatting, vandalism and interest rates are constantly in the headlines. The Government, recognising the difficulties for owners leaving their homes and wishing to encourage the private landlord, introduced the Housing Act 1988 which came into force on 15 January 1989. This Act simplifies the many provisions of the various Rent and Housing Acts from 1965 to 1987. Landlords now have a choice between an assured tenancy and an assured shorthold tenancy. It is not possible here to define the various differences between these two forms of tenancy, but there are specific areas of which the owner-occupier needs to be aware. However, lettings to large companies where the occupier is a genuine employee being housed by the company temporarily are excluded from the Act. It should be noted that a letting to a member of the Diplomatic Corps who has immunity is inadvisable, as the individual would be outside the jurisdiction of British courts. It is essential, therefore, for the owner to obtain legal advice before deciding which form of tenancy to opt for.

Assured tenancies

1. An assured tenancy may be for a fixed term or periodic, ie month to month.
2. The tenant must be an individual, not a limited company.
3. The tenant must occupy the house or flat as his or her only or principal home.
4. There are various terms which should be provided in the agreement and in particular a provision for the rent to be increased by notice in writing.

The benefits of an assured tenancy are as follows: there is very little

---

* Adapted from *Working Abroad: The Daily Telegraph Guide to Working and Living Overseas*, 15th edition (Kogan Page).

rent control; there is no restriction on the initial rent; premiums can be taken (although this is unlikely to be a marketable facility); rents can be increased during the tenancy, provided there is a term in the agreement; and even where not so provided the landlord may serve notice under the Act to increase the rent. In the latter instance, the tenant may go to the Rent Assessment Committee who must fix the rent at a 'market' figure, not at the previous imposition of what was perhaps unfortunately called a 'fair' rent.

Possession of the property can still be obtained by virtue of former owner-occupation and the service of the appropriate notice on the tenant before the commencement of the tenancy. Additional provisions for a mandatory possession order have been included in the new Act, such as three months' arrears of rent, and there are a number of discretionary grounds on which possession can be granted, even if the owner does not wish to return to the house. However, there is one specific disadvantage with the Act if the owner is unfortunate enough to have a tenant who refuses to leave when the owner wishes to reoccupy. This is the provision under the Act where the owner is obliged to serve two months' notice advising the tenant that the owner requires possession and on what ground(s) prior to any proceedings being commenced. This undoubtedly will extend the period needed before a possession order is granted by the Court and owners would be well advised to take out one of the various insurance policies now available to cover hotel costs, legal fees, etc and as a minimum to make sure that either alternative accommodation is temporarily available in the event of a return home earlier than expected or the tenancy is terminated well before the projected date of return.

Assured shorthold tenancies

1. These must be for a minimum term of six months without provision for a break clause, although after this period there can be two months' notice provided.
2. A notice must be served in the specified form at least four or five working days before the commencement of the agreement.
3. The tenant may apply to the Rent Assessment Committee during the period of the tenancy to fix the rental at a 'market' figure. However, on the expiry of the original term, the owner is entitled to require the tenant to pay a higher rental and the tenant is not entitled to go back to the Rent Assessment Committee. It is therefore preferable to have relatively short lease periods.
4. Two months' notice has to be served that the landlord requires possession before or on the day the fixed term comes to an end

and, if the tenant refuses to leave, the Courts must grant
possession, after the expiry of the notice.

As must now be obvious to the reader, the rules do nothing to
encourage the owner to attempt to let the property or manage the
home him or herself while away, and the need for an experienced
property management firm becomes even more important than in
the past. A solicitor might be an alternative but, although more
versed in the legal technicalities than a managing agent, a solicitor
will not be in a position to market the house to the best advantage
(if at all) and solicitors' practices do not usually have staff
experienced in property management, able to carry out inspections,
deal with repairs, arrange inventories and to handle the many and
various problems that often arise.

Having retained a solicitor to ensure that you have the correct
form of tenancy, you now need to find an experienced and reliable
estate agent (ideally, a member of the Royal Institution of Chartered
Surveyors, the Incorporated Society of Valuers and Auctioneers,
The Association of Residential Letting Agencies or the National
Association of Estate Agents) specialising in property management
who will be well-versed in both the legal and financial aspects of the
property market.

Property management

Property management is a rather specialised branch of estate agency
and you should check carefully that the agent you go to can give you
the service you need, that he or she is not just an accommodation
broker, and that the agent is equipped to handle the letting,
collection of rental and management of your property, as well as the
more common kinds of agency work. Your solicitor should be able
to advise you here, but to some extent you will have to rely on your
own judgement of how ready and satisfactory the agent's answers
are to the sort of questions you are going to want to ask. There are
several specialised firms well equipped to deal with your affairs. One
such firm is Anderton & Son of Croydon (with offices in
Beckenham and Cheam), which supplied much of the information
upon which this chapter is based.

In the first place the agent you instruct should have a clear idea of
the kind of tenant you can expect for your property, and preferably
be able to show you that he or she does have people who are looking
for rented accommodation of this kind. Obviously, the rental and
the tenant you can expect will vary with what you have to offer. A
normal family house in a good area should attract someone like the

executive of a multinational company who is in a similar, but reverse, position to your own: that is, a person working here on a contract basis for a limited period who may well provide a stable tenancy for the whole or a substantial part of your absence. A smaller house or flat would be more likely to attract a younger person who only wants the property for a limited period or who, at any rate, might be reluctant to accept a long-term commitment because of the possibility of a change in professional circumstances or marital status.

For your part you should bear in mind that tenants, unlike house purchasers, are usually only interested in a property with almost immediate possession, but you should give the agent, wherever possible, at least two or three months' warning of your departure in order that interest may be built up by advertising, mailing out details, etc over a period of time.

Rent

How much rent you can expect will also vary with what you have to offer and where it is, but the point to bear in mind is that rents are not usually subject to bargaining like a house price. Bargaining, if there is to be any, is more likely to occur over the terms of the lease which are set out below. Do not, therefore, ask for an unrealistically high figure in the expectation that the tenant will regard this as a starting point for negotiation.

Your agent, if he or she knows the job, will be able to advise you on the rental you should ask, though if you have not had previous dealings with the agent it might be advisable to have your solicitor check out the figures or to ask the agent to give you some instances of rentals being charged for similar accommodation. On the other hand, an offer which is a bit less than you had hoped for, but from a good tenant, might be worth taking in preference to a better one from somebody who, for various reasons, looks more doubtful.

Terms of agreement

A property management agent should have, or be able to produce fairly quickly, a draft agreement to cover the specific situation of the overseas landlord. You should show this to your solicitor and how well it is drafted will again be a pointer to how effective the agent concerned is likely to be. The document should cover at least the following points:

1. The intervals of payment – monthly or quarterly – and the length of lease.

2. A prohibition from assigning the lease without your express permission; likewise from keeping animals on the premises or using them for other than residential purposes.

3. An undertaking by the tenant to make good any damage, other than fair wear and tear, to fixtures, fittings and furniture and to maintain the garden.

4. An undertaking by the tenant to pay for telephone and other services from the commencement of the lease.

5. An undertaking to allow the landlord, or agent, regular access to the property for inspection and repair; and two months before the expiry of the lease to allow the landlord to take other prospective tenants or purchasers round the property.

6. A clause stating that the lease is terminated if any of the other clauses are broken although the wording has to be carefully drafted to avoid invalidating the agreement.

7. What you, as landlord, are responsible for in the way of repairs: usually the maintenance of the structure and furnishings of the property together with anything left in the property (eg the central heating boiler). You can exclude some items, such as the television, from your responsibility, but generally the tenant is only liable for specific damage to items left in the house and not for their general maintenance.

8. Any special restrictions you want to impose: if, for example, your house is full of valuable antiques you may wish to specify 'no small children'.

9. The conditions under which the tenancy can be terminated prior to its full period having run and without any breach having taken place.

10. Notice must be served under Schedule 2, Ground 1 of the Housing Act 1988 which notifies the tenant that you are an owner-occupier within the meaning of the Housing Act. This gives the landlord and those members of the landlord's family who occupied the house before it was let the right to reoccupy it when the lease expires or is terminated.

11. Notice under Sections 47 and 48 of the Landlord and Tenant Act 1987. The former should be on all rent demands; the latter, notifying the tenant of an address in England and Wales at which notices can be served on the landlord, need only be served once on a tenant at the beginning of a tenancy.

Although the agreement is probably the central document in the transactions involved in letting your house, it does not bring to an end all the things you have to think about. For instance, there is the important matter of the contents insurance.

Letting your home to a third party is probably not covered in your policy and you will have to notify your insurers (and the people who hold your mortgage) that this is what you are doing. In many instances, insurance companies will not insure the contents if property is to be let, and you will need to check carefully that you have cover and can switch to another company if it becomes necessary. At the same time you would be wise to check that the contents insurance covers the full value of what you have left in the house. This check could be combined with making a proper inventory of the contents which is in any case essential before tenants move into a furnished property. Making an exact inventory is quite a time-consuming business and you should bear in mind that it will also have to be checked at the end of the lease, when you may not be there. There are several firms that provide a specialist inventory service at both ends of the lease, covering dilapidations as well as items actually missing, for quite a modest charge which, incidentally, is deductible from the tax due from the letting. Any good property management agent should be able to put you on to one of them.

Since 1 March 1993 it has been an offence to supply furniture which does not comply with fire resistance regulations. Upholstery and loose covers must pass a cigarette test, a match test and an ignitability test. There is a transition period for furniture supplied and used in the same property prior to 1 March 1993, but after 1 January 1997 *all* furniture must comply with the regulations.

Finding the tenant and getting the tenant's signature on the agreement marks the beginning rather than the end of the property management firm's responsibilities. Broadly, these fall under two headings: the collection of rental and the management of the property. The rent is collected from the tenant, usually on a standing order basis, under the terms – monthly or quarterly – as set out in the agreement; and, in the event of persistent non-payment, the agent will instruct solicitors on your behalf to issue a county court summons.

What can you expect from the agent?

Management is a more complex subject but an experienced property management agent should be able to supply you with a list of the services that he or she can undertake. It is, therefore, also a checklist of the kind of eventualities that may crop up in your absence which, broadly speaking, relate to the collection of rent, the payment of charges such as service charges and insurance, arrangements for repairs to the fabric of the building and its contents, garden maintenance or when forwarding mail.

Thus, apart from the basic business of collecting the rent, the agent can also pay, on your behalf, any charges on the property (eg ground rent, water rates and insurance) that your contract with the tenant does not specify should be paid by the tenant. There may also be annual maintenance agreements to pay in respect of items like central heating plant and the washing machine.

Then there is the question of what to do about repairs. As we have indicated earlier, whatever you manage to get the tenant to agree to take care of under the terms of the lease, there are certain responsibilities for maintenance and repair that you have to accept by virtue of your status as a landlord. If repairs are necessary, you will simply have to trust the agent to obtain fair prices for you.

On the other hand, except in the case of essential repairs which affect the tenant's legal rights of enjoyment of the property, you can ask your agent to provide estimates for having the work carried out, so that your approval must be obtained before the job is put in hand. Bear in mind, though, that in certain parts of the world the postal system may not be all that reliable. You may, therefore, find it a good idea to put a clause in the management contract giving the agent freedom to proceed with the best estimate if the agent does not hear from you within a specified period. For the same reason it is also wise to ask the agent to send you a formal acknowledgement of receipt of any special or new instructions you have given the agent. An example of this might be an instruction to inspect the property at regular intervals.

Depending on how many concessions you have to make to the tenant to get him or her to sign the lease, there may be other articles for which repair and maintenance remain your responsibility. These may include washing machines, TV and the deep-freeze. Such responsibilities should be set out in the management contract and you should give the agent the details of any guarantees or maintenance contracts relating to them and photocopies of the actual documents for reference. If no such arrangements apply, you should list the manufacturers' names and the model number and age of each item so that the agent can get the manufacturer to send the repair people along equipped with the right spares.

It is very important that a third party, other than you and the tenant, should be in possession of all this information, particularly when there is likely to be more than one tenancy during your absence; and it is a competent management agent, rather than friends, relatives or even a solicitor, who will be best equipped in this case to find new tenants, to check their references, to draw up new agreements and supervise the hand-over of the tenancy.

Costs and tax

The costs of all these services vary according to the nature of the package you need. The professional societies already mentioned recommend charges, which would be applicable in most circumstances. For example, letting and collection is usually 10 per cent of annual rental. In the case of management services, expect to find additional charges made (usually 5 to 7 per cent of the annual rent). These are reasonable fees for the quite considerable headaches involved. We have shown enough of them here to indicate that not only is it virtually impossible to administer a tenancy yourself from a distance, but also that these are not matters to be left to an amateur – friend or relative – however well intentioned. In real terms the agent's charges may be reduced because they are deductible against the tax levied in the UK against rental income.

Expatriates letting their houses also derive a further benefit in respect of capital gains tax. Generally, if you let your principal residence, when you come to sell it you can claim exemption from CGT only for those years in which you lived in it yourself. However, if you let it because you are absent abroad this does not apply, provided you come back to live in the house before you sell it (see pages 33–4).

Finally, in this context, it is worth pointing out that some building societies are now prepared to consider giving mortgages to expatriates for the purchase of a property in the UK *and* to allow them to lease that property for the period of their stay overseas. Up to 90 per cent of the purchase price is available at normal building society rates of interest.

This is an attractive proposition for expatriates, particularly for young executives and professional people who have not yet bought a home in the UK but are earning a substantial income in, say, the Middle East, and for older expatriates perhaps thinking of a retirement home in the UK.

Some agencies supply details of the building societies offering this facility, or you could approach a society directly and explain your position. Should you buy a house as an expatriate and then let it until you return, the earlier recommendation that you leave the management of the property to an experienced and competent agent still applies.

You should note that if a UK property is bought purely as an investment, you would have to time its sale carefully to avoid liability to CGT.

Taxation is a complex subject and varies considerably in its effects on the individual; such advice as can be offered is found on pages 18–48, and we stress the necessity of employing the services of an accountant in your absence. Changes in the Budget allow the use of personal allowances against property income, subject to some restriction, while the Revenue have tightened up the method and timing and collection of tax due in each year, with stiffer penalties for late payment, and refusal to accept postponements except on specific grounds. Should you have an agent collecting the rent, whether this is a professional firm or a friend, the agent will be liable to pay tax on your behalf and, without an indemnity from a UK-based employer or a chartered accountant, may be obliged to deduct tax from each monthly or quarterly rental payment, to enable payment of the amount requested by the Revenue on 1 January.

Similar liabilities now fall on an agent collecting the rental in respect of the Council Tax. The owner will be responsible jointly with the agent to meet the standard charge if the property is empty, or where the property is let for less than six months to an individual. In these cases expect the agent to retain sufficient money to meet this commitment on your behalf.

Insurance

One important point that is often overlooked by people who let their house or flat is the necessity of notifying the insurers that a change of occupancy has taken place. Insurance policies only cover occupancy by the insured, not the tenants, though it can be extended to do so on payment of what is usually only a small premium. As already mentioned, many insurance companies will not insure the contents of let property, so notifying the company becomes even more important.

What worries insurance companies much more is if the house is left unoccupied for any length of time. If you look at your policy you will see that it lapses if you leave your house empty for more than 30 days or so – a point that is sometimes forgotten by people who go away on extended holidays. If you are going abroad and leave the house empty – maybe because you have not yet succeeded in finding a tenant – the insurers will usually insist that you turn off the main services and that the premises are inspected regularly by a qualified person. That means someone like a letting agent, not a relative or friend who cannot be relied on 100 per cent. Even if you have let the house without an agent, it may still be advisable to get one to look after the place. A situation could easily occur where the tenant moves out, leaving the place empty and without satisfactory steps having been taken from an insurance point of view. Furthermore, if the worst happens and the house is broken into or damaged, it is imperative that the insurers are notified right away. The effects of damage can be made worse unless they are rapidly attended to, and insurers do not hold themselves responsible for anything that happens between the time the insured eventuality occurs and the time they are notified of it. For instance, if your house is broken into and, a few days later, vandals get in through a broken point of entry and cause further damage, you would not be covered for that second incident unless the insurers had been notified of the first break-in.

Valuable contents are best put into storage and insured there: Pickfords, for instance, charge a premium of $7\frac{1}{2}$ per cent of the storage charge. For very high value items, safe deposit boxes are becoming popular, but from an everyday point of view, the important thing is to make sure you are insured for full values. If you insure contents for £15,000 and the insurer's assessors value them at £20,000 you will only get three-quarters of your claim. To keep insured values in line with rising costs, an index-linked policy would be the best buy for anyone contemplating a long stay abroad. A policy specially written for expatriates is available from the Europea Group: the Expatriate UK Home Owners' Insurance Contract. They also offer expatriate motor insurance on private cars being used overseas.

Insuring at full value, incidentally, is equally important when it comes to insuring contents and personal belongings in your residence abroad. Many items will cost much more locally if you have to replace them than they did at the time they were originally bought. It is possible to effect such insurance in the UK, but from the point of getting claims settled quickly it is better to insure in the country concerned, where possible.

Finally, but most important, you should insure against legal and hotel costs when letting your house. Although in principle the legal instruments for quick repossession exist, events have shown that a bloody-minded tenant with a committed lawyer can spin things out to his or her advantage for an almost indefinite period. Premiums, which can be offset against rental income, are in the region of £50 a year. A typical policy covering legal costs is the DAS Homeowners Legal Protection Policy.

Chapter 4
Learn a Language

Please learn the native language of the country where you intend to settle, even if you are of retirement age. Surely it is just good manners to speak even a few halting words of the language of your host country when you go to live there permanently or even just to spend long vacations?

You will enjoy the many benefits of closer contact with your neighbours, in business relations or with tradespeople. They will appreciate your efforts to communicate with them and will often go out of their way to help you, not only to learn the right words but also giving assistance in solving problems while shopping, visiting banks and post offices or dealing with officialdom.

There are many different methods of learning a language and if you persevere your efforts will be rewarded, although care should be taken to choose a method that will provide you with the up-to-date language you will require.

Before you go to live abroad, why not take a series of evening classes at a local college of further education or enrol for a 'crash course' at one of the many language colleges?

Other sources of spare-time language education include the Linguaphone system, which offers a wide variety of courses using cassettes or compact discs, together with books containing exercises and further tuition. It is one of the longest-established organisations specialising in teaching foreign languages, and is based at the Linguaphone Institute Ltd, 50 Poland Street, London W1E 6JJ. It has a range of 30 languages. Advanced courses in French, German, Italian, Spanish, Arabic, Chinese, Russian and Swedish are also available.

Using audio cassettes supplemented by an excellent series of books, the courses are designed for students who want to learn in their own time and place. Some can speak quite fluently in just three months. An advisory service is available free of charge and a panel of language experts are able to answer students' linguistic or general study questions.

Hugo's Audio Language Courses take absolute beginners

through to a good working knowledge of written and spoken language. Fairly proficient students also find the courses invaluable for revision and advancement. Each course includes a copy of the appropriate 'Three Months' book.

There are 17 titles in the series, covering Arabic*, Chinese*, Czech*, Danish, Dutch, French, German, Greek, Hebrew, Italian, Japanese*, Latin American Spanish*, Norwegian*, Portuguese, Russian*, Spanish, Swedish and Turkish*. These books set out the rules of grammar which enable students to gain a practical knowledge of the language in a short time. Conversational sentences and selected idiomatic phrases are also included.

In addition to the book there are four tapes with about four hours of recorded time and an instruction leaflet.

Students should first immerse themselves in the sound of the language by listening to a tape for a few minutes, and then repeat the sound while reading the relevant section of the book. They should study in depth the instructions, attempt the written exercises and check their answers against the key in the back of the book. At the commencement of each day's work, students should revise briefly the material learnt on the previous day.

With self-discipline and regular periods of study, Hugo's are certain that it is possible to learn a language within three months.

Prices for the courses are £32.95, except for the less popular courses, which are marked on the list with an asterisk. These sell for £36.95. Orders should be sent to Hugo's Language Books Ltd, Old Station Yard, Marlesford, Woodbridge IP13 0AG.

Hugo's also publish phrase books covering 23 different languages (prices £2.50) and 23 travel packs, each of which contains a phrase book and a cassette of the phrases which are designed to help the traveller to understand and speak the language by familiarisation, without having to learn a lot of grammar. These are priced at £7.95 each. The books can be purchased from bookshops or directly.

Other audio courses with cassettes and books are produced by Berlitz, and there is the Hodder & Stoughton 'Teach Yourself' series. They cost around £10 each, are available in several languages and can be purchased from bookshops.

Linguarama Ltd offer individual face-to-face instruction in many different languages. Intensive or part-time tuition is available with teachers who are native speakers of the languages. Study can be in the UK, France, Spain, Italy, Germany, Holland, Belgium, Finland or Japan. For details, contact David Thompson at Queen's House, 8 Queen's Street, London EC4N 1SP; 071-236 1992.

Videos

Video encourages participation by students who can work at home and retain a stronger interest in the subject than by studying from books alone.

The BBC have produced Spanish and French language-learning packages incorporating videos, audio-cassette material, a course book, user guide and activities book in the standard editions. De luxe editions contain additional video and cassette material and books including a dictionary. There is also a CD de luxe edition. Prices range from £99 to £229 and the packages are only available direct from BBC Enterprises Ltd, Milton Keynes MK6 1HW.

BBC Training Videos comprise a language library of quality videos in French, Spanish, German, Italian and Japanese. Each package concentrates not only on the language element but also on the cultural and social aspect, to create a greater understanding of the customs and characteristics of each country. The package comprises a complete self-contained course with four VHS video-cassettes, between two and five audio cassettes, teachers' notes and a text or workbook. Each language course costs from £249 plus VAT and is obtainable from BBC Training Videos, PO Box 77, Wetherby, West Yorkshire LS23 7HN.

The BBC also market a useful business language series of videos covering French, German, Spanish, Italian and Eastern Europe (Poland, Hungary and the former Czechoslovakia).

Berlitz also have videos in French and Spanish, which give about 60 minutes' basic tuition, at a cost of about £16 each.

Knowledge of a foreign language has other practical advantages, especially if you need to communicate with local authorities such as the police. If you are stopped by a traffic patrolman for an alleged infringement of the law, such as speeding in, say, southern Europe, it is very difficult to plead your innocence if the officer cannot speak your language and you are unable to understand his. In this sort of situation you may well decide to pay the fixed penalty rather than become more deeply involved; if you can speak the local language you may save yourself a fine.

If your home is burgled and you need to report the event to the upholders of law and order, you may find it necessary to pay for the cost of an interpreter to explain all the details to the police. A basic knowledge of the local language could avoid this problem.

Chapter 5

Taking Your Pets With You

Many families are very fond of their pets, particularly cats and dogs, and are loath to leave them behind when they go to live abroad. Import regulations vary from one European country to another and a summary of these rules is given below.

Do remember, however, that if you take a cat or dog to a place outside the British Isles and then want to bring it back, it becomes an imported animal as far as the Rabies Act 1974 is concerned and will have to undergo a period of quarantine.

France

No import permit is required, but dogs and cats not intended for sale in France have to be accompanied in transit, or met at the port of entry by the owner. You will be expected to verify that the animal is not for sale. A maximum of three animals, one of which may be a puppy, is permitted; all must be at least three months old.

An export health certificate should accompany all cats and dogs exported to France. To obtain this, form EXA1 (obtainable from the Ministry of Agriculture Fisheries and Food, Hook Rise South, Surbiton, Surrey KT6 7NF) should be completed and sent to your local Animal Health Office, who will issue the certificate to the applicant's nominated Local Veterinary Inspector who will complete the certification. Rabies vaccination is only compulsory for animals entering the island of Corsica or being introduced to holiday parks, camping grounds or those participating in shows being held in areas affected by rabies.

It is recommended that dogs should be vaccinated against distemper, pervovirus and depatitus, and cats against infectious lecopenia, but this is not compulsory.

Greece

A permit is not required to import a cat or dog into Greece from Great Britain. Animals must however be accompanied by the following certificates:

1. A bilingual health certificate issued by a local veterinary inspector

of the MAFF (Ministry of Agriculture, Fisheries and Food), confirming the breed and species of the animal, that the inspector has examined the animal and that it is in good health, free from symptoms and signs of contagious disease and it has been treated for echinococosis within 30 days of the proposed shipment date. The certificate will only be valid for 10 days from date of issue.

2. For dogs only, a certificate is required stating that the animal has been vaccinated against rabies not less than 15 days before or not more than 12 months before importation into Greece.

It is not necessary to have a dog under three months of age vaccinated against rabies before importation into Greece, provided it is vaccinated on reaching the appropriate age after entry.

Italy

The Italian authorities do not require an import permit for cats or dogs, but the animals must be accompanied by documentation as follows:

Animals accompanied by travellers

A bilingual (Italian and English) certificate of health is required from the local veterinary inspector of MAFF, indicating that the animal was examined on the day of issue of the certificate and found to be free of any clinical signs of disease, and that it was vaccinated against rabies not less than 20 days and no more than 11 months prior to the date of issue of the certificate.

Accompanied animals which have not been vaccinated against rabies, or were vaccinated outside the qualifying period mentioned above, can be imported into Italy provided that they have a veterinary examination at the point of entry into the country.

Unaccompanied animals

Animals that are unaccompanied are exempt from rabies vaccination, but must be examined by an Italian veterinary officer at the place of arrival in Italy and be found to be free of disease in order to qualify for admission.

Portugal, Madeira and the Azores

An import permit is required for dogs and cats entering Portugal, together with appropriate certificates. The first is a health certificate issued by a local veterinary inspector of MAFF not more than 14 days prior to export, stating that the animals are free of signs of contagious or infectious diseases including distemper and rabies. Also required is the Ministry's export certificate issued not more than 14 days prior to export, declaring that rabies has not existed in any of the districts from which the animal originates and that it has remained in the area of origin since birth or for six months prior to the date of shipment.

A health certificate has to be sent to the Ministry at Surbiton for authentication.

On arrival in Portugal, dogs have to be kept in the home under the supervision of the Animal Health Services. The period of restriction may be specified on the import permit or by the Animal Health Services. All dogs in Portugal over four months of age must be vaccinated against rabies; this is undertaken during the period of home quarantine.

Spain, Canary and Balearic Islands

Animals exported to Spain for commercial purposes only will require import permits, but all cats and dogs destined for Spain require a certificate of health in duplicate from a veterinary inspector authorised by MAFF, indicating that the animals are healthy and have no signs of contagious or infectious diseases, and are not suspected of suffering from rabies. The certificate has to be issued not more than two days prior to the animals leaving Great Britain.

Vaccination against rabies is not required for animals under two months of age, or for those that are native to Great Britain and are domestic pets. Other animals which are aged three months or more and which have been imported to Great Britain from a country which has not been rabies free within the last six months must be vaccinated not more than 12 months, or less than one month, before importation into Spain. Where vaccination is required, a certificate by a local veterinary inspector stating that the dog or cat has been vaccinated is necessary. An export certificate issued by MAFF is required which states that no disease to which the species is liable, and which is compulsorily notifiable under the Animal Health Act 1981, has existed at the address where the animal has normally been kept over the past two years.

An Export Health Certificate must accompany cats and dogs exported from Great Britain to Spain and a maximum of two pets may accompany travellers. Rabies vaccination is not compulsory for accompanied pets or for animals less than three months of age. If rabies vaccination has not been carried out on animals for commercial export, they may be placed in quarantine for 14 days in Spain, after which they will be vaccinated and released. All quarantine and vaccination costs will be borne by the owner. Commercial exported animals can only be consigned to an approved sporting or commercial establishment or zoological unit.

Belgium, the Netherlands and Luxembourg

Cats and dogs exported to or in transit through the Benelux countries must be vaccinated against rabies at least 30 days before export and not more than 12 months in advance.

It is advisable to have a health certificate by a veterinary surgeon issued within seven days before export. This document should state that the cat or dog has been examined by the veterinary surgeon and found free of contagious and infectious diseases and is fit to travel.

Denmark

Dogs and cats accompanied by travellers from Great Britain, Australia, the Faeroes, Finland, Iceland, the Irish Republic, Japan, New Zealand, Norway and Sweden can be imported into Denmark without restriction, provided that they travel direct to Denmark from the countries listed.

Accompanied animals from other countries require a rabies vaccination certificate.

Unaccompanied animals require a certificate indicating vaccination against rabies at least one month and at most 12 months before importation. They will undergo inspection immediately on arrival at specified Customs houses by the veterinary surgeon and must be in good health before being allowed entry to Denmark.

Unaccompanied cats and dogs from the countries listed in the first paragraph are granted entry without a rabies vaccination.

Germany

An import permit is not required to take dogs and cats into Germany, if not more than three animals, accompanied by the owner or the owner's representative, are imported for transit through the country or are imported because of a change of residence. Also, not more than three animals can be imported by air, accompanied or unaccompanied, because of a change of residence.

A permit is required if the animals are intended for sale or going to a different person following arrival in Germany. In these cases the import permit must be obtained from the Veterinary Authority of the Federal State (*Land*) in which the border crossing point is situated, prior to importation.

A bilingual certificate from an authorised veterinary surgeon is necessary, indicating that the animal has been vaccinated against rabies not less than 30 days and not more than one year prior to the date of export.

Furthermore, no import permit is required if the animals are over eight weeks old and have been vaccinated against rabies at least 30 days and not more than 12 months prior to their arrival.

Northern Ireland, Republic of Ireland, Isle of Man and the Channel Islands

Unrestricted movement of cats and dogs between Great Britain, Northern Ireland, the Republic of Ireland and the Channel Islands is permitted and no documents are required.

Arranging for rabies vaccination

Although the use of rabies vaccination is not normally allowed in Great Britain, arrangements have been made for vaccine to be available for animals being exported. The owner or exporter may choose a veterinary surgeon to undertake the work and the surgeon should contact the Divisional Veterinary Officer well in advance of the export date, giving a description of the animal and its destination, and requesting that vaccine be released so that it can be administered. The owner must provide documentary evidence to the vet that the animal is being exported.

Chapter 6
Education Overseas

Parents who go abroad for business reasons or retirement when their children are still of school age often arrange for their offspring to continue their education at a boarding school in the UK, so that they see them only during the holidays or at half-term.

This is a pity because it tends to break up the family and can be very expensive. What is more, it is not really necessary as there are excellent English-speaking establishments in most European countries where pupils learn not only the subjects normally studied in Britain, but also a wider curriculum which introduces them to the international scene.

Very young children who commence their education in a foreign country also have the opportunity of mixing naturally with local youngsters and soon become bilingual. (Some even become fluent in three languages if their parents are of different nationalities and the country where they reside speaks a third tongue.)

A long-established advisory service for UK education is offered by Gabbitas, Truman & Thring of 6–8 Sackville Street, Piccadilly, London W1X 2BR. This includes free impartial advice on the selection of independent schools throughout the UK. A careers counselling service is available on a fee-charging basis and a full guardianship service is offered in the UK for children whose parents live abroad.

The firm publishes annually *Which School*, an 800-page book listing schools in the UK. It costs £12.95 plus £3.25 postage and packing and can be obtained from the above address.

For more advanced students Kogan Page Ltd publish *Higher Education in the European Community*.

The Independent School Information Service, 56 Buckingham Gate, London SW1E 6AG, is another useful source of information.

A brief selection of schools in Europe for English-speaking children is given below:

Cyprus

Nicosia

American Academy, 3A, M Parides Street, PO Box 1967, Nicosia; tel: 02 462886.
Primary and secondary school for boys and girls; also a junior school.

Ecole St Joseph, PO Box 1546, Nicosia.
Secondary school for girls only.

English School, PO Box 3575, Nicosia; tel: 02 422274.
Secondary day school for boys and girls.

Falcon School, PO Box 3640, Nicosia; tel: 02 424781.
Reception, primary and secondary school for boys and girls.

GC School of Careers, PO Box 5276, Nicosia; tel: 02 448187.
Secondary school for boys and girls.

Grammar School, Anthoupolis Highway, PO Box 2262, Nicosia; tel: 02 621744.
Secondary school for boys and girls; also a junior school and reception class.

Junior School, PO Box 3903, Nicosia.
Junior school for boys and girls.

Terra Santa College, PO Box 1546, Nicosia.
Secondary school for boys and girls.

Limassol

American Academy and Junior School, Limassol; tel: 010 3575 337054.
Boys and girls, 5–16 years.

Limassol Grammar School (Foley's), Homer Street, Ayios Nicolaos, Limassol.
Junior and secondary school for boys and girls.

The Logos School of English Education, Nikocleous Street, PO Box 1075, Limassol.
Secondary school for boys and girls.

Private Grammar School (Gregoriou), PO Box 1340, Limassol.
Secondary school for boys and girls.

St Mary's School, Grivas Digenis Avenue, Limassol.
Primary school for boys and girls.

Larnaca

American Academy, Afxentiou Avenue, PO Box 112, Larnaca.
Secondary school for boys and girls.

St Joseph, Mich. Parides Square, Larnaca.
Secondary school for girls.

Paphos

Anglo-American International School, 24–26 Hellas Avenue, Paphos.
Primary and secondary school for boys and girls, 5–18 years.

France

American School of Paris, 41 rue Pasteur, 92210 Saint Cloud, Paris.
Boys and girls, 5–18 years.

British School of Paris, 38 Quai de l'Ecluse, 78290 Croissy-sur-Seine, Paris.
Boys and girls, $4\frac{1}{2}$–18 years.

International School of Paris, 6 rue Beethoven, 75016 Paris.
Boys and girls, 3–8 years.

Marymount School, 72 Boulevard de la Saussaye, 92200 Neuilly-sur-Seine.
Boys and girls, 3–14 years.

Greece

Athens College, PO Box 5, Psychio, Athens.
Boys and girls, grades 1–6; boys only, grades 7–13.

Italy

Ambrit International School, Via Annia Regilla 60, 00187 Rome.
Boys and girls' kindergarten and primary school.

International School of Naples, Mostra d'Oltremore, 80125 Naples.
Boys and girls, $4\frac{1}{2}$–17 years.

St George's English School, Via Cassia, Km16, 00123 Rome.
Boys and girls, $2\frac{1}{2}$–18 years.

Malta

Chiswick House School, Sliema.
Junior school for boys and girls.

St Edward's College; De La Salle College; St Aloysius College.
Typical secondary schools with GCSE and A-level courses for pupils up to 18 years old.

The Netherlands

British School in the Netherlands, Tapijtweg 10,
2597KH The Hague (junior school); Jan van Hooflaan 3,
2252BC Voorschoten.
Boys and girls, 3–18 years.

British School of Amsterdam, Jekerstraat 86,
1078MG Amsterdam.
Boys and girls, 3–12 years.

International School of Amsterdam, A J Ernststraat 875,
Amsterdam 1081HL.
Boys and girls.

Portugal

Barlavento English School, Espiche 8600, Lagos, Algarve.
Boys and girls, kindergarten.

British School, Oporto (founded 1894).
Prepares pupils for Cambridge and London Boards and Common
Entrance.

Casa dos Santos Infant School, Quinta do Relógio, 2710 Sintra.
Nursery school for boys and girls, 1–6 years.

Escola Espartana, Sagres.
Boys, 12–16 years.

International Preparatory School, Rua do Boror 12, Carcavelos,
2775 Parede.
Pupils, 5–13 years.

International School of the Algarve, Porches, near Lagoa, Algarve.
Boys and girls, 4–16 years. Centre in southern Portugal for
Cambridge University GCE examinations.

Nursery Class, Rua da Arriaga 39, 1200 Lisbon.
Boys and girls, 3–6 years.

O Pincho Kindergarten, Quinta de S Joao, Rebelva, Carcavelos.
Boys and girls, 2–6 years.

Prince Henry International School, Vale do Lobo, Almansil,
Algarve.
Boys and girls, 3–16 years.

St Anthony's International Primary School, Avenida de Portugal 11,
2765 Estoril.
Boys and girls up to 12 years of age.

St Dominic's College, Rua Outeiro da Polima, 2780 Arneiro.
Catholic school for boys and girls, 4–16 years.

St George's School, Vila Conçalves, Quinta dos Loureiras, Estrada Nacional, 2750 Cascais.
Boys and girls, 3–13 years.

St Julian's School, Quinta Nova, Carcavelos, 2775 Parede (about 10 miles from Lisbon).
Boys and girls, 3½–18 years.

Spain

A large number of British schools have been established in Spain and many of these are members of the National Association of British Schools in Spain: Chairman, Mr Norman Roddon, English Montessori School, Madrid. A list of establishments in major resort areas is given below. Further information can be obtained from the schools direct.

Costa del Sol

Aloha College, 'En Angel', Nueva Andalucia, Marbella, 3–17 years.

Calpe College, San Pedro de Alcantara, Marbella, 3–18 years.

English International College, Urbanizacion Ricmar, Ctra. de Cadiz, Km 189, Marbella, Málaga, 3–18 years.

International School, Apartado 15, Sotogrande, Cadiz. Offers day/boarding facilities, 3–18 years.

St Anthony's College, Apartado 119, Los Boliches, Fuengirola, 4–18 years.

Sunny View School, Apartado 175, Cerro del Toril, Torremolinos. Co-educational, 4–18 years.

Swan's International Primary School, Villa Capricho 2, 29600 Marbella, 2½–11 years.

The Young English School, Avenida Miraflores del Palo 26, 24018 Malaga, 2½–6 years.

Costa Blanca

Caxton College, Carreterra de Barcelona, 46530 Puzol, Valencia, 3–11 years.

Lady Elizabeth School, Apartado 298, Javea, Alicante, 2–18 years.

Sierra Bernia School, La Caneta San Rafael, Alfaz del Pi, Alicante, 3–18 years.

Barcelona

Anglo-American School, Paseo de Garbi 152, Casteldelfels, Barcelona, 3–18 years.

Kensington School, Carrer dels Cavallers 31, Barcelona, 4–18 years.

Oak House, San Pedro Claver 12, 08017 Barcelona, 3–17 years.

St Peter's School, Eduard Toldra 18, 08034 Barcelona, 15–18 years.

Madrid

British Council School, Urb. Prado de Jomosagnas, 28223, Pozuelo de Alarcon, Madrid, 3–18 years.

English Montessori School, Calle Triana 65, Madrid, 3–17 years.

Hastings School, Paseo de la Habona 204, Madrid, 3–14 years.

International Primary School, Rosa Jardon 3, Madrid, 3–14 years.

Kensington School, Avenida de Bulares, Pozuelo de Alarcon, Madrid, 3–16 years.

King's College, Urb. Soto de Vinuelas, Madrid 28790, 3–18 years.

Numont PNEU, Parma 16, Madrid, 2–11 years.

Runnymede College, Camino Ancho 87, La Moraleja-Alconbendas, 28100 Madrid, 3–18 years.

St Anne's School, Jaroma 9, Madrid, 4–18 years.

St Charles College, Tambre 3 (El Viso), 28002 Madrid. Business and secretarial College.

Schiller International University, Rodriguez San Pedro 10, 28015 Madrid. Full- or part-time study for a variety of degrees.

Valencia

Cambridge House, Campo Olivar, 46110 Valencia, 3–11 years.

Caxton College, Ctra de Barcelona 74, Puzol, Valencia, 3–14 years.

English School Los Olivos, Avenida Pino Panera, 46110 Godella, Valencia, 3–14 years.

Plantio International School of Valencia, Urbanizacion El Plantiori Calle 233, s/n 46353, La Canada, Valencia, 3–11 years.

Canary Islands

American School of Las Palmas, Apartado 15, Tarifa Alta, Las Palmas, 3–18 years.

British School of Grand Canary, PO Box 11, Tarifa Alta, Las Palmas, 4–16 years.

British School of Lanzarote, Jose Antonio 80, Arrecife de Lanzarote, 3–16 years.

British Yeoward School, Parque Taoro, Puerto de la Cruz, Tenerife, 3–18 years.

Canterbury School, Juan XXXII 34, Las Palmas, 3–18 years.

Colegio Hispano-Britanico, Apartado 228, 35500 Arrecife de Lanzarote, 3–18 years.

Oakley College, Tafira Alta, Las Palmas, Gran Canaria, 3–11 years.

Trinity School, Camino Montijo 16, La Carrera 38410, Los Realejos, Tenerife, 2–11 years.

Wingate School, Mirador de la Cumbrita 10, Cabo Blanco, Arona, Tenerife, 4–17 years.

Balearic Islands

Academy International College, Apartado 1300, Palma, Majorca. Co-educational, 2–14 years.

American International School, Oratorio 4, Portals Nous, 07015 Majorca. Co-educational, 3–18 years.

Baleares International School, San Agustin, Palma, Majorca. Co-educational day and boarding, $3\frac{1}{2}$–18 years.

Bellver International College, José Costa Ferrer 5, Cala Mayor, Palma, Majorca. Co-educational, 3–18 years.

Queens College, Juan de Saridakis 64, Palma, Majorca, 3–18 years.

Switzerland

Aiglon College, 1885 Chesières Villas.
Boys and girls, 11–18 years.

Brillantmont International School, Avenue Secretan 16, 1005 Lausanne. Boys and girls, 14–19 years.

International School of Berne, Mattenstrasse 3, 3073 Gumlegen bei Bern.
Boys and girls, 3–18 years.

St George's School, 1815 Clarens, Montreux.
Girls, 11–19 years.

Chapter 7

Health Benefits and Insurance

Pensioners living in any of the EC countries are entitled to claim medical and health facilities that are available to nationals of the country concerned.

Benefits include free dental treatment, sickness benefit, free medicine and drugs. Widows' benefits are also payable on the death of a husband. Generally speaking, the benefits are available to pensioners who were, at some time during their working lives, employed in any of the 12 EC countries, but there are exceptions. Details are given in the Department of Social Security leaflet SA29, *Your Social Security, Health Care and Pension Rights in the European Community*, available from your local Social Security Office or direct from the DSS Overseas Branch, Newcastle upon Tyne NE98 1YX.

Those drawing their pensions from the Department of Social Security should receive a copy of Form 121 whereon the Newcastle authorities certify the pensioners' entitlement and this is sent to the appropriate social security authority in the country of residence.

Pensioners, or younger members of the family who stay temporarily in an EC member state, can obtain full medical and hospital treatment if taken ill in that country but they must obtain Form E111 before they leave home and give it to the appropriate health authority in the country where they are staying.

A leaflet which gives information for nationals moving permanently, or temporarily, to another member state can be obtained free from: The Office for Official Publications, Commission of the European Communities, 8 Storey's Gate, London SW1P 3AT.

More information about individual countries is given in Part 4.

Although these free medical benefits are available, delays in obtaining treatment in hospitals and consulting doctors can be lengthy, as in the UK. Also, hospital wards often lack the desired privacy when a patient is seriously ill.

It is therefore highly recommended that those living permanently in an overseas country should subscribe to a private medical insurance scheme.

Wherever you work or retire, you don't have to go without BUPA.

When it comes to overseas healthcare, you'll find BUPA goes to the ends of the Earth to help.

A Survey of Current Expatriate Medical Schemes

Benefits	*Private Patients Plan (PPP) International Health Plan (Prestige Option)*	*BUPA International Senior Lifeline* (Typical Scheme)
Overall maximum	£500,000	£200,000
Hospital accommodation	Full refund	Full refund
Home nursing	Full refund up to 28 days	£600/full refund, depending on circumstances
Surgeons' and anaesthetists' fees	Full refund	Full refund
Operating theatre fees	Full refund	Full refund
Hospital (non-surgical) treatment	Full refund (outpatients £2500)	Full refund (outpatients £1000)
GP treatment	£2500	£15 per visit (max 6 visits per annum)
Maternity care	Complications only (full refund) Normal childbirth available on prestige option and corporate groups > 10 employees	—

BUPA International Lifeline (Typical Scheme)	Exeter Friendly Society (Middle range)	Europea – IMG Ltd Expatriate Health Care
£200,000	None	£500,000 any one person, in respect of all events occurring during the period of insurance.
Full refund	£1000 per week (Europe), £825 per week (outside Europe)	Unlimited cover up to maximum above
£600 on specialist's recommendation	£200 per week (10 weeks max.)	Maximum 14 days and one condition. Unlimited costs up to maximum above.
Full refund	£1000 per operation* plus £300 for anaesthetists' fees	As above
Full refund	£400 per operation*	As above
Full refund (outpatients £1000)	Various inpatient charges are covered up to specified limits (outpatients £1000 per annum)	As above
—	Optional extra	As above
Complications only	Complications only	Up to £3000

*Plus additional grant
of up to 100% for
complex major
operations

A Survey of Current Expatriate Medical Schemes

Benefits	*Private Patients Plan (PPP) International Health Plan*	*BUPA International Senior Lifeline* (Typical Scheme)
Emergency dental treatment	Covered under Prestige option	—
Emergency evacuation/ repatriation	No overall maximum	No overall maximum
Premium	Varies according to age and area[1] (PPP operate a series of five-year bands). Lower range: *Europe* Adult 40–44: £444.60 Child: £162.20 *World excl. North America* Adult 40–44: £537.10 Child: £200.90	Varies according to age. (No cover for USA and Canada.) Excluding tax relief 50–65: £1117 65–69: £1373 70–74: £1721 75+: £2591

Key
S = single
M = married
F = family

1. Higher premiums apply for the USA and Canada. Rates quoted are for individuals. Company paid groups are lower.

BUPA International Lifeline (Typical Scheme)	Exeter Friendly Society (Middle range)	Europea – IMG Ltd Expatriate Health Care
£400 per person per annum	—	£500 per insured person
No overall maximum	Not covered but the Society has negotiated a special arrangement with a repatriation insurer	Unlimited cover up to maximum above
Varies according to age. (Higher premiums for USA and Canada.)	Rates do not vary with age[1]	Varies according to area.
Lifeline Gold[1] Under 21: £202 21–29: £420 30–39: £484 40–49: £670 50–64: £910	S: £620 F: £879	Insured: from £550 Spouse: from £475 Child: from £300
Standard Lifeline approx 20% less than Gold; Essential Lifeline (excluding outpatient cover) average 20% less than Standard		
1. Individual cover only.	1. New members over 65 pay a once only extra joining fee	

Simply the best health Insurance Money can buy.

Over the years International Health Insurance danmark a/s has incorporated all the elements demanded by people who, when it comes to matters of health, need the ultimate protection.

INTERNATIONAL HEALTH INSURANCE danmark a/s
This card certifies that the holder is insured as shown below against expenses in connection with illness and injury.
POLICY NO.: 160750-8881
CO-INSURED CHILDREN: MEDICAL EXPENSES
COVERAGE: INCLUDED
MEDICAL EVACUATION: £230,000
INSURANCE AMOUNT PER YEAR PER PERSON GBP: 31/12/94
EXPIRY DATE:
PETER JONES
Insured's Name and Signature

Our wealth of international experience gives our clients confidence, of course, and our long-standing position as the pioneer of high quality health insurance has not precluded us from being innovators, too. By listening to our clients, and closely monitoring all their health needs when they're away from home, we are able to respond with plans to suit each and every individual. These range from the most comprehensive cover it is possible to buy, to a simple "top-up" plan which elevates the sort of plain insurance provided by an employer or a local scheme to the worry-free level of excellence that IHI danmark a/s is renowned for.

Fill out the coupon today and discover how the world's best health insurance can help you to face the future with confidence.

International Health Insurance danmark a/s.
64a Athol Street, Douglas, Isle of Man, British Isles.
Tel: +44 624 677412. Fax: +44 624 675856.

The card that gives credit to your health

Name _____

Address _____

_____

Country _____ Tel _____

Nationality _____ Age _____

International Health Insurance danmark a/s

64a Athol Street, Douglas, Isle of Man, British Isles.
Tel: +44 624 677412. Fax: +44 624 675856.

A worldwide private health insurance plan for expatriates in retirement abroad is also available from Exeter Friendly Society, Devon (see pages 79 and 81). This organisation is a registered friendly society and a member of the International Federation of Voluntary Health Societies.

The Society widened its scale of operations in the early 1960s with the aim of giving lifetime protection against the high cost of medical treatment abroad, and members are guaranteed the right to renew cover every year throughout their life irrespective of their claims record.

As treatment charges vary from one country to another, the scheme gives subscribers a choice of several scales of benefit covering average costs, or a super scale for areas where charges are higher. The hospital accommodation benefit within each scale can be increased by buying extra accommodation units.

The scales cover a wide selection of treatments in addition to hospital costs. Claims may be submitted in respect of convalescence, private health checks, body scans, private outpatient treatment, qualified nursing at home, surgical appliances and so on.

Details of annual subscriptions can be obtained from Exeter Friendly Society, Beach Hill House, Walnut Gardens, Exeter EX4 4DG.

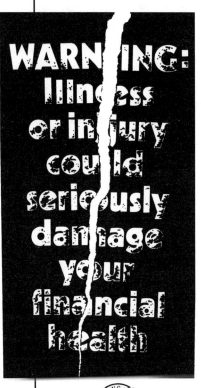

WARNING: Illness or injury could seriously damage your financial health

international
HEALTHPLAN

PPP International Health Plan is specifically designed for expatriates. Non-expatriates may apply subject to any applicable governing laws or exchange control regulations.

What would happen if you or your family needed medical treatment whilst living abroad?

Are the local health care facilities accessible and adequate? If not, is private medical treatment affordable - probably not!

Membership of the International Health Plan from Private Patients Plan (PPP), the UK's second largest medical insurer is the solution.

It ensures financial peace of mind and provides access to the best medical facilities for you and your family.

There is a wide range of options from which to choose, so you'll be able to select a scheme that's just right for your needs and budget.

For full details return the coupon by fax to (44) 892 515167 or by post to:

**PPP International
PPP House,
Tunbridge Wells,
Kent, TN1 1BJ
United Kingdom**

Alternatively, and if you require immediate cover, telephone any time, day or night:

☎ **(44) 81 667 9988**

TITLE: Mr ☐ Mrs ☐ Miss ☐ Ms ☐ Dr. ☐ Other ☐

SURNAME:

FORENAME:

ADDRESS:

COUNTRY:

TEL NO: FAX NO:

CURRENT SCHEME: RENEWAL DATE:

Daily Telegraph Guide

MS 6041

85

WPA Health International offer three full health schemes for expatriates with worldwide cover including USA/Canada and also excluding these two countries. In addition they have a cash plan which provides money benefit when in hospital, or towards dental, optical, consultation fees and maternity benefit.

The expatriate scheme includes hospitalisation, emergency medical evacuation and a no-claims bonus of one year free after five consecutive years without a claim.

On permanent return to the UK members can be transferred to a WPA UK policy with no change in registration conditions.

A new service offered by Private Patients Plan (PPP) to subscribers to their overseas medical insurance scheme is the provision of a number for a telephone help-line to those living or working abroad, where they can be put in touch with medical service providers in the area where they are residing. This will include names and addresses of local English-speaking doctors, dentists and dental clinics. Where possible the names of two or more contacts will be given. Information on opticians, ophthalmologists and suppliers of contact lenses will also be available.

Subscribers to the PPP low-cost travel insurance option under their International Health Plan can also secure pre-travel information on visa requirements, vaccinations, climatic conditions, health warnings, currency and driving regulations, and also banking hours for any country they are visiting.

Both help-lines are available round the clock, 365 days per year.

Part 2
Moving Out, Settling In and Coming Back

Chapter 8
Moving Overseas

Moving house can be a traumatic experience at the best of times. At worst, with careless planning and trying to cut costs, it can be a disaster!

Before the actual move there are always weeks of preparation; bringing down old boxes from the loft and poring over their contents to see if they are worth keeping; clearing out the garage and throwing away the odd bits of wood and junk that you were keeping in case they proved useful. Ask any remover – we've all got much more in our homes than we think.

So imagine the additional problems facing a householder who is moving abroad. He (or usually she) has to go through the family's possessions and ruthlessly pare them down to manageable proportions for packing into a container for shipping or air freighting to perhaps the other side of the world.

Difficult decisions have to be made, such as whether to take the three-piece suite and dining room table/chairs or to buy new ones once you are settled in your new home. How do prices compare? Whom to ask?

Invaluable help can be provided by a reputable international remover who will be able to advise you as to what is best left behind and replaced at destination and what should be taken to save expense or because of supply difficulties and so on. It costs nothing to invite a remover to survey your household goods and personal effects and to provide an estimate of the removal costs; and it could also save you a lot of time and energy.

The first main danger which people can suffer is sending their possessions through a freight forwarding agent who delivers only as far as the port of entry of the destination country. This means that you will have to arrange Customs clearance and also find someone to transfer your belongings from the port to your new home or, if that is not ready, into store. Without knowledgeable help, finding proper local storage facilities is no easy task in a strange country.

Second, a surprising number of people rely on a remover with no financial or other backing who nevertheless quotes extremely attractive prices. Unfortunately, in the past this lack of financial

HOW TO ORGANISE YOUR INTERNATIONAL REMOVAL

The first steps you should take are to determine which of your household furniture and personal possessions you wish to take with you to your new home, and which you are going to leave behind, perhaps in storage until you return.

It is often useful to find out something about the kind of property available at your destination. Is it likely to have fitted wardrobes? Do UK electrical appliances work in the country you are moving to? If not can they be adapted and if so how much will this cost? The answers to these kind of questions can help you reach a decision. What is the value of items of furniture at your destination? If the item is expensive to buy new at your destination and the secondhand value in the UK is not good then it makes sense to take it with you. As a general rule furniture that has been purchased within the last five years, and all types of antique furniture are well worth taking with you as their value overseas is often greater than it is here.

When you have decided which items are going with you then it's time to phone your removal company and arrange for their representative to come to your home to survey your household effects. During the survey the representative will compile an inventory of the items that you wish to take with you, assess the packing requirement and estimate the weight and volume of your possessions. The weight and volume will be crucial to the overall price paid and is usually expressed in Cubic Feet/Lbs or Cubic Metres/Kilos.

Once the remover has completed the survey a cost estimate for the removal of your possessions can be prepared.

An international removal is comprised of three important steps. Firstly there is the packing of your possessions (the origin service) which involves carefully ensuring that all items are wrapped in protective materials and all small articles eg glassware, are boxed in sturdy export cartons and cases. For delicate items of furniture, eg a grandfather clock, a special custom built crate may also have to be made. Once the packing has been completed your possessions can then be loaded and for surface transportation this will be either into a removal van or a 20ft or 40ft steel container. For air transportation, and for some surface destinations the loading will be into a wooden case, often referred to as a lift van. A lift van gives additional protection to high value possessions and is constructed so that it can fit neatly inside either a removal van or a steel container.

The second step to be carried out is the transportation which will either be by road, sea or air. The remover will select the most appropriate vehicle, ship or aeroplane according to the route and your final destination.

Once the transportation has been completed and your possessions have arrived at their destination the third step (the destination service) can begin. The remover will, through his colleague at your destination, arrange customs clearance, delivery and unpacking of your effects into your new home.

In other words the reverse of the packing services at origin will take place during the destination service.

Many of the leading international removers are shareholders in OMNI, Overseas Moving Network Incorporated, which is a consortium of the leading removers of the World welded together into a tight knit organisation designed to give high quality service at many worldwide locations. If you choose to move with an OMNI remover then smoothness and quality should be the passowrds of your relocation. John Mason International, with offices in London, Liverpool and Manchester, are one of the leading OMNI members in the United Kingdom.

base has often meant the remover going bankrupt and being unable to carry out the move for which the remover was contracted. In this case, the hapless customer, who will already have paid the first remover, will have to pay yet again for someone else to complete the move. Regrettably, the chance of redress is so limited as not to be worth considering.

Both these circumstances can be avoided if you choose a contractor from among the Overseas Group members of the British Association of Removers (BAR). All international member companies have links throughout the world with equally reputable removers, through their international trade association, the Federation of International Furniture Removers (FIDI).

Membership of FIDI means that a contractor can arrange a door-to-door international removal, working with a reliable and knowledgeable firm in the destination country who will deal with the formalities relating to Customs clearance and (if pets are involved) quarantine regulations, store the consignment as long as necessary and finally deliver it to your new address.

While these relationships offer a comforting level of expertise, the BAR Overseas Group also provides tangible security, through its guarantee of the financial soundness of its members. Its BAR-IMMI advance payment scheme provides a written guarantee that, should a member company fail to fulfil its commitments to a customer, the removal will be completed at no extra cost or the money refunded.

So people moving overseas who use a BAR Overseas Group member need have no fear of settling in their new home with only the clothes they stand up in while the rest of their belongings are stranded in Britain – something which has happened to many people using non-BAR Overseas Group members which have gone out of business.

In addition, a qualified remover can also guide you through the minefield of documentation relating to import/export licences and Customs regulations.

Electrical appliances may not be compatible with voltages in your destination country and your TV and video will probably not be suitable. If you are moving to a warmer climate you will definitely need a larger fridge/freezer, so, unless you have recently bought a new one, the freezer, or fridge, is not worth taking. Many houses have built-in furniture, so you may not need your wardrobes either.

On the other hand, there are some items which cost less in Britain than elsewhere and it may be worth buying these before you go. Under the government's personal export scheme, people who are emigrating or who intend spending at least 12 months out of the country are allowed to buy certain goods free of VAT charges. Your remover will be able to give you details of this.

Take good carpets, high-quality furniture and fine china/glass if you wish, and remember to include some articles of winter clothing. Even in warmer climes the evenings can be chilly.

Take your tool kit too, as tools are costly to replace wherever you live. But think twice about taking cane furniture as this is viewed with grave suspicion in most countries. As a precaution the quarantine authorities may decide to have the furniture fumigated at your expense, and the cost is high.

English books are often expensive in foreign countries, so you may wish to take not only your present collection, but also some for future reading and reference.

Special provision usually has to be made for pets and cars. In some countries both may be banned; in others (such as the USA) the car will have to comply with exhaust emission legislation.

Finally, do not forget to make a complete inventory of everything to be moved and to give your remover a copy. Any discrepancy between the list and the contents of your consignment could result in Customs officials delaying clearance – and although there may be the temptation to slip a few 'extras' in, don't try it; Customs searches are rigorous and the penalties severe.

For more hints about moving abroad, a free leaflet is available by sending a stamped and self-addressed envelope (preferably 9 x 4 in) to the British Association of Removers, 3 Churchill Court, 58 Station Road, North Harrow HA2 7SA. There is also an easy-to-use audiovisual programme available free of charge to local associations which gives complete advice on how to go about a removal.

Removal checklist

Don't forget to arrange a UK contact address and to tell the following that you are moving abroad:

Your bank.

Income Tax Office. Notify the Inland Revenue, giving the exact date of departure.

National Insurance/DSS. For benefits, allowances, pension. Send your full name, date of birth, full National Insurance number, details of country to which you are moving and duration of your stay to the DSS Overseas Branch, Newcastle upon Tyne NE98 1YX.

Vehicle licence. If you are taking your vehicle abroad for longer than a year this is regarded as a 'permanent export'. In this case you should return your existing (new style) registration document to the Vehicle Licensing Centre, Swansea SA99 1AB, filling in the 'permanent export' section. Alternatively, you can apply to your local Vehicle Registration Office for the necessary forms.

Driving licence. You should retain your British driving licence (European Communities Model). Many countries, in addition to those in the EC, recognise it as valid; a list of those which do not is available from the AA.

International driving licence. An international driving licence is obtainable from the AA (even if you are not a member) and is valid for one year. The licence is not valid in the country where it is issued so you must obtain it before leaving the UK. Most countries require residents to hold a local driving licence, so check whether this is the case on taking up your new residence.

Motor insurance. Notify your insurers of the date of your departure – your insurance should be cancelled from that date and you should obtain a refund for the rest of the insurance period. Ask your insurance company for a letter outlining your no-claim record to show to your new insurer.

Life and other insurances. Notify the companies concerned or your insurance broker if you use one.

Dentist. Let your dentist know you are moving, as a matter of courtesy; it will save him or her posting useless check-up reminders.

Optician. It may be useful to take a copy of your prescription with you.

Private health insurance. Notify subscriber records department.

Gas. If you use it, notify your local gas showroom, giving at least *48 hours'* notice. They will give you a standard form to fill in with details of the move and any current hire-purchase agreements. If appliances are to be removed the gas company requires as much notice as possible to arrange an appointment; there is a disconnection charge.

Electricity. Notify your local office or showroom at least *48 hours* before moving. Arrangements are much the same as for gas.

Water. The local water supply company should also be notified at least *48 hours* before the move. Drain tanks and pipes if the house is to remain empty in winter.

Telephone. Notify your local telephone sales office, as shown in the front of your directory, at least *seven days* before the move.

Local authority. Notify the town hall of your departure. You may be entitled to a partial refund of your Council Tax.

Libraries. Return books and give in tickets to be cancelled.

Professional advisers. Solicitors, accountants, stockbrokers, insurance brokers etc. Make sure they have a forwarding address.

Stocks and shares. Write to the company registrar at the address on the last annual report or share certificates.

Organisations and clubs. Any business, civic, social, cultural, sports or automobile club of which you are a member. For the AA write to Membership Subscription and Records, PO Box 50, Basingstoke, Hampshire, for the RAC write to RAC House, Lansdowne Road, East Croydon, Surrey.

Credit card companies. Advise them that you are leaving the country.

HP companies. Notify the office where repayments are made. You will need to settle your accounts.

Local business accounts. Department stores, newsagents, dairy, baker, chemist, dry cleaner, laundry, motor service station.

Publications. Cancel postal subscriptions to magazines, professional and trade journals, books and record clubs etc, and orders for newspapers.

National Health Service. Return your NHS card to the Family Practitioners' Committee for your area, giving your date of departure, or hand in the card to the immigration officer at your point of departure.

Pension schemes. If you have a 'frozen' or paid-up pension from a previous employer be sure to notify the pension trust of your new address.

TV and video. If you have rented equipment, make arrangements to return it.

Post Office. Notify day of departure and UK contact address, as letters can be forwarded for a fee.

Personal Giro. The Post Office have a special SAE for this.

Premium Bonds. Anything rather than join the sad list of unclaimed prizes! Contact Bonds and Stocks Office, Lytham St Anne's, Lancashire FY0 1YN to check the current position, because in a few countries Premium Bond holdings may contravene the lottery laws.

Save As You Earn and National Savings Certificates. It is important to notify any permanent change of address, particularly for index-linked retirement issue certificates and SAYE contracts. Advise the National Savings Certificate Office, Durham DH99 1NS, quoting the contract number(s).

National Savings Bank. Notify at Glasgow G58 1SB.

Your landlord. If you are a tenant, give the appropriate notice to quit.

Your tenants. If you are a landlord, that UK address you've organised will be needed.

Your employer. Give new address details, or a contact address, in writing.

Schools. Try to give your children's schools a term's notice that they will be leaving. If you wish your children's education to be continued in Britain contact your local education authority or the Department for Education, Sanctuary Buildings, Great Smith Street, London SW1P 3BT, for advice.

Make sure your *removers* have any temporary contact address and phone numbers for you, both in the UK and abroad, so they can get in touch with you if need arises. It is also useful to them if you can tell them when you expect to arrive in your new country.

Reproduced by courtesy of Allied Pickfords Ltd.

Taking a car abroad

After a virtual lifetime of driving on the left, British people still tend to prefer right-hand drive and will therefore consider buying their car here and taking it with them. First check at the embassy of the country you propose to live in that private car imports are permitted.

Probably the best way to plan this is to make a list of what you will want your car to do. You may no longer be using it to commute, so there will be less stopping and starting; the road surfaces may be less good than those you are used to, so you may consider taking a good second-hand car rather than a brand-new one. You will not then be so worried about driving through very narrow streets. In some places drivers actually park by shunting the cars ahead and behind!

In the Channel Islands small old cars are fine if your budget is tight. The road network will limit the amount of driving you are likely to do and a good used car with a guarantee can be bought from a reputable dealer.

If you are used to driving a large, comfortable car in this country, when you go abroad you may feel happier with a new, luxurious, well-appointed small car rather than a very old model. If you buy a new car in the UK before going abroad, you can use it here for six months, run it in and have your first service before you take it overseas.

Check the servicing facilities in the area where you plan to live. It would be unwise to take a car abroad if the nearest dealer service is 70 miles away. This factor may well limit your choice.

A big car will be expensive on petrol consumption and difficult to park. If you will be living in an apartment and there is no garage, the car will usually be left in the street and possibly for long periods at that. Consider carefully the security of your car and what you may have in it. Choose a model with locking wheel nuts and high-quality locks so that it is hard to get into without smashing the windows. Radio thefts are prevalent in some countries; therefore you may wish to consider a demountable radio.

Should you decide to take a small car to a hot country, buy one with a sun roof because the smaller cars carry no air conditioning.

Lead-free petrol is now widely available and you should check whether your engine will take this quality. Some engines need minor adaptation.

If you plan to put small pieces of furniture in the car for your move abroad, a hatchback is easier. On the other hand, an economical way of organising a move to the Continent is to hire a transit van, load it up with your furniture and drive it there, returning with the empty van to pick up your own car and any remaining luggage, but make sure you have the correct documentation (see page 93).

Personal export of new cars

Those who wish to buy a new car and use it in the UK before they go abroad to live can take advantage of a special scheme which allows the purchase without payment of VAT or car tax. Motor cycles and motor caravans can also be purchased under the scheme. UK citizens who use the scheme may have the use of the vehicle in this country for up to six months before it is exported.

Form VAT 410, obtainable from UK manufacturers and foreign manufacturers' sole selling agents approved by Customs and Excise to operate the scheme, must be completed and returned to the manufacturer or agent. Customs and Excise will need to approve the application, after which the vehicle can be delivered to you. It is wise to allow plenty of time for the procedure. Only the applicant may take delivery of the vehicle, and there are restrictions on who can drive it while it is still in the UK. It must not be disposed of in any way before it is exported.

The vehicle may be taken abroad temporarily before the export date shown on the documents, but must be declared to Customs on its return to the UK, and the documentation produced. If the car is not exported by the due date for any reason (even if it is stolen or damaged), then VAT and car tax will become payable on its value when new, so it is vital to insure it for its full value as soon as it is delivered to you.

It is worth making shipping arrangements well in advance of the due export date, to avoid last-minute problems which could involve you in payment of VAT and car tax. These payments will also be levied if the car is brought back into the UK within six months of the export date on the documents.

Details of the scheme are explained in Notice 705, available from your local Customs and Excise Office.

It is possible to take delivery of a new car outside the UK free of VAT and car tax if you do not want to use it before you go abroad to live; this is a direct export and the manufacturer or sole selling agent of a foreign manufacturer in the UK will be able to supply full information.

Taking your existing car abroad

If you take the car you own at present abroad for longer than 12 months, this is regarded as a permanent export and the procedure is described in leaflet V526, obtainable from your local Vehicle Licensing Office.

The following procedure applies to exports from England, Scotland, Wales and the Isles of Scilly only – not to Northern Ireland or the Isle of Man where cars are registered separately.

Complete section 2 on the back of the Vehicle Registration Document, entering the proposed date of export, and send the document to your local Vehicle Licensing Office or to the Driver and Vehicle Licensing Centre. This should be done well in advance of your departure.

You will receive back a Certificate of Export (V561) which in effect confirms your vehicle registration.

A different procedure applies in Northern Ireland as vehicles are registered locally; it is necessary to register and license a car taken *to* Northern Ireland permanently as soon as the current British tax disc expires, if not before. The Certificate of Export mentioned above will still be necessary.

Motoring services in Europe

The International Touring Alliance has its headquarters in Geneva, and driving clubs throughout Europe, including the Automobile Association, are affiliated to it. These clubs provide a wide range of services to each other's members travelling abroad, so membership of one is worthwhile.

Austria
Osterreichischer Automobil Motorrad and Touring Club (OAMTC)

Belgium
Touring Club Royal de Belgique (TCB)

Cyprus
Cyprus Automobile Association (CAA)

France
Association Française des Automobilistes (AFA). (The Automobile Association has a Continental Emergency Centre at Boulogne-sur-Mer.)

Germany
Allgemeine Deutscher Automobile Club (ADAC)

Greece
Automobile and Touring Club of Greece (ELPA)

Italy
Automobile Club d'Italia (ACI)

Luxembourg
Automobile Club du Grand-Duché de Luxembourg (ACL)

Netherlands
Koninklijke Nederlandse Toeristenbond (ANWB)

Portugal
Automovel Club de Portugal (ACP)

Spain
Real Automovil Club de España (RACE)

Switzerland
Touring Club Suisse (TCS)

Turkey
Turkiye Turing Ve Otomobil Kurumu

Chapter 9
Settling In

After the excitement of the move and the traumas of starting a new life in a foreign country, a period of calm ought to be enjoyed while settling down in your newly acquired villa or apartment.

Unless you are very experienced in uprooting your family and shifting them to an entirely new environment you are almost certain to have a few problems to solve before you are really accepted as a 'local' by your neighbours in your adopted country, so here are a few tips on the subject of settling in.

Documentation

Most countries require the completion of some documentation by new residents from overseas. It may be as simple as having an up-to-date British passport, so make sure that yours has at least one year to run before it expires in order to give yourself a breathing space prior to having it renewed by the local British Consul or the passport office in Britain. The one-year passport which can be obtained from post offices in Britain is not a satisfactory document for emigrants as its life is too short and it is not always acceptable to overseas authorities.

If you already hold a pink driving licence issued in the UK and endorsed 'European Communities model', you do not need to obtain any other licence to drive a car in any EC country.

The International Driving Licence issued by the AA or RAC contains translations in nine languages plus an identity photograph of the holder. This impresses officialdom in some countries, particularly if you are stopped by the police, but many nations now require new residents to apply for a local driving licence. This may involve the completion of a simple form and the payment of a fee, but in some instances it is necessary to pass a driving test and to repass that test on achieving the age of threescore years and ten or some other arbitrary figure.

Residence permits are required in many countries and before these are issued, certain qualifications need to be fulfilled. These may take the form of satisfactory certificates from the police or legal bodies in your homeland regarding social or crime-free behaviour. Bank certificates are also often necessary to prove that you have sufficient income and/or capital to sustain an appropriate standard of living, so that you will not become a burden to your host country.

Take care regarding technical terms used in some countries. For instance a *permanencia* is not a permanent permit to reside in Spain but temporary permission to remain in Spain for a further 90 days after the first 90 days granted to tourists have expired. A *residencia* is a permit to reside in Spain.

If you are hoping to take up some form of employment in your new home country, examine the laws regarding work permits. In areas of high unemployment these are often very hard to obtain and permission to work in your own business which you are planning to set up is sometimes required. Professional people such as doctors, lawyers and accountants may need to be accepted into membership of the local professional guild before being permitted to practise their particular skill and foreigners do not always find it easy to qualify, particularly if the profession is already over-staffed.

In EC countries mobility of labour should be unrestricted but this ideal situation has not yet been achieved throughout the Community.

Remember, it is never worthwhile, in the long run, to flout regulations; if you are caught, a large fine can be imposed or you may be banned from living in the country of your choice.

The fees charged by local consultants such as the *gestor* (an administrator who can deal with many financial and legal problems) or *abogado* (lawyer) in Spain are generally money well spent when dealing with officialdom, for it is much better to solve any problem first time round.

Finances

Before departing for your new home make sure that you have settled your financial affairs and that your income will be sufficient for your requirements. The cost of living in countries with a temperate climate can be lower than in northern Europe as far less has to be spent on home heating and warm clothing. But food is more expensive if you insist on eating familiar brand names imported from the UK or America.

In planning your finances do ensure that you have a reasonable reserve fund to cover unexpected or unplanned expenditure on setting up home, for it is impossible to anticipate each and every need for a new life-style.

Keeping your vote while living abroad

On moving abroad, you retain your right to vote in UK and European parliamentary elections; however, there are a number of conditions of which you should be aware. To be eligible you must be a British citizen and satisfy *either* of two sets of conditions:

Set 1

- you have previously been on the electoral register for an address in the UK;
- you were living there on the qualifying date;*
- there are no more than 20 years between the qualifying dates for that register and the one on which you now wish to appear.

Set 2

- you last lived in the UK less than 20 years before the qualifying date for the register on which you now wish to appear;
- you were too young to be on the electoral register which was based on the last qualifying date before you left;
- a parent or guardian was on the electoral register, for the address where you were living on that date;
- you are at least 18 years old, or will become 18 when the register comes into force.

You have to register every year on or before the qualifying date and you may continue to register while overseas for 20 years from the qualifying date for the last electoral register on which you appeared as a UK resident.

How to register

To register you must fill in an Overseas Elector's Declaration form which you can get from the nearest British consular or diplomatic mission. The following information will be required: your full name and overseas address, the UK address where you were last registered and the date you left the UK. The first-time overseas elector will have to find someone to support the declaration who is aged 18 or over, has a British passport and is a British citizen, is not living in the UK, and who knows you but is not a close relative. First-time

---

* The qualifying date each year is 10 October in England, Scotland and Wales and 15 September in Northern Ireland. This is for the electoral register which comes into force on 16 February of the following year and remains in force for 12 months from that date.

overseas electors who left the UK before they were old enough to register will also have to provide a copy of their full birth certificate and information about the parent or guardian on whose registration they are relying.

How to vote and remain registered
You do not have a postal vote. Instead you must appoint a proxy who will vote on your behalf. He or she must be a citizen of Britain, the Commonwealth or the Republic of Ireland, a UK resident, and willing and legally able to vote on your behalf. The application form for appointing a proxy is attached to the Overseas Declaration form. Your declaration, proxy application and, if required, birth certificate should be returned to the electoral registration officer for the area where you were last registered. The electoral registration officer will write to tell you whether you will qualify as an overseas elector and be included on the register: if you do not, he or she will explain why. You will be sent a reminder each year, enclosing another declaration form.

Where to shop

Countries with an outdoor way of life mostly have regular weekly markets in the main square or some other convenient location in each town and many villages.

These are the places where you can learn to shop for fruit, vegetables and other products and get good value for money, but you do need some linguistic ability if you are going to have any meaningful conversation with the local traders.

Supermarkets abound in towns with a sizeable local or tourist population. These establishments may be a little more expensive than the markets, but they do stock prepacked products, all individually priced, which means that you can serve yourself to packs that suit your requirements and know immediately how much they cost.

Although you will miss familiar foods, local products are often just as satisfactory and fruit and vegetables are particularly good value. Fish caught fresh from the sea is much tastier than frozen slabs of produce whose origins are far distant from the area of consumption. Meat producers are also more skilled in marketing cuts of joints, chops and other meat products than in former years. Even British-type sausages can be found in some shops.

Specialised shops covering ironmongery, shoes, clothes, pharmaceutical products and many other household requirements demand a little more courage for shoppers unskilled in the local tongue, but practice makes perfect; if you do not make the effort to use these establishments you will never make progress in shopping, and some of the staff may be able to talk your language!

It is well worth while taking advice from local people when planning the purchase of luxury items such as leather goods and jewellery as they should know the shops which offer the best value.

Local relationship

If you are ever to become accepted by your neighbours you must endeavour to mix and talk with them, irrespective of whether they are of the same nationality as yourself.

The apparent reticence of British people, particularly those from the large towns and cities, must be overcome when living abroad; otherwise new residents will find it almost impossible to establish the friendships which are so essential to a happy life in a new environment away from familiar places and people. Loneliness must be avoided if at all possible.

Much can be learned from those who have lived in a particular area for a number of years or a lifetime.

Domesticity

Running a house in a strange country can produce problems for the housekeeper. Different types of food, new styles of catering, a much warmer climate, strange shops with unfamiliar product brands can all produce periods of uncertainty during the first months of residing in a different country. It is during this period that each partner should show a greater interest in the household routine by trying to assist with daily chores and shopping, to the detriment, if necessary, of work in the garden or even giving up a round of golf!

Hobbies and sports

Most people should have interests that not only entertain them but also, if possible, produce some useful end results.

Woodwork, photography, painting, model making, needlework, floral decoration, sewing or music are just a few suggestions for acquiring or improving useful skills to occupy leisure hours, all year round.

In the summer everyone can enjoy walking, gardening, bird watching and nature studies in the open air. Those able to participate in sport will find opportunities for lawn bowls, swimming, archery, tennis and riding plus extensive opportunities for golf in an ideal climate.

Many of these activities have their own clubs which enable members to mix and meet.

Voluntary work

In every country there are opportunities for voluntary welfare work among the young and the old, and also for looking after the welfare of animals. This can be a most rewarding full- or part-time occupation and the need is great, particularly with local underprivileged children and the elderly, who are often housebound and lonely. For them a regular weekly visit to do some shopping or just to have a chat is a kindness which is much appreciated. All able-bodied people should keep an eye on those who are physically handicapped or elderly, and frequent visits will help to allay their fears of being taken ill with nobody near to help them.

Organisations of expatriates often establish a service through their members to undertake this valuable welfare work and this should receive willing support from those who are capable of looking after others as well as themselves.

Clubs and social organisations

In almost every location where there are a number of expatriates living in fairly close proximity, clubs covering a wide variety of activities become established.

These might include simple lunch clubs for males, females or both sexes, where a wide variety of topics can be discussed and differing opinions aired over a meal and a glass of wine or other refreshment. From this might emerge a debating club, or specialised clubs covering subjects such as gardening, music, chess, bridge, darts, amateur dramatics, film societies and table tennis to mention but a few.

Apartment blocks in Spain generally have a Community of Owners, so that individuals can have a say in the management of the communal facilities, public parts or gardens, and the expenditure on external maintenance, caretaking staff, refuse disposal and so on. These regular gatherings of owners provide an opportunity to meet other owners in the development, which might not occur in the normal way where there are a large number of units in the scheme.

Exploration

Please do not settle too permanently in your new home, for there are almost certainly many sights to be seen and territory to be explored within easy reach of your base.

All who are active in mind and body should take the opportunity of visiting all the noteworthy historical monuments and modern 'wonders of the world' within, say, 30 miles of their home, so as to be aware of local attractions and knowledgeable about the history, flora and fauna of the territory where they live. This will make life much more interesting and it is to be hoped that the knowledge acquired can be passed on to newcomers who are ignorant of the local attractions.

Many of the foregoing remarks have been devoted to urging expatriates to get out and about, and to help not only themselves but others less fortunate. However, a word of warning – do not overdo these activities or undertake too many obligations which will make them all onerous. Just take life steadily so that you enjoy the daily round without getting too tired or exhausted. If you do this you will have greater enjoyment from all your activities.

Appointments and punctuality

Do remember that you need a degree of patience when dealing with those who have a Latin or Mediterranean temperament. In business or even domestic life you may have considered punctuality to be vital, but those fortunate enough to live a more placid, easygoing life do not consider this trait to be of such great importance.

If you reside in, say, Portugal or Spain, you will soon discover that a meeting planned for 10 am may not take place until noon, or even the following day. No discourtesy is intended for 'there is always tomorrow for things not done today'. A charming philosophy if you can get away with it and one that gradually becomes acceptable when you get to know your contacts better.

Chapter 10

Coming Back to the UK

The biggest single event which causes emigrants to return to their native country is the death of one partner, when the survivor feels that he or she just cannot cope with life alone in another country.

Elderly people come to realise they are less able to care and cater for themselves with the passage of time and they feel that they would prefer to reside near the family and old friends in their declining years.

Another factor that makes people decide to give up the 'new life' and return to their former living conditions is the discovery that they are not really happy in a strange environment with all its contributory features such as different weather conditions, unfamiliar food, new traditions and ways of life, or perhaps just a deep dissatisfaction with the property purchased in the sun, or with one's neighbours.

There is no disgrace in admitting defeat and returning home, but there are certain factors which must be considered in advance of any plans to move. These include the following:

Sale of the overseas property

For the best results, appoint a well-established, legally constituted estate agent to sell your home. He or she will value it for you and undertake the marketing. In some areas a speedy sale can be effected if the price is right, but remember agents' commissions are much higher on the Continent compared with the UK. Ascertain the agent's terms before giving instructions to sell and don't be surprised if you are quoted commission figures of between 5 and 10 per cent of the purchase price.

Once appointed, let the agent get on with the sales campaign, but make sure that you keep the house neat and tidy at all times so that it will look its best to any unexpected prospective buyers, no matter what time they call.

Grant a sole agency for a limited period whenever possible and leave the agent to appoint a sub-agency if this is thought desirable.

The CLUB WITH AN INTERNATIONAL DIMENSION

for both men and women

*T*he Royal Over-Seas League provides the ideal club for internationally minded men and women. *Its London clubhouse, Over-Seas House, comprises a beautiful period property in the heart of St James's, overlooking Green Park and offering an exceptionally wide range of superb facilities.   There is a second clubhouse in Edinburgh and members enjoy reciprocal facilities with other clubs worldwide.*

The London clubhouse facilities include:

❏ Convenient central location close to London's West End shops and theatres.
❏ 72 quality bedrooms with satellite TV.
❏ Renowned restaurant and buttery, also bar and drawing room.
❏ Superb Garden adjoining Green Park.
❏ Open 7 days a week. Car Park.
❏ All facilities at club prices.
❏ 7 conference and banqueting rooms with capacity ranging from 15 to 200 and full business facilities. *(Membership not required. Please send for details).*
❏ Reciprocal sporting and exercise arrangements with local clubs.

Photos of Over-Seas House, London (Top to bottom):
The Central Lounge. The Garden. The Main Entrance.

The Royal Over-Seas League's clubhouse in Princes Street Edinburgh, overlooking the Castle, provides similar facilities and there are regular social, international and cultural events organised at both venues.   Membership includes access to 57 reciprocal clubs in 16 countries worldwide.

 Royal Over-Seas League

Over-Seas House, Park Place, St James's Street, London SW1A 1LR
Tel: 071 408 0214.   Fax: 071 499 6738.
Enquiries: 9.30am-5.30pm Monday-Friday.

Membership of the Royal Over-Seas League is available to British subjects, Commonwealth citizens and associated membership to various other nationals

To:- **Membership Secretary,**
Royal Over-Seas League, Park Place, St James's Street, London SW1A 1LR.
Please send me details of membership of the ROYAL OVER-SEAS LEAGUE.

Full Name (in Capitals)..
....
Residential Address (in Capitals) ....
....
Tel No .... [DTG]

Subscription Rates

London £157
Edinburgh £123
Country £89
Overseas £68
Younger Members £46

An initial joining fee of half the annual supscription is also charged.   Corporate rates are available to a large number of associations, institutes and societies.   Please ask the Membership Secretary for details.

In this case a commission-sharing arrangement will be worked out between the two firms.

Next, ascertain the current regulations regarding the repatriation of the sales proceeds and any capital gains. Make sure that permission will be granted to remit the money received from the sale back to the UK. Generally this is allowed but sometimes you have to produce evidence that foreign currency was imported to pay for the property in the first place.

An alternative is to sell the property to a non-resident of the country where it is located and have the proceeds remitted to your normal UK bank. This procedure works quite well and obviates the necessity for applications which need to be approved by official-dom. The change of ownership must, of course, be registered at the local Land Registry; also local legal fees and tax will have to be paid.

Check up on current procedures for pension and other receipts. Give the bank and other officials adequate time to make the appropriate arrangements.

Taxation

On returning to the UK after a number of years abroad, your status for taxation purposes will probably change quite dramatically and it is essential to seek full advice from an accountant or tax expert.

Exchange control

Restrictions on the export of capital are imposed by a few countries. If you have substantial capital invested in shares or a local bank account, check the procedures and restrictions (if any) about the repatriation of your funds. A comprehensive review should be undertaken of all investments, with the aid of expert advice.

It is sensible to re-examine testamentary provisions on return to the UK, particularly if a will has been drawn up in a foreign country. Don't forget to advise relations, friends, business contacts and insurance companies of your new address on returning to the UK. Work through the removal checklist on pages 93–6 in case it applies to your move back.

Chapter 11

The End

Death comes to us all eventually so it is wise to have made some plans in advance if you are living in a foreign country, and the following notes may be of some help to prepare for the ultimate eventuality.

A surprising number of people fail to make a will, or do not update one when it has become inappropriate because of the passing of the years and the arrival of new circumstances.

Everyone, no matter how large or small their estate, should make a will, properly drawn up by a lawyer; the fee expended on this advice is money well spent if it avoids any complications after death.

Both wife and husband should make wills and everyone moving abroad or retiring to a new country should take advice on the rules of what constitutes a valid will in the country in which they propose to reside in the future.

In some countries there are laws which protect the family of the deceased and, as a result, the estate has to be divided so as to ensure that the surviving spouse, and also any children, are adequately catered for; after this the testator can deal with the remaining estate in accordance with any particular wishes.

Every responsible person should compile a 'What I own and where it is kept' list giving details of investments, insurance policies and property etc. This will save next of kin and executors much work and worry, eventually.

As far as the actual arrangements for the burial are concerned, those who wish to be interred in the UK should realise that the cost of sending the body back to the homeland can be substantial, so adequate financial arrangements should be made in advance to cover this by setting up a separate fund, or taking out a special insurance policy.

If you are being buried in the place where you die, the arrangements regarding interment may vary from one country to another. Cremation is not always available in every country, so it may be necessary to purchase a plot in a cemetery.

Spain

On the death of a person in Spain, it is necessary to register the fact immediately at the local Civil Registry. This is generally undertaken by a friend or a relative who will need to have a doctor's certificate stating the cause of death. On receipt of a Spanish death certificate, this should be taken to the nearest British Consul's office who will then register the death and issue a British death certificate.

A lawyer should be instructed immediately to deal with the payment of inheritance taxes, for the assets of anyone dying in Spain cannot be distributed until taxes have been paid.

Most cemeteries in Spain are Catholic, but people of any religion may be buried there. In fact, by tradition, bodies are often not buried, but placed in sealed niches above ground. There is a British cemetery at Malaga and an International cemetery at nearby Benalmadena. The latter has burial plots for those who prefer them. The law states that bodies must be interred within 72 hours of death, but not before 24 hours of the sad event. Those who prefer cremation will find that these facilities are scarce, but there are establishments at Madrid, Seville and Malaga. The ashes can be placed in an urn, which can easily be transported back to the UK.

It is advisable to have a Spanish will, but if this does not exist the estate can be distributed in such a way that it complies with the deceased's British will. Those who die intestate will have their estate distributed to the next of kin in accordance with Spanish law.

France

In France, a death has to be registered at the local *Mairie* within 24 hours and a doctor's certificate obtained from the doctor who attended the deceased person, or from a medical person who is retained by the local council.

It is not permitted to close a coffin within 24 hours of death; this act can only be undertaken with the authority of the official by whom the death is registered.

In France, cemeteries belong to the local authorities, who issue licences to undertakers to carry out the actual burial. Despite the fact that there are no separate Jewish or Protestant cemeteries, a tradition has grown up whereby parts of many cemeteries are used only by specified religious groups.

For religious reasons cremation has not been popular in France in the past, but it is now being used more frequently and there are a growing number of crematoria.

Portugal

The tradition in Portugal is for burial to take place very quickly, generally within 24 hours of death. There are undertakers in many towns who have experience of arranging funerals for foreigners; deaths have to be registered at the local Civil Registry where a doctor's certificate showing the cause of death has to be produced.

It is recommended that the British Consulate be informed of the death, especially if a British death certificate is required.

In places where there is a substantial foreign population, cemeteries permit both Catholic and non-Catholic people to be buried.

There is a British cemetery in Lisbon, but space is very limited and only former parishioners of local Anglican churches can now be buried in this cemetery. Some Portuguese cemeteries permit graves to be occupied for only five years, so it is desirable to ascertain that the choice of final resting place is a permanent one. Cremation is permitted in the recently opened Lisbon crematorium.

Italy

In Italy deaths should be registered within 24 hours at the local *municipo* in which the person died. The next of kin usually undertakes this duty, but anyone can do it. Two witnesses are required and a death certificate should be signed by two doctors. Coffins are closed within 24 hours of death and burials should take place within 48 hours.

Cremation is quite common, particularly in the north of the country, and special documents are required. Costs tend to be higher than for ordinary burial.

There are communal cemeteries in most communes, where residents have the right to a free plot when they die.

One final, essential point is the choice of a storage place for your will. Make sure that your next of kin know where this is located, and try at all times to arrange your affairs in a neat and tidy manner so as to make your executor's task as simple as possible.

Often the family solicitor keeps the will and it would be useful if information on bank accounts, insurance policies and so on is also deposited with your legal adviser.

Part 3
A Home Overseas

Chapter 12

Try Before You Buy

As already explained, nobody should consider the purchase of a permanent home abroad without carefully investigating the facilities, amenities and life-style of the chosen district in considerable detail before entering into any commitment to purchase a property.

Without doubt, the most satisfactory way to do this is to rent a property for a period of several months in the area where you think you would like to reside, if possible in the low season when most of the holiday-makers have gone home and the seasonal attractions are no longer available. This will enable you to experience life with local people and get to know some of the foreigners and your own compatriots who have already settled in the area.

From them it should be possible to obtain information and useful tips about the best places to shop, local medical facilities, clubs for the British or other nationalities, sporting amenities and a whole host of other useful data.

With the advantage of local knowledge and contacts, you will soon become experienced at living in a foreign country and have the opportunity of deciding whether you like the life-style or whether in fact you would do better to remain at home.

During the winter months there is generally a good selection of top-quality apartments and villas available for renting at very reasonable prices and information on these can be obtained from local estate agents or firms in the UK who specialise in self-catering holidays. Beach Villas (Holidays) Ltd, 8 Market Passage, Cambridge CB2 3QR (0223 311113) publish an excellent guide to villas and apartments in Spain, France, Greece, Portugal, Cyprus, Turkey, Italy and Florida, USA, which are available through them for holidays; both winter and summer editions are issued, and prices quoted include return air flights, insurance and transportation from the airport to your property.

The *Villa Guide* is a useful publication produced six times a year and available, price £2.25, from Private Villas, 52 High Street, Henley in Arden, Solihull, West Midlands B95 5AN. It lists private villas which are available for renting direct from the owners or their agents. Here again, an inclusive package can include flights from the UK.

Whichever method you adopt to rent a property, do make sure that you are aware in advance of the terms offered by the owner or the letting company. Points well worth checking are the following:

1. Does the quoted cost include maid service?
2. Do you need to take towels?
3. Are gas and electricity charges included in the rental, or do you have to pay the owner's agent for energy consumed during the time in residence?
4. Location of shops and amenities.
5. How far are the sea and airport from the selected property; are there satisfactory transport arrangements made on your behalf?
6. If your flight is delayed and you arrive later than expected, can you gain access to the property?
7. Does the owner or agent provide a starter pack of food for use on arrival at the property? (This is especially important if you travel at weekends.)
8. Brochures often describe a property as, say, 'sleeping six'. What extra charges will be levied if only three people travel and use the accommodation?

Some developers arrange to have a limited number of properties available on larger sites for renting to prospective purchasers; the use of this service is well worthwhile and is generally quite economical.

Having made the momentous decision to purchase a home abroad, do not charge into the transaction blindly, even though it is an exciting proposition which you feel you want to fulfil at the earliest possible moment.

Time will be well-spent reflecting on your immediate and future needs and may well ensure that you do not make any hasty decisions that could turn out to be disastrous later on.

Some people purchase an apartment in their favourite resort, and this may be an excellent choice for annual vacations. But will it be large enough for permanent living? And will you really enjoy residing during the summer months in a building where transient occupants provide a constantly changing scene, with no opportunity to make permanent friends and with the recurring problem of late-night parties? Arrivals and departures can disturb the early hours of the morning because of the whims of charter flights to the UK and other parts of Europe.

Security should be adequate in an apartment block with a resident concierge, but the winter life could be very lonely if there are only one or two year-round owners in residence.

If you buy an apartment, make sure that the block has one or more adequate lifts – as you get older, climbing several flights of stairs may become almost impossible and then you will be dependent on others to fetch your shopping and to undertake errands such as a visit to the bank or post office.

Villa ownership, especially if the property is detached, offers greater privacy, some protection from undue noise and a feeling of true ownership which never seems to come with an apartment.

Many overseas houses have patios or balconies and most have gardens, sometimes large and sometimes small. When you retire you will have more time to potter around your 'estate', but make sure it is planned and laid out so that gardening tasks do not become a burden as you grow older.

The exterior maintenance of any home is an important point to consider in advance. Many units are finished in cement rendering which requires an application of white or coloured emulsion paint every year or two. This is easy to apply on a single-storey dwelling, but requires more effort for a two- or three-storey villa. You may need to employ some professional skill if you find the work too tiring, but the cost should not be too great and it will help to keep costs down if the job can be completed in a few hours.

Even a small villa can easily be made into a permanent home and the purchase price is often not a great deal higher than that of a flat. However, take particular care in your choice of location, for an isolated villa away from shops and facilities could prove particularly inconvenient and lonely, especially if you become less mobile with advancing years and do not possess a car.

How much?

Undoubtedly your very first consideration should be how much you can afford to spend on your new home.

Prices in the sunniest countries of southern Europe vary immensely. It is still possible to purchase a modest studio flatlet near the Mediterranean coast of Spain for not much more than £15,000 – but it will be very small and not in a prime position or of top-class construction. It could fulfil the holiday needs of a couple who want to escape from the uncertainty of Britain's summer climate for two or three weeks annually, but it might well be completely useless as a permanent home or for stays of three months or more.

Opportunities to acquire a large flat or a new detached luxury villa costing £35,000 or more are plentiful in many parts of the sun-belt. If you are very well-off, there should be no difficulty in spending £1 million or more on a modern villa or an old mansion by the sea or in the country in, say, Spain, Portugal or France. Here you can enjoy privacy and live in an elegant style for short or long periods.

After some day-dreaming about your ideal residence, a home which you soon discover is beyond your means, re-examine your finances and decide on a sensible sum that will not eat too deeply into your capital or cost you an excessive amount to maintain.

Abbey National has established Abbey National (Gibraltar) Ltd at 237 Main Street, Gibraltar to provide a UK-style mortgage service to clients purchasing a home on the Costa del Sol and Costa Blanca, Costa Brava, Almeria, Tenerife and Majorca, in Spain, Portugal's Algarve, also Italy. Advice on insurance and other matters is also available.

Some overseas builders and developers are willing to offer short-term loans, generally for not more than 60 per cent of the purchase price and for periods not exceeding five years. Interest rates tend to be high.

Many older home-owners in the UK have considerable equity locked up in their main residences, with little or no mortgage outstanding. They are in the fortunate position of being able to re-mortgage their property and use the proceeds to buy a home abroad or use the house as security for a loan.

Sheltered housing

Sheltered housing schemes for the elderly on the Continent are gradually becoming more numerous. McCarthy & Stone, the UK's largest developer in this category, has two schemes on the Côte d'Azur, France – at Grasse and Juan-les-Pins with limited availability. They also specialise in the development of second or holiday homes in selected coastal or mountain locations in the South of France.

A sheltered housing retirement complex on Spain's Costa Blanca is the Colina Club, near Calpe. It claims to be the first of a series of Golden Life retirement resorts, with 50 one-bedroom apartments, swimming pool, bowling green and a surgery visited each day by a medical practitioner. Round-the-clock nursing care is available if necessary in the 20-bed nursing home. Twenty-year leases are offered from £31,000 and there is an annual service charge. There are substantial additional charges for use of the nursing home.

Sheltered housing schemes in Spain include Interpares, near Malaga on the Costa del Sol. This self-governing community, a non-profit organisation, comprises 73 spacious apartments, mostly individually owned and each having central heating and air conditioning. Services include restaurant and meal delivery, housekeeping and laundry, alarm bell and intercom, handyman and medical assistance. There are extensive gardens and a swimming pool. A nursing service for up to six weeks per illness per year is included in the monthly charges which are based on the size of the apartment. Apartments are for sale from 7.5 million pesetas or may be leased for life-time occupation.

Costa Care near Mijas, Malaga, provides sheltered housing for the more independent and those requiring personal assistance round the clock in a complex providing luxury accommodation with maid service and the provision of meals.

Nearer to England, Pinewood Residential Home, Mont Millais, Jersey in the Channel Islands offers UK standards of care for the over 60's in first-class accommodation with qualified nurses in attendance 24 hours per day.

Chapter 13
Property Organisations

When purchasing an overseas property there are inevitably greater risks than when buying a home in the UK.

Different laws, contracts in foreign languages, varied financial arrangements, local building methods and firms whose authenticity is difficult to check, all add difficulties and hazards to property transactions.

How can members of the public, who are sometimes very gullible and quite ignorant of procedures in the country they have chosen as a place for their home, be protected?

Currently there is one UK trade association of agents and developers who specialise in marketing property overseas. This is the Federation of Overseas Property Developers, Agents and Consultants (FOPDAC).

FOPDAC requires its members to comply with a code of conduct and to fulfil certain entry qualifications. It investigates complaints by the public against members and takes disciplinary action against member firms who are proved to be treating clients in an unsatisfactory manner.

Many problems arise because members of the public fail to take adequate legal and financial advice before committing themselves to a purchase. The very thought of owning a home in a chosen resort or country area seems to cause normally sensible business or professional people to throw caution to the wind. As a result, legal documents in a foreign language are often signed without recourse to proper expert advice and substantial sums of money are paid over to relative strangers, either individuals or firms, before any check has been made about their bona fides.

To minimise the risk of an unsatisfactory transaction, careful preliminary planning and caution throughout the acquisition period should be adopted by all buyers.

Federation of Overseas Property Developers, Agents and Consultants (FOPDAC)

FOPDAC was formed in 1973 with the aim of establishing a code of conduct for its members in their dealings with the public and to try to educate prospective purchasers of overseas residential property on the dos and don'ts of buying villas and apartments outside their native land.

During the recent recession FOPDAC has used the time to restructure itself in preparation for the expected market recovery in the 1990s, as well as to bring itself more into line with the aims and objects of the Single European Act.

The Federation is now a full member of CEI (The European Confederation of Estate Agents).

Chartered surveyors, architects, planners and developers, as well as tour operators, travel experts, lawyers and, of course, selling agents and builders, are now included in the membership. Areas covered by the membership include mainland Spain, the Balearic Islands and the Canaries, Andorra, Cyprus, France, Italy, Greece, Malta, Portugal, Switzerland, Austria and South Africa.

To join FOPDAC, firms or individuals must have well-established businesses and have an integrity that is beyond reasonable question. Principals of companies are required to have sufficient professional expertise and experience to meet the strict requirements of the Federation's code of ethics, a summary of which is given below:

Members shall make honesty and integrity the standard in all their dealings with their clients and customers. They shall avoid misleading property descriptions, concealment of pertinent information, and exaggerations in advertising. They shall not market property for specific purposes if that property is not accessible and usable for such purposes. Members shall comply with all financial and legal obligations relating to their transactions in overseas property and their clients or customers.

Members shall use their best endeavours to enlist all the professional talents available to them in the fields of ecology, engineering and architecture for the design of a development that strives for the best employment of the land and protection of the environment. They shall use their best endeavours to encourage developments with due consideration for open space and proper environmental controls. Members shall report in writing any violation of the by-laws, whether their own or those of others, whether members or not, to the Committee.

Where Federation members accept clients' money for payment, whether partial or full, for land or property, they must maintain a legally separate client's account which must be properly conducted and disclosure must be given, to the Secretary of the Federation, of the name and address of the bank at which the account is maintained.

Should any member of the general public conducting business through a member of the Federation complain that the member has not acted in accordance with the code of ethics, then the committee will investigate the complaint and arbitrate where necessary. If the committee should decide that a member is in default and the member subsequently fails to rectify the matter, then the member would be liable to immediate expulsion from the Federation.

The Federation symbol is displayed on all advertisements and literature distributed by members.

As part of their efforts to help the house-buying public, the Federation occasionally publishes a free newspaper entitled *Update*, as well as several very useful leaflets, including a general guide to 'Buying Property Overseas' plus fact sheets on legal procedures for property purchase in Spain, France, Italy, Switzerland, Malta and Portugal. These latter can be obtained (price £2) from the Secretary, FOPDAC, PO Box 3534, London NW5 1DQ.

Before inspecting any overseas property the Federation suggests that each prospective buyer obtains answers to the following questions:

1. (a) Is the property being offered by its owner, its developer or an agent acting on their behalf?

   (b) Does the British agent have an association with an agent or agents in the chosen locality who is legally licensed in that country? Does the British agent represent the vendor or the purchaser?

   (c) What are the risks in dealing with an unlicensed local agent?

2. Is the property being offered with clear title? Is it 'free and unencumbered'?

3. (a) Are the costs of connecting water, electricity and drainage included in the selling price of a new home? If not, what are these costs likely to be?

   (b) What are the acquisition and conveyancing costs usually incurred by the purchaser under the traditions and regulations of the locality?

4. (a) What are the formal stages of property purchase in the country in which the property is situated?

   (b) Is the purchase contract binding? Is it in a foreign language?

   (c) What essential points should be covered by the purchase contract to ensure that both parties are adequately protected?

5. (a) Should legal advice be sought on the purchase of an overseas property?

    (b) Must a solicitor draw up the conveyance of an overseas property?

    (c) Can the overseas property be sold freely and the proceeds transferred abroad without difficulty?

6. (a) What are the annual costs likely to be incurred by the owner of the property in the country or area chosen?

    (b) If the property is in a development complex are there any charges for communal facilities?

    (c) What is a Community of Owners? Is membership obligatory? What are the benefits? What are the costs? Are the statutes in a foreign language?

7. Can a bank account be opened locally? What are the advantages of having a local bank account?

8. Can the property and its contents be insured? What are the rates of premiums to be expected?

9. Can the property be let to friends? Can a formal rental agreement be made with a rental agency? What return can be expected? Will this restrict the owner's use of the property unduly? Is tax payable on rental income?

10. Could the view from the property or its amenities be affected by unsightly future development? Is there a zoning plan for the surrounding area?

11. Are there any local regulations which affect the purchase of property by foreign nationals? If so, what are the formalities?

12. (a) If a plot of land is bought on which to build in future, are there any conditions of building permission? Are there time limits for such building? Are there height or size limitations?

    (b) Must a local architect be used? Must an architect be used who is nominated by the vendor? Must a nominated building contractor be used?

    (c) Are there any other formalities which should be observed when building a home on a plot purchased?

13. (a) Is furniture included in the price of the property, or does the owner arrange to furnish it? What is the approximate cost of furnishings to a basic or a high standard?

    (b) If the property has a garden, is the cost of planting included in the sale price? If not, what is the cost likely to be? Who maintains the garden in the owner's absence? Could a garden be planned and planted which requires little or no maintenance?

    (c) How much external maintenance is the property likely to need? Who is responsible for this maintenance? How much is it likely to cost?

    (d) Can a company be appointed locally who will manage the property during the owner's absence and supervise cleaning etc for the owner and guests when they visit?

14. What is the most economical and reliable means of travel to the property? Are there privileges to be obtained for owners and their guests?

Ahead of all the happenings in Europe expected to take place after 1993, FOPDAC began appointing European representatives in countries where members transact business, namely France, Greece, Italy, Portugal, and Spain and its islands. At a later date representation will be established in non-EC areas such as Austria, Malta and Switzerland.

The main object of these appointments is to provide two-way feedback on legislation which affects FOPDAC members and their clients.

Other organisations of interest to overseas property owners include:

The Royal Institution of Chartered Surveyors

Some UK estate agents who operate overseas property departments are members of the Royal Institution of Chartered Surveyors. They are subject to a strict code of conduct and are bonded, so far as their operations in the UK are concerned, but this protection does not cover transactions or work undertaken abroad.

However, a degree of security for buyers does exist, as the majority of individuals who are members also have well-established practices in England, Wales, Scotland or Ireland and are unlikely to jeopardise their reputation and professional qualifications by involving themselves in unwise foreign deals.

The Institute of Foreign Property Owners

This organisation was founded in 1983 by Norwegian-born Per Svensson and has had considerable success in helping foreigners who are planning to buy or who have already purchased a home in Spain. Per Svensson is the author of an excellent book entitled *Your Home in Spain*, which is published by Longman in the Allied Dunbar Money Guides series.

Membership of the Institute now exceeds 24,000. The membership fee for the first year is £50, then £44.50 on renewal. Further details are available from Instituto de Propietarios, Avenida Fermin Sanz Orrio 15-2-9, 03590 Altea, Alicante, Spain.

Chapter 14

Timesharing

In a book on living abroad this chapter may seem slightly out of place, but timesharing is a method of acquiring experience in living abroad for short periods without the expenditure of large sums of money.

This method of property ownership has been in existence for over 27 years. The first scheme was offered in a French Alpine ski resort in 1967. In the following year timesharing was offered by a co-ownership scheme in Spain promoted by two British businessmen who had built and sold two blocks of apartments in the main street of Javea, on the Costa Blanca, and then decided to construct a third block whereby clients could purchase part-ownership of a freehold, two-bedroom flat with names registered on the deeds. The cost of the use in perpetuity of a two-bedroom unit for a fortnight in June was £250, or £500 would purchase the use for all the winter months from November to March. This scheme is still operating successfully. Resales now fetch about £3000 for a week in the summer.

In the UK, a pioneer scheme was started 17 years ago in the Highlands of Scotland, at Loch Rannoch. This operates very successfully, with nearly 100 units ranging from luxury three-bedroom lodges with huge living areas on the first floor enjoying the fine views across the Loch, down to small apartments. Features on the site include a dry ski slope, hotel and club, boating and fishing opportunities, swimming facilities and various other sports and pastimes.

It is estimated that more than 120,000 families now own timeshare weeks in about 80 resorts spread throughout the UK from the north of Scotland to Wales, the Midlands, the South Coast and the West Country.

The term 'timesharing' originated in America and has also been called 'interval ownership', 'vacation ownership' and 'co-ownership'. There can be up to 50 owners of a single unit of accommodation, each having purchased seven days or more at the time of year when they wish to use their accommodation.

Having paid the purchase price, which can sometimes be spread over two or three years, no further capital payment is required but

TIMESHARE IN PORTUGAL — LUGGAGE IN FLORIDA
(AND WE DIDN'T MIND A BIT!)

When we retired a couple of years ago my wife and I took a well deserved holiday at a beautiful resort in the Algarve.

Smart villas completely fitted out, swimming pool, tennis courts and 3 restaurants with one of the best golf courses I have ever played right next door.

The timeshare salesman tried to persuade us to buy weeks in a new villa and we were seriously tempted.

Fortunately we mentioned this to some friends who already owned at the resort. They laughed and said that it was a good job we had told them because we would get a much better deal if we bought a resale from a private owner. He suggested that we contact PrimeShare when we got home.

Eventually we bought two high season weeks. PrimeShare completed all the legal formalities and I looked forward to our first holiday. My wife however had other ideas.

"Harold" she said "I know we've bought our timeshare in Portugal but we can go there anytime —

why don't we go to Florida instead this year?"

"Wonderful," I thought, "I buy a timeshare in Portugal, and she wants to go to Florida!" Fortunately, PrimeShare had suggested that we join RCI (the worldwide timeshare exchange club). My wife had already done her homework and arranged a fabulous exchange into a Florida resort near Disneyland.

Maybe next year I'll get a round or two of golf in the Algarve, or perhaps we'll head for the Caribbean.

PrimeShare is the ideal way to survey the timeshare market from your armchair, with literally thousands of choices in the most favoured countries and best developments around the world, many at less than half current new prices. And remember, timeshare can be left on to your heirs like any other asset.

Call us now on 0449 616055 or send the coupon below.

PRIMESHARE
THE TIMESHARE ESTATE AGENTS

there are annual maintenance charges which range from about £50 to £200 per annum at the time of writing and these cover maintenance and management expenses.

In the UK and some other countries it is not possible to transfer legal title to the freehold ownership of a property to more than four people. To overcome this problem many timeshare developers adopt the club trustee system, whereby an independent trustee is appointed to hold the land and buildings on trust for the timeshare owners. Should the promoter get into financial difficulties, time-share owners' rights are not affected and title cannot be taken away by creditors of the bankrupt company.

An alternative method is to grant a 'right to use' licence. Here the developer who holds the legal title provides the timesharer with a licence which permits use of the accommodation for the period purchased, over an agreed number of years or in perpetuity, the maximum in England and Wales being 80 years.

Normally at least two weeks in the year are not sold by the developers in order to provide a suitable period to cover maintenance and redecoration of properties. The average period of time purchased is between two and three weeks.

To ensure proper management of the scheme, and to spread general outgoings over sufficient owners, a minimum of 16 units is considered to be necessary and, if this is achieved, maintenance fees can be kept to a reasonable level.

Variations to the standard scheme include 'floating weeks' whereby there is no entitlement to a selected week each year and it is necessary to book your period in advance. Those wishing to take a holiday in the peak season may find availability a problem.

Four-owner and six-owner schemes provide occupation of the selected villa or apartment for three or two months each year respectively. The time segment is usually divided into several periods, so that each owner can enjoy peak weeks, mid-season and low-season periods each year. The periods allocated generally rotate so that each participant has the opportunity to enjoy holidays at differing times each year over, say, a four-year time span.

An objection that some people raise about the purchase of holiday accommodation is that they may tire of going to the same place year after year. This is not a problem experienced with timesharing, for most developments are in membership with one of the two major exchange organisations whereby owners can exchange their accommodation for similar size and quality apartments or villas in upwards of 1000 timeshare developments in most parts of the world.

The best-known organisations are Interval International and Resort Condominiums International. They both have offices in the UK, as well as in the USA where they were originally founded. They carry out quality checks on all the schemes which apply for membership and have been known to reject a number of sites which do not come up to their strict standards of quality.

Resort Condominiums International, which now has over 2000 resorts in 70 countries worldwide, has its European headquarters at Kettering. In 1992 it operated over 250,000 exchanges for European members. Its staff arrange for the publishing of directories in 12 languages and maintain computer links between the 12 RCI offices in Europe and the group's headquarters at Indianapolis, USA.

To ensure that a development will be a success and will sell readily throughout most of the year, a wide variety of facilities, including sporting activities, shops, restaurants, health clubs and live entertainment, is essential.

Every bit as important as the amenities is the standard of furnishing and the design of the properties themselves. All furniture should be very hardwearing, and attractive in appearance; kitchens should be furnished and equipped to luxury standards; bathrooms should be designed and equipped to first-class specification.

In recent years, a number of well-known firms in the building industry, including Barratt, have purchased existing or established timesharing schemes in the UK and overseas. The involvement of these firms has helped considerably to build the public's confidence in timesharing.

During the boom years between 1984 and 1988 some of the timeshare marketing firms adopted hard-sell tactics to persuade reluctant members of the public to commit themselves to the purchase of time segments which they often could not afford or did not, on reflection, really want. Methods adopted included inducing holiday-makers to visit sales centres and show properties with promises of valuable free gifts, which were not always honoured, or complimentary meals and drinks for attending sales presentations which often lasted up to three hours. Participants were then expected to sign contracts and pay deposits without any opportunity for reflection or consultation with professional advisers.

Salespeople were often over-zealous and persuasive and contact agents frequently pestered holiday-makers on the beaches, in shopping centres or at tourist airports.

There are many bona fide timeshare developments in the UK and overseas where prospective and actual clients are treated fairly, but the black sheep have brought the whole industry into disrepute. As a result, in 1989 the Parliamentary Under-Secretary for Industry and Commerce asked the Director of Fair Trading to investigate the problems of timesharing.

Sir Gordon Borrie's report, published in July 1990, stated that he had no quarrel with the concept of timesharing for he believed it provides, for the most part, a high standard of holiday accommodation and brings economic benefit to the resorts where schemes are situated.

Nevertheless, he considered that there was a need for effective legislative controls to deal with problems such as unacceptable selling techniques, the use of false or misleading statements, and to ensure that the public have adequate information and time to consider propositions before committing themselves.

In 1993 The Timeshare Act was passed by Parliament to ensure that buyers of timeshares who sign contracts in Britain, are given a 14-day 'cooling-off period' during which they can have their money refunded should they decide not to proceed with the purchase.

Properly organised, developed and managed timesharing schemes will undoubtedly prosper in the future, for they do give families and individuals a safeguard against the escalating cost of vacations. It should be borne in mind that timesharing is not an investment in money terms, simply in future holidays.

Although capital profits have been achieved by many owners who invested at the early stages of the most successful schemes, no capital appreciation should be expected for, say, five years, or while the developers are still selling the units.

Other specific points to bear in mind, before signing any documents which commit you to purchase, are as follows:

1. Adequate management and maintenance of the development are of vital importance to the future. Ascertain who is going to undertake this work and the proposed charges, including any increase in costs in future years. Will they be based on the cost of living index, or will the figure be fixed annually at the whim of the management organisation?

2. Get details in writing of the facilities that will be offered on the site and, if possible, ensure that these will be available as soon as occupation is offered on timeshare units.

3. Details of the furnishings, fixtures and fitments to be included in each unit should be presented to each buyer in inventory form. Check the maximum number of people permitted to use each timeshare unit.

4. If you are paying cash, you may be entitled to a discount if settlement is made by a specified date. If you are financing the

purchase on credit, check up on the interest rates to be charged for the period over which repayments are permitted.

5. Investigations into the track record of the project developers are a wise precaution; with already completed developments, endeavour to speak to one of the existing owners and get his or her opinion about how well the scheme is organised.

6. Check the terms on which the scheme is being offered, ie either freehold or club trusteeship, and whether segments are sold by the week or multiple weeks, whether they are for a fixed period every year or for a floating period whereby the weeks vary or rotate each year.

Under a Spanish Wealth Tax law passed during 1991, owners of timeshares in Spain were technically liable to pay an annual tax of 0.2 per cent of the value of their weeks. However, as a result of representations made by the Timeshare Council to the Spanish government, the tax has been waived for those owning under the 'Club Trustee' legal system. Further representations are being considered on behalf of those owning under the second Spanish legal system, *escritura*, where effectively the proposed levy is a property tax.

Selling your timeshare

Having owned a timeshare segment for several years, it is likely that some owners will decide they would like to dispose of their existing entitlement and purchase in another location, while others may want to recoup some or all of the money they have invested, due to changed circumstances.

When marketing of new timeshare schemes was at its height during the 1980s, it was not always easy to find a buyer for a 'second-hand' period, but now there are a number of firms who specialise in handling resales. Generally, they operate like estate agents and compile details of timeshare units which owners wish to sell and advertise these in the press and elsewhere to find purchasers.

As with all real estate transactions it is advisable to ascertain the *bona fides* of any organisation through whom you propose to try and sell your property. Some agents have been known to charge a substantial, money-back guarantee fee for achieving a sale within a stated period, then make no attempt to find a buyer and suddenly disappear at the end of the period, with all the fees.

Among the reputable firms is PrimeShare Estate Agents of 41 Bury Street, Stowmarket, Suffolk IP14 1HA, who were established in 1987 and are a founder member of the Timeshare Council. They have achieved timeshare sales of more than £2.5 million and now operate throughout Europe, the USA, the Middle East, Australasia and the Caribbean. They advertise their resales exstensively in the national press and local media.

Their charges are reasonable and they arrange the transfer of titles to the new buyer on behalf of the vendor. They are also able to arrange finance facilities for purchasers which can encourage sales.

From the purchaser's point of view a resale is almost always cheaper than buying new from a developer because the latter is heavily involved in marketing and promotion costs which can amount to around 40 to 50 per cent of the original purchase price. The individual owner, on resale after say five years, is not involved in such heavy expenditure and can therefore accept a figure well below the current 'new' price, thus offering an attractive proposition.

Companies handling resales operate outside the Timeshare Act and do not have to provide a cooling-off period, but PrimeShare offer a 21-day money-back promise.

European Timeshare Federation

This Federation was established in June 1991, to represent the interests of all those involved in timeshare activities on a pan-European basis. The Federation is lobbying in particular for a fair and equitable European Timeshare Directive which will provide wide consumer protection without being unduly industry punitive. Currently, the Federation comprises 11 industry bodies representing 15 European countries and covers over 90 per cent of all timeshare schemes across Europe.

The Timeshare Council

The Timeshare Council was established in October 1990 to protect the interests of both the consumer and the developer and to re-establish the credibility of the industry after a period of bad press reports and unsatisfactory experiences involving members of the public.

A substantial drop in demand for timeshare, caused by the worldwide recession of the early 1990s, has resulted in the departure of many less desirable operators in the industry. Nevertheless the Council has found it necessary recently to expel one member firm for failing to comply with its requirements.

The membership includes timeshare developers, marketeers, agents, management firms, finance organisations, solicitors, consultants, owners' associations and also leisure and hotel operators with timeshare interests.

One of the Council's aims is to represent the industry in dealings with UK government departments, the EC and elsewhere, also with the media, the public and various other trade organisations.

Useful information and advice leaflets on timesharing are produced by the Council. Copies can be obtained, together with a list of members, by sending a large stamped addressed envelope to The Director, The Timeshare Council, 23 Buckingham Gate, London SW1E 6LB.

Holiday Property Bond

The Holiday Property Bond, marketed in the UK by Villa Owners Club Ltd, HPB House, Newmarket, Suffolk CB8 8EH, is not timesharing but an excellent alternative method of investing a capital sum to provide self-catering holiday accommodation in the UK and overseas each year.

The scheme comprises a lump sum investment of a minimum of £2000, in a life assurance policy with the Isle of Man Assurance Co Ltd. Part of the money is invested in securities, to provide an income towards management and maintenance costs and the balance is used for the purchase or construction of holiday properties.

Established for 10 years, the bond now holds investment exceeding £100 million for 17,000 investors, and owns nearly 600 high-quality properties in a wide variety of countries including Austria, Portugal, France, Spain, Italy, Cyprus, the USA, England, Scotland and Wales. These range from delightful cottages in the English Lake District, an 18th-century *manoir* in France, a hilltop hamlet in the Dordogne, holiday homes in Tenerife, apartments near ski facilities in Austria, attractive villas in Florida, a converted castle in Wales and one of the latest schemes is the redevelopment of the famed Trossachs Hotel in Scotland. Many of these sites have exceptional holiday facilities such as swimming pools and all are equipped to luxury standards. In order to extend still further the range of accommodation, a tenancy programme has been launched to provide holidays in Madeira, Crete, Turkey, Tenerife and the USA.

A points system (one point per £1 invested) is operated and the points value of each self-catering holiday home varies according to location, size of accommodation and time of year booked. The points allocation to each investor is at least the same every year, so it is possible to afford the same standard of accommodation each year, regardless of inflation, in perpetuity. There is no fixed annual charge, just a no-profit 'user charge' when a bond property is occupied, which helps to cover cleaning and utility costs.

Hard-sell tactics are not employed when marketing the bond and in fact there is a 28-day cooling-off period for each investment and the money is paid to the bond's trustees. A buy-back guarantee is available after two years. A property advisory committee, comprising an independent chairman and a number of owners, provides the management with information about the availability of suitable additional properties and keeps in touch with bondholders to ascertain their preferences regarding new locations for possible property purchase by the bond.

Premium Leisure Bond

Premium Life Assurance is offering the Premium Leisure Bond. The resources of the investors are used to buy holiday properties. At present, they own six properties in France and Portugal, but investors can use their points to use properties offered through Beach Villas.

The minimum investment is £2000 and a points system is used with 100 points granted for every £100 invested. These can be used to book holiday accommodation when four months have elapsed after joining the scheme. The number of points required for a week's holiday varies according to the accommodation, the resort and the time of year chosen. It is considered that an investment of at least £4000 is necessary to secure a week's accommodation during school holidays.

A charge of £10 per week per person is made for cleaning and utilities. This may be increased in the future.

Details can be obtained from Premium Life House, 37–39 Perrymount Road, Haywards Heath, West Sussex RH16 3BN.

Pierre & Vacances Paris Timeshare Scheme

Paris-based builder and developer Pierre & Vacances is offering a timeshare scheme in luxury accommodation in the popular Porte de Versailles district of Paris. Studios (to sleep two people) and one-bedroom apartments (sleeping four) are well-equipped and include fitted kitchen and bathroom, and there is covered parking space for each unit.

Owners can purchase one or more weeks and may, if they wish, exchange their week or weeks for a similar period in any one of 50 specially designed and built Pierre & Vacances holiday centres in

French skiing areas and resorts bordering the Mediterranean and Atlantic. It is also possible to exchange with one of over 700 quality holiday destinations around the world through Interval International, a major timeshare exchange organisation. Further details can be obtained from Pierre & Vacances UK agents, PrimeShare Direct, 41 Bury Street, Stowmarket, Suffolk IP14 1HA.

Chapter 15

Title Insurance and Trustees

In the USA, title insurance is an important aspect of house purchase procedure and there is a considerable number of companies which offer this facility at a relatively modest cost. This precaution has not received the same acceptance in the UK. A number of insurance companies have endeavoured to market schemes in Britain without conspicuous success, although at least one firm has persevered and is gaining ground gradually in respect of properties in the UK and, more especially, on the Continent.

Title insurance is, in effect, an insured statement of the condition of a title to a property which is being transferred to a new owner. It has two advantages, namely that the company issuing the insurance pays for any losses incurred should the title subsequently be found defective, and also that it will provide an additional cover for the cost of any litigation in defending claims. Purchasers do not have to prove negligence.

For timeshare schemes, both in the UK and abroad, where a divided freehold exists, title insurance provides the purchaser with an independent assurance, backed only after detailed investigation of the title, enforced by a financial guarantee that the title being passed on by the developers is all that it appears to be.

A title company has the right to guarantee its findings via a bank guarantee programme or insurance bond on properties under construction. On finished properties, whether new or a resale, a certificate of documentation and completion is issued.

Timeshare Trustees

One of the largest trust companies operating in the European timeshare field, Timeshare Trustees (International) Ltd (TTI) provides a service to developers and committees of timeshare clubs in the UK and Europe. One of the duties of this organisation is to ensure that taxes are paid and buildings insured for all properties held in trust. Computerised records are maintained regarding ownership of weeks and payments for time purchased.

TTI is the parent company of a wholly owned subsidiary in the

UK, known as Holiday Property Trustee Ltd, which is an authorised custodian trustee under the UK Public Trustee Rules. The main purpose of TTI is to make sure that purchasers of timeshare obtain and always have a good legal title to occupation of a completed timeshare property and to maintain the good legal title throughout the period of trust.

Developers are requested to transfer clear legal titles to fully completed properties to TTI, who holds them on behalf of timeshare owners. Before transfer of the title to TTI, all money actually paid by the purchasers to TTI is held in a blocked account and not released to the developer until the title is transferred or, alternatively, until satisfactory completion guarantees have been given.

TTI also helps management companies to collect maintenance charges from owners and ensures that annual accounts of property-owning companies are audited satisfactorily. It will also organise general meetings of the clubs on behalf of the owners committee. Although TTI does provide important services to timeshare resort operators, it is primarily responsible to owners and cannot be replaced except by a vote of the owners themselves at a general meeting of the club.

Further information regarding Timeshare Trustees (International) Ltd can be obtained from the Legal Director, TTI-Europe, Bourne Concourse, Paul Street, Ramsey, Isle of Man, Tel. 0624 814555 or fax 0624 811823.

Chapter 16

Flights for Owners

To get maximum benefit from their overseas homes, many owners are keen to obtain the most reasonably-priced flights to their chosen destination, not only for themselves but also for their tenants, when they rent out their property in the summer. There are a number of clubs which provide members with low-cost travel by air and other benefits.

The Owners Travel Club is part of Owners Abroad, the largest publicly-quoted travel company, which has been established for 20 years. Membership of the Club costs £20 per year and benefits include priority access to reduced price seats before they are offered on the open market, a no-surcharge guarantee, free delay insurance, low-cost holiday insurance, reductions on car hire and parking, a reduction on overseas property insurance, and a discount club card giving considerable reductions in restaurants and bars, and on perfume, clothes etc.

Seats are booked on different airlines, and services are to Spain, Malta, Portugal, Cyprus, Switzerland, France, Italy, Greece, Turkey, Canada and the USA (Orlando). The company also has its own airline – Air 2000 – with departures from Gatwick, Birmingham, Bristol, Manchester and Glasgow.

Further details of the Owners Travel Club can be obtained from Owners Abroad, Astral Towers, Betts Way, Crawley, West Sussex RH10 2GX.

For those who prefer to cross the Channel or Bay of Biscay with their car to reach their second home in France, Spain or Portugal, the Property Owners Club may be of interest. This is operated by Brittany Ferries who have a fleet of seven passenger ships operating out of Portsmouth and Plymouth to St Malo, Caen and Roscoff, and from Poole to Cherbourg, France. They also have a service to Santander in northern Spain, which departs from Plymouth in the summer months and Portsmouth during the winter.

Their largest vessel, the *Val de Loire* (32,000 tons) launched in 1992, can carry 1700 passengers and 600 cars, with onboard accommodation for 1700 passengers. It serves the Plymouth–Roscoff and Plymouth/Portsmouth–Santander routes.

Club members receive discounts of up to 30 per cent on the normal fare, plus reductions on on-board meals and facilities, as well as reductions for members' guests. For membership application forms and timetables, telephone Brittany Ferries, 0752 227941.

The alternative to club membership is to use one of the cut-price flight specialists, many of whom publicise their offers in the national press. However, it is advisable to ascertain if the flight you select is operated under an ATOL number (Air Transport Operators' Licence) and whether the agent making the offer is a member of the Association of British Travel Agents (ABTA). The reputation of certain uncontrolled 'bucket shops' (as they are known in the trade) has been poor, because of irresponsible behaviour over cancelled flights, late surcharges, unreliable aircraft, and even bankruptcies which have left holiday-makers stranded abroad.

Another firm able to offer low-price flights to the more popular European holiday destinations and to Florida is Skybargains, 29-31 Elmfield Road, Bromley, Kent BR1 1LT. In the summer they have flights from 13 UK airports to Spain, Portugal, Austria, Malta, Italy, Greece, Cyprus, Turkey, Tunisia and Florida. They also have a winter programme, which is not quite so extensive.

They are so confident that the prices they quote are the lowest that they offer a guarantee that if a client finds a comparable flight for less than their price, within 14 days of booking with them, they will either (at their discretion) beat that price or accept a cancellation with full refund of the value of their flight.

The Air Travel Advisory Bureau, with offices in London and Manchester, offers a data system which discloses details of the operators offering the best-value seats, at the time of application, to numerous destinations. Information can be obtained by telephoning 071-636 5000.

Tour operators also dispose of surplus seats from time to time to selected destinations in southern Europe. Many airlines operating scheduled services are prepared to quote reduced fares to stand-by passengers, but the snag here is that you can rarely be certain that you will depart on the flight of your choice until the last minute and you may have to wait patiently for several days at the airport.

Chapter 17
Security and Safety

Unfortunately vandalism, violence and burglary are on the increase in most countries, so it is wise to take appropriate countermeasures if you own a property abroad or intend to live overseas.

As far as property is concerned, the precautions you take with an overseas home are much the same as in the British Isles. If you live in a block of apartments with a full-time caretaker your problems are substantially solved, provided that the person in charge is reliable and conscientious. Of course, it is wise to have good strong locks on all external doors, plus a spy hole for use when you are in occupation and an unexpected visitor arrives at the front door. Then you can see who is calling, and if you have a chain you can open the door a little without allowing direct access.

The concierge or a close friend should have door keys when you are away, so that the property can be aired regularly and checks made to ensure that there is no problem with water, either from a leak in the pipes or a flood from a neighbouring property.

Villas, particularly if they are in a somewhat isolated position, require more detailed planning. In addition to a high standard of door locks, every window that is accessible from the ground should be fitted with security locking devices. In Spain and some other countries metal window grilles are installed as decoration; these also become effective deterrents to housebreakers and burglars.

Anyone living alone should have a telephone to call emergency assistance, plus an alarm system with panic button. A loud whistle could also be useful, plus a well-trained house dog.

One of the first tasks on settling into a new home is to ascertain the best methods of alerting the security authorities. Discover the telephone number of the local police station and find out if it is manned 24 hours a day. Place this information in a prominent position in the dwelling so that it can always be found, and add to it instructions for contacting the fire and ambulance services. List the nearest doctor and hospital in case of sudden illness.

On some modern estates where there are perhaps more than 50 dwellings, a private security service is provided permanently and paid for by the owners as part of their community charges.

Chapter 18

Household Insurance

Prudent owners of overseas property make sure that they have adequate insurance cover not only for the building but also for the contents.

When considering insurance for overseas holiday homes, it is perhaps natural for the average Briton to feel happier with a policy underwritten in the United Kingdom and prepared in the English language. In the event of either a major or minor disaster to the property, the policy conditions can be fully understood and perhaps, more important still, communication with those whose job it is to resolve the problems is streamlined.

However, the single market of the European Community has now imposed regulations which decree that property in an EC country, owned by a UK resident, must be covered by an insurance company that is licensed to underwrite in the country where the property is situated. Furthermore, the taxes and charges that are applicable to that country must be paid. Britain is the only country in the EC that does not pay fire brigade charges etc on insurance premiums.

The style of policy that is available within the UK market, which meets all the criteria, is similar to the familiar UK home policy and can be obtained from a specialist company – Holiday Insurance Services (Homes) Ltd, Unit 2, Midland Court, 109–113 Victoria Road, Romford, Essex RM1 2LY. This firm has provided cover for holiday homes for the past two decades.

During the past year a new contract to meet all the requirements of the EC has been made available, with the policy document being issued in English, premiums and claims paid in sterling, but with full translation into the language of the country where the property is situated. The contract is arranged with a major UK insurance company in conjunction with their European partners.

A specimen quotation to cover a building in France for a sum insured of £37,945, with liability indemnity of £750,000 and £600 emergency travel expenses, would amount to about £137. The French national premium tax and common fund for victims of terrorism, included in the annual premium, amounted to just over £12.

To cover an apartment in Spain for £30,000, plus contents of £5000, indemnity liability of £750,000 requires an annual premium of £135, included in which is Spanish fire brigade charges and taxes of £6.48.

In both quotations there is a policy excess of £25 on each claim, but this is not applicable to fire, cash in meters or emergency travel claims.

An annual Holiday Homes Travel and Medical Insurance policy is also available from the above address. Cover is provided for the holiday home owner and family for trips to a destination outside the UK from the time of leaving home or place of employment until return home, with a maximum duration for any one trip of two months. The premium is £95 annually.

You can, of course, place your insurance with an insurance company overseas, but you might have difficulties in understanding the proposal form and the policy in a foreign language. However, some companies now provide English translations of documents. Another point to remember is that policy wording is not always as wide as that obtainable in the UK; however, companies such as Commercial Union, Guardian, Royal, Royal Exchange and Sun Life are represented in most European countries.

The Home Owners Abroad Emergency Travel policy devised by Marcus Hearn & Co Ltd provides useful cover for owners of homes in Europe, the USA and Canada which they do not occupy permanently. In the event of the property being seriously damaged by fire, explosion, earthquake, storm, flood, theft or break-in, which causes any room in the property to be unusable, the policy will cover travelling expenses by the owner to the site to deal with the emergency, rental of alternative accommodation for up to 15 days, the loss of personal baggage during the journey and the cost of any medical expenses for emergency treatment while attending to the damaged property abroad, for up to 15 days.

The premium is £15 per person per annum and the policy is underwritten by underwriters at Lloyds in conjunction with Europ Assistance Insurance Ltd. Further details are available from Marcus Hearn & Co Ltd, 65–66 Shoreditch High Street, London E1 6JL.

Chapter 19

Letting Your Overseas Property

Many families purchase an overseas home with the intention of using it for perhaps only four to six weeks a year for annual holidays and, perhaps at a later stage, when retirement is in prospect, plan greater use by the parents as they have more leisure time. Grown-up children can possibly have the advantage of using a family-owned property overseas at certain times of the year.

The property will not improve if it is closed up for long periods and not inspected and aired at regular intervals. Damage may occur as a result of freak weather, so some owners decide it is worth going to the trouble of letting their property on a commercial basis.

It should be realised that, generally speaking, this can involve quite a lot of work and the annual return will perhaps not be more than 5 or 6 per cent after all expenses have been paid. To achieve satisfactory results, it is essential to have a good local agent on the spot to see that the property is in a satisfactory condition and ready for occupation as tenants arrive and that it is tidied up after they depart, ready for the next tenant.

Cleaning and maintenance are of great importance, and having a local person available at all times to deal with any emergencies such as electricity breakdown or a malfunction of domestic appliances is highly desirable.

Some new developments have their own management service which they offer to purchasers for a competitive fee, and in the main resort areas there are firms willing to undertake management on behalf of individual owners as a specialist service.

It is unlikely that a property, even in a popular resort, will be let for more than about half of the year. Villas in country or remote locations will probably be occupied even less frequently.

The reputation of the management organisation is of paramount importance as it is not unknown for dishonest or careless operators to find a tenant for a week or more and not report the letting to the owner; thus the opportunity is there for them to pocket the rent themselves.

Before deciding finally on letting your property for the weeks or months that you don't require it for yourself, draw up a list of conditions for tenants and have these incorporated in any publicity material that you prepare to assist you in letting the property.

Decide on the maximum number of people you want to occupy the property. Do you expect tenants to pay an additional charge for gas and electricity consumed, or do you include this in the rent? Decide on arrival and departure times for tenants and ensure that there is adequate time between the two to allow for the property to be prepared satisfactorily for the arrival of the new occupants.

If you arrange lettings through a major tour operator there will probably be quite a wide assortment of people using your home and possibly a fairly quick turnover. However, these companies wish to protect their reputation and will ensure a high standard of maintenance and cleanliness. In any case, can you really expect higher standards from people recommended to you than from strangers? Even friends in whom you have complete faith sometimes have lapses and leave places in a horrible mess.

An alternative, although not always a satisfactory one, is to ask a neighbour to manage the property for you in your absence. This means relying on that person's goodwill to undertake the job properly. Don't forget that the neighbour may want a holiday away from home, just at the peak period when you have several tenants arriving within a short period. Will the job be done to your satisfaction if your 'volunteer' suffers a period of illness, and how much should you pay as recompense for his or her trouble? In the long run, professional management is probably more satisfactory.

In some countries, such as Malta, Cyprus and Florida there are government restrictions on letting holiday property, so check the facts in advance. Also, do not forget that the tax collector will demand a share of your 'profits'.

Chapter 20

Look Before You Leap

As a final reminder, the following checklist should be studied by everyone before buying a property in a foreign country.

1. Visit the property you plan to buy wherever it is situated. If it is not already completed, ask to see a similar design that is furnished and ready for occupation. Check on the materials and finishes being used and get assurance that any proposed amenities such as swimming pools or tennis courts will be available for use immediately the building programme is completed.

2. Before signing any documents or paying over substantial sums of money, seek advice on the contract, the specification and the terms of business from a qualified legal expert and an accountant. Ask the developer or agent for English translations of all documents which commit you to purchase.

3. Don't be in too much of a hurry to buy a property. The vendor will obviously encourage you to make a quick decision and sign up during your first visit, but it is better to lose the opportunity of purchasing a property which seems to attract you immediately than to make a hasty decision which you may regret later.

4. When purchasing an apartment, obtain written confirmation of maintenance charges and management arrangements.

5. Where estate facilities such as swimming pools, clubs and tennis courts are promised in brochures and publicity, but have not been provided at the time you purchase your property, get confirmation that these will be available within, say, 12 months. In some countries, developers are required to provide the bulk of the amenities and access roads before they launch the sales programme.

6. Ensure that you obtain a proper title to the property you are buying and, where a Land Registry exists, that there are no encumbrances, such as a mortgage, registered. Where a legal expert is employed, these checks will be part of his or her routine work.

7. A completion date in the sales contract is very desirable, but not always easy to obtain.

8. At an early date, compile a list of costs and taxes you will be expected to pay when you purchase the property – then you should not suffer any shocks.

9. When buying a new property still under construction or not yet started, obtain information about stage payments as the work proceeds and check if you are permitted a 5 per cent retention for six months to cover any building faults and if any guarantees are offered for, say, two years to compensate for bad building.

10. Make sure you comply with the fiscal rules of the country of your choice so that you can repatriate your capital on the sale of the property. Also examine the regulations regarding taxation of foreign residents, payment of pensions, medical facilities and so on.

Part 4
Country Surveys

Rates of exchange quoted are those applying
on
22 March 1994

Readers are advised to check information about the
country they are particularly interested in, as
changes occur daily.

Chapter 21

The Islands Around Britain

The Isle of Man and the Channel Islands are offshore islands around the coast of Britain that offer interesting financial benefits but, sadly, lack a climate which is significantly better than on the mainland.

However, they do attract considerable numbers of tourists and some new residents each year. The very strong protective legislation imposed in Jersey means that this island is virtually closed to new residents.

Isle of Man

The Isle of Man lies in the Irish Sea midway between the Republic of Ireland and Scotland. It has an area of 572 square kilometres (221 square miles) and a population of 69,750, a third of whom live in the capital, Douglas, which is on the east coast. Other towns of importance include Ramsey, Peel, Castletown and Port Erin.

The island has never been a part of the United Kingdom and has its own two-tier parliament known as the Tynwald, which was founded over 1000 years ago by the Vikings.

The Isle of Man has a special relationship with the European Community which guarantees free trade in goods with the rest of the Community, but there is no involvement with the Community's budget so contributions to the EC are not required and no financial assistance is available. Long-term objectives to harmonise tax, social and employment legislation are also not applicable.

As an important part of a programme of economic development, the government is keen to attract new residents and there is a positive welcome to families who would like to live on the island. The aim is to encourage those who will integrate well into Manx society, and will make a contribution to the island's economic well-being.

Why should the Isle of Man government wish to increase the population? The simple answer is that there is ample room for expansion on the island, for the population density is about some six or seven times less than that in the Channel Islands. Also the

Tynwald prides itself on the quality of its health, education and social services and it is clear that these services could cope readily with an increase in population of 10,000. In fact, many services, particularly electricity supply and other public utilities, benefit greatly from an increase in the number of consumers. Furthermore, the various amenities provided for tourists require a strong domestic market to thrive, and increased consumption by residents will improve the standard of retailing and restaurants available for visitors. In addition, the recreational facilities, such as golf, sailing, rambling and fishing, have substantial spare capacity to cater for additional demand.

Business people establishing new enterprises in the island are encouraged by the favourable taxation and a loyal, hard-working labour force, plus good communications with the UK and Europe.

Expatriates and retired people enjoy the relaxed way of life and the sophisticated financial facilities, plus the absence of taxes on capital. Domestic labour, as in most developed countries, tends to be scarce, but is available. There is a low crime rate. A sizeable industrial sector provides jobs for skilled engineering craftspeople.

The fact that everyone on the island speaks English and uses a similar currency to the mainland are other advantages. The system of law in the Isle of Man is common law and therefore Anglo-Saxon based. This is helpful to people who have been brought up in a business environment or home environment of English law and, although separately administered by the Isle of Man judicature, the laws generally follow those of England. This makes understanding house purchase, wills, etc, quite easy.

Residence permits

There is complete freedom of entry and abode to all citizens who have full permanent residency rights in the UK or Irish Republic. Overseas nationals are affected by immigration regulations, details of which can be obtained from a British Embassy or Consulate.

Tax and exchange control

The standard rate of income tax is 15 per cent on the first £8500 of taxable income of resident individuals and 20 per cent on the balance. Broadly speaking, the Isle of Man government does not seek to tax non-residents, either private or corporate. There are no wealth or capital gains taxes or death duties.

As a tax haven, the island has numerous financial institutions of both local origin and national renown. The island finances all its own services and makes a contribution to the UK for defence and diplomatic services. VAT is charged at 17.5 per cent on all goods and services, except those which are zero rated.

Currency
The island issues its own £1 notes and pence coinage which are at par with £1 sterling.

Politics
The stability of the Tynwald is enhanced by the absence of party politics and its history of more than 1000 years of independent rule.

Health services
Health, education and social services are of high quality.

Cost of living
The cost of living, excluding housing, is about 2 per cent lower than in the UK. The rate of inflation is similar to that in the UK.

Communications
Air services to London, Manchester, Blackpool, Belfast, Glasgow, Edinburgh, Dublin, Birmingham, Liverpool, Leeds/Bradford and Newcastle. London journey time 60 minutes. Sea ferries to Heysham, Belfast, Dublin, Liverpool and Fleetwood.

Property purchase
There are no restrictions on non-islanders purchasing property in the Isle of Man.

A wide range of homes is available at prices up to £45,000 for a converted two-bedroom flat to over £300,000 for a large luxury residence on an exclusive site with views. Considering the size of the island it is pleasing to discover that some of the country properties have extensive grounds of up to about 50 acres.

All title deeds (including mortgages and other charges) are recorded and held in the Isle of Man deeds registry. There is a charge for registering but no stamp duty is imposed on conveyancing. Legal fees are controlled by a scale of charges imposed by the Tynwald.

Guernsey

Guernsey (population 59,500) is the second largest Channel Island. It does not attract as many holiday-makers as its neighbour Jersey, but is a very pleasant place in which to live. Excellent shopping facilities are available in St Peter Port and there are plenty of recreational facilities.

Economy

The financial sector has expanded, and Guernsey is an offshore tax haven. A large banking sector with over 70 institutions is licensed to undertake deposit business. Many well-known financial institutions have local offices.

Tourism is the second largest industry, together with a very active conference business. Light industry has developed into an important employer and exporter. Fishing and 'high-tech' industries are also of importance.

Taxation

Income tax – 20p in the pound – has not changed in the past 30 years; there is no VAT, corporation tax, capital gains tax or inheritance tax. There is a double taxation agreement between the UK as well as Jersey. A special relationship with the European Community exempts Guernsey from most of Common Market law, and there is no need to harmonise taxation and other internal policies with those of the EC.

Medical

There is no health service, but there are no nursing or maintenance charges in general hospitals. Patients pay fees to their own doctor while in hospital. Private medical insurance is recommended.

Education

Administered by the States Education Council and broadly similar to England. There is a £6 million grammar school for boys and girls. Well-known private schools include Elizabeth College for boys and Ladies College for girls. There are also some small fee-paying schools and a college of further education.

Housing

New residents may occupy 'open market' properties only. These are inscribed on the Housing Control Register and amount to about 10 per cent of total housing stock (19,600). The aim is to protect bona fide locals from speculative purchasers of lower-priced properties. A wide variety of properties is available, ranging from larger town houses to country residences. Little scope exists for new building owing to land shortage.

Period or Victorian-style homes or estate houses cost approximately £180,000 to £250,000, while good-quality, detached houses in pleasing locations usually range between £400,000 and £600,000.

There is also a limited number of superior properties costing up to around £4 million.

Conveyance charges amount to approximately 4.25 per cent of purchase price. Rates are very low and in three categories: occupiers' rates levied by the parish, tax on rateable value payable annually to the States, and quarterly water rate. Open market houses with a market value of £250,000 pay combined rates, including water, of about £200 per annum.

The Bristol & West Building Society has an office in Guernsey. The laws of inheritance differ from those of the UK and it is advisable to make a new will on taking up residence. Advice should be obtained from a local advocate.

Purchasing procedures

Verbal contracts are legally binding in Guernsey. The purchaser is represented by an advocate who undertakes the title search and drafts the conveyance. Completion normally takes about six weeks and is effected by appearance before the Royal Court. A *congé* of 2 per cent of the consideration is payable on conveyance plus a document duty at varying rates depending on the value of the property.

Jersey

This is the largest of the Channel Islands and the most southerly of this group of islands.

It is a very popular resort for holiday-makers from the mainland and attractive as a low tax area for wealthy individuals and international businesses. The island has also become a major international banking community with a wide selection of banks, mainly in St Helier.

Property purchase and residency

In order to protect local people and to maintain a balance between economic development and the preservation of the environment, it has been necessary to impose severe restrictions on the movement of people into the island.

This is achieved by local licensing laws which prevent individuals who do not have birth or marriage qualifications from buying or leasing freehold or leasehold residential accommodation unless approved by the Jersey Housing Committee.

One way of obtaining this approval is to be essentially employed in one of what are considered to be the most important professions such as medicine, accountancy and banking.

Having obtained the Committee's permission, the employing company can then purchase or rent a property for the employee to live in. The individual cannot buy a property in his or her own name unless resident in the island for 20 years or more.

The only other way of obtaining a residence permit is as a wealthy immigrant. Each application is considered on its merit and requirements do vary. As a general guide, an annual tax liability of £100,000 is required and total wealth in the region of £10 million. Very few people of this status are accepted each year, and they must spend a minimum of £750,000 on a property.

Under Jersey law the legal title to property does not depend on deeds. Title passes only when the Royal Court of Jersey decrees. The Court will do this only when the parties have indicated their mutual agreement to the terms and have also previously satisfied the Housing Committee that the proposed new occupant has the necessary residential qualifications. Thus the housing purchase regulations are enforced without undue difficulties.

Alderney

Alderney is the most northerly of the Channel Islands and lies only eight miles off the French Normandy coast. It has a population of about 2400 and is the third largest in the group (measuring $3\frac{1}{2}$ by $1\frac{1}{2}$ miles). Many of the inhabitants are of French descent and some of the street names are in French, but English is the common tongue. This is a location where peace and serenity can be enjoyed in abundance, amid some delightful scenery. There is much natural beauty with fine sandy beaches, attractive bays, cliff walks and country lanes.

St Anne, 'the town', is little more than a sleepy village with cobblestone streets, colour-washed cottages and a surprising variety of small shops. It is inland, yet within easy walking distance of the harbour at Braye.

There are a number of clubs and 9-hole golf courses.

Administration

Alderney is a self-governing territory and one of the constitutive islands of the Bailiwick of Guernsey. The legislature known as the States comprises a President and 12 elected members. Each person who has lived on the island for at least one year is entitled to vote and is qualified to stand for the States after three years in residence.

The Court of Alderney, which is administered by six Jurats and a Chairman, deals with all civil, criminal and company law matters.

Economy
Tourism is important during the summer, yet the island is never overcrowded and visitors are made very welcome. Local crafts include pottery, spinning, weaving and knitwear, and also fishing.

Like its larger sister islands, Alderney is now an offshore financial centre and has the same modern banking, insurance and investment laws as Guernsey. The island has its own company law with about 500 firms currently registered. Costs of forming and operating a company compare favourably with the other Channel Islands. There are three branches of UK clearing banks and Alderney Trustee Savings Bank, who act as local agents for Barclays.

Taxation
There are no death duties or capital gains taxes for residents. VAT is not charged and local rates are minimal for they average between £5 and £20 per annum. Income tax is 20 per cent, with allowances similar to those in the UK. Other revenue comes from modest import duties on alcohol, tobacco, petrol and the sale of the island's own postage stamps.

Medical
The UK Health Service does not exist in the Channel Islands, so the majority of residents are covered by either the Western Providence Association, which has a special local scheme, or BUPA.

There is a small modern hospital on the island but patients have to pay for treatment by doctors and dentists. Newcomers likely to require geriatric treatment immediately or in the near future are advised to stay away as legislation is being considered to restrict demand on these services.

Education
Children between the ages of 5 and 16 can attend the modern local school where nationally recognised examinations can be taken. Further education can be taken in Guernsey where there are excellent schools for girls and boys. Alderney also has nursery schools and playgroups for under-fives.

Work permits
For non-islanders wishing to settle and work in the island an employment permit system operates, but certain categories of

occupation are exempt. Further information can be obtained from the Chief of the States Office.

Importations

Domestic pets from other Channel Islands, the Isle of Man and the UK mainland can be imported without a permit. All other animals require a permit and may be quarantined. The maximum length of cars allowed on the island is 4.67 metres. Caravans cannot be imported.

Housing

There are no restrictions on the purchase of houses or bungalows by UK or EC passport holders, and there is always a selection of homes for sale. Small terraced houses range from about £80,000. Town houses and compact bungalows suitable for retirement are available for between about £120,000 and £180,000, while family homes with four or more bedrooms generally sell for in excess of £190,000.

Building plots rarely come on the market for much of the island is designated green belt where development is prohibited. New building is strictly controlled and the few permits granted each year are normally given to local people providing an essential service to the community.

Purchasing procedures

Verbal contracts are legally binding having signed the conditions of sale. No advocate is required but a title search should be undertaken. Completion generally averages four to six weeks and is effected by appearance before the Alderney Land Registry.

Expenses comprise *congé* (the local property purchase tax) – 4 per cent of the purchase price – and a stamp duty of 1.5 per cent.

Communications

There are scheduled air services throughout the year from Southampton, Jersey, Guernsey, Cherbourg and Dinard. During the summer, passenger services by sea are available via Guernsey to Poole, Weymouth and France. There is also a weekly car ferry with passenger accommodation from Alderney to Cherbourg throughout the year.

Chapter 22

Europe and the Mediterranean

Andorra

General information
Status. Co-principality
Capital. Andorra la Vella
Area. 465 sq km (180 sq miles)
Population. 40,000 (approx)

Location
Latitude 43°N; longitude 0°E. Landlocked territory in the Eastern Pyrenees, surrounded by France and Spain, roughly the same size as the Isle of Wight and having very mountainous terrain.

Political stability
Excellent, for it has a unique record of diplomatic non-intervention in European affairs stretching back for 700 years. As a co-principality it has been run largely on feudal lines with the President of France and the Bishop of nearby Spanish town of Seu d'Urgell as joint sovereigns. At a referendum held early in 1993, Andorrans voted in favour of a more democratic constitution, allowing the country to make its own foreign policy and to join international organisations. Political parties have been formed and a general election was held in December 1993. As a result no party won an overall majority so a coalition has been formed among three of the parties. Local opinion considers that there is little chance of any radical legislation being passed and in some quarters fresh elections are being predicted within a year.

None of the parties supported the idea of direct taxation, so wealthy expatriates can heave a sigh of relief.

Economy
Currency. The French franc and the Spanish peseta comprise the official currency as Andorra does not have its own monetary unit. Coins and bank notes of these two countries circulate freely and travellers' cheques in various currencies can be cashed at local

banks. Access, Amex and Visa credit cards are accepted by many traders. Credit Andorra, a local bank has 10 branches with English-speaking staff and there are seven other Andorran banks, but foreign banks are not permitted to operate locally.

There are no exchange control restrictions.

Cost of living. This compares favourably with many other European countries. Food and other living expenses are roughly on a par with Spain, while fuel costs are very competitive as electricity is generated by hydro-electric power. Telephone charges and property insurance are not high, while luxuries such as alcohol, jewellery and electrical goods are quite cheap due to low import duties.

Taxation. With no tax on incomes, wealth, profits, inheritance tax or VAT, Andorra is a tax haven. The main source of income for the government is a small excise duty levied on all goods imported for sale into the country. A treaty with the EC in 1990 provides non-member status with agreed customs regulations.

Exchange rate. As for Spanish pesetas and French francs.

Exchange control. None.

Language
Catalan, Spanish and French are the main spoken languages, but English is spoken and understood in some areas, especially tourist parts.

Expatriate community
Only about 25 per cent of the population are native Andorrans, the rest being about 18,000 Spanish residents, 8000 from France and the rest a mixture of other nationalities including about 1000 Britons.

Because of the large immigrant community, Andorrans are obviously welcoming in their attitude.

Security
Andorrans are generally law-abiding citizens, with a few 'black sheep' who are mostly visitors and foreign workers. The crime rate is very low and the country itself has no army.

Residence permits
To be granted a residence permit (*residencia*) applicants must own or rent a property in Andorra and genuinely want to live in the country and become active members of the community. They must also have sufficient private income, so that it is not necessary to seek

employment in the principality. Permits are issued annually initially, but longer extensions may be granted subsequently. Applications often take some time to be considered and have to be submitted in Catalan.

Work permits
People wishing to seek employment face great problems in gaining a work permit.

Personal effects
No duties are payable.

Housing
Only about 8 per cent of the country's total area is available and suitable for residential development, so there are restrictions on how much property a foreigner may own. Currently this comprises one unit, ie one apartment or villa or one plot of land not exceeding an area of 1000 square metres. Husband and wife count as one entity in this respect, but children over the age of 18 may register a property in their own name.

Many ski apartments and some excellent villas have been built for foreign owners over the past three decades, so there is a good selection of resales on the market, also some newly built homes. Prices range from about £40,000 for a one-bedroom ski apartment.

Buying on property
A property can be reserved verbally, but once a 10 per cent deposit has been placed with the vendor's agent, the purchaser is committed and will lose the deposit if the deal is not completed by the buyer. A receipt for the deposit is issued and, about six weeks later, after the necessary enquiries have been made and government approval (*suplica*) has been obtained, both parties appear before a local notary to sign the purchase contract. At this time the balance of the purchase price is paid over and the title deeds are then issued.

Fees charged by the notary amount to about 1 per cent of the purchase price. There is a fee for the *suplica* and probably a once-only charge of about £20 per square metre based on the area of the property.

Where to live
The best residential districts include Arinal, Erts, La Masana, Sispony and Sant Julia. Avoid areas near the highway which traverses the main valley through the country as this is used by heavy goods traffic and is consequently noisy.

Inspection flights
Not available, but independent travel facilities are adequate (see below).

Communications
Air. Daily air services from Heathrow and Gatwick to Barcelona (flight time about two hours), which is about 130 miles south of

Andorra. Then a road journey by an excellent public shared taxi or minibus at a reasonable fare. Alternatively, it is possible to fly to Toulouse in France and continue the journey by train or hire car.

Rail. By train, the journey from London via Paris and Toulouse to Hospitalet, close to the Andorran border, takes about 24 hours.

Road. The journey by car is via the trans-Pyrenean highway which links Toulouse with Barcelona and passes within 40 km of Andorra la Vella, the capital. From the Channel ports the distance is about 600 miles and with a morning crossing it is possible to cover about two-thirds of the journey on the day of departure, spend a night in a hotel *en route* and arrive in Andorra about the middle of the next day.

Recreation and residential amenities

Andorra is a mountainous country with more than 60 peaks over 7500 feet high. Even the 'lowlands' are about 4000 feet above sea level, so there are plenty of opportunities for winter sports. From December to April there are excellent facilities for skiing with a number of excellent ski stations and over 130 pistes suitable for all levels of the sport. Enthusiasts can undertake snow-biking, surf-skiing, heli-skiing and mono-skiing. After an outdoor session it is possible to enjoy swimming in Olympic-size pools, visit an ice rink, play squash and tennis, athletics and football.

Walking, hiking, biking and horse riding can be enjoyed in summer through beautiful scenery and along the banks of numerous rivers.

There are a number of sports clubs and a new Water Palace. Nightclubs and dance halls are also open.

The main shopping centre is at Andorra La Vella. Here there is an excellent range of retail establishments including some large department stores.

BBC World Service Radio enables residents to keep in touch with happenings in other countries. TV addicts can watch BBC programmes and ASTRA with satellite dishes. Local French and Spanish TV programmes can also be received.

Health services

The healthy climate is beneficial to those suffering from chest complaints and the two modern state hospitals have resident English-speaking doctors. A comprehensive social security plan is available.

Climate

Spring (April–May). Maximum temperature 22°C, minimum 4°C. Generally warm but with variable rain or snow showers.

Summer (June–September). Maximum temperature 26°C, minimum 10°C. Mostly dry hot days, with cooler nights. No humidity.

Autumn (October–November). Maximum temperature 18°C, minimum 2°C. Clear skies, fresh mornings and evenings. No fog.

Winter (December–March). Maximum temperature 15°C, minimum 7°C. Snow on most higher altitudes, mostly sunny days and not damp.

Austria

General information
Status. Republic
Capital. Vienna
Area. 83,855 sq km (32,367 sq miles)
Population. 7,555,338

Location
Latitude 48°N; longitude 10°E to 16°E. Austria is situated in southern central Europe, covering part of the eastern Alps and the Danube region. Though landlocked, the country has a wide variety of landscape, vegetation and climate, ranging from Alpine highlands, through the foothills, to lowland plains.

Political stability
Despite a history of political and territorial instability, post-war Austria has gained a reputation for comparative continuity and stability. It is a federal republic, which effectively gives considerable autonomy to the regions. Party politics, although well-developed, have created some problems.

Austria's position of neutrality helps to enhance the policy of cordial relations with all nations. In economic matters, Austria is also non-aligned as it is not a member of the European Community.

Economy
Cost of living. The Austrian economy is undoubtedly very stable. Prudent policies and efficient industry have combined to produce a high level of employment and, generally, a high standard of living for most of the inhabitants. Prices are high when compared with the UK but this is compensated for by good wages.

Taxation. A double taxation agreement between Britain and Austria does exist. VAT varies, depending on the type of goods, from 8–10 per cent to 32 per cent (luxury goods). Income tax varies from a minimum of 10 per cent to a maximum of 50 per cent.

Exchange rate. Austrian schillings 17.76 = £1.

Exchange control. There are no limits to the amount of foreign currency which can be imported or exported. The Austrian schilling is one of the most stable currencies in the world.

Language

The language of 98 per cent of the population is German, so a knowledge of the tongue would be useful. However, knowledge of English is fairly widespread in Austria, especially among the well-educated.

Expatriate community

There are few expatriate Britons in Austria.

Security

Austria is a secure nation and faces no specific problems.

Residence permits

A residence permit may be granted only on specific authorisation from the Ministry of the Interior. Material independence is usually required. Where family reunion is concerned, the name, nationality and address of the relatives are required too. A temporary visa for six months can be acquired but all applications must be made in the mother country.

Work permits

Work permits can only be applied for prior to departure from the UK. They are issued in line with existing conditions in Austria, and so, because of the unemployment situation, are currently very hard to get. A sound knowledge of German is required.

Personal effects

Household goods may be imported duty free, so long as they are accompanied by a household goods inventory (see Chapter 8).

Housing

In order to protect local inhabitants from growing shortages and escalating prices of residential property, a quota system has been imposed on the purchase by foreigners of homes in certain regions. As a result, it is virtually impossible to purchase property in some regions of the country if you are not Austrian. In other communities the restrictions are not severe. In the centre of the country the Styrian Salzkammergut district offers good opportunities for property purchase. Ski lodges and apartments appeal most to the British. Small studios can be acquired for around £30,000.

One-bedroom apartments cost around £35,000, while those with three bedrooms realise in the region of £75,000. Two-bedroom ski chalets can be purchased from approximately £80,000. Individual country houses with four bedrooms are available from between £275,000 and about £500,000.

Buying property

The property agreement is written in German, with an English translation, and this can be signed in either Austria or the UK. A copy is given to the purchaser. The lawyer acts for both parties and can have power of attorney to act on behalf of the purchaser. He or she can also prepare a mortgage agreement if a loan is required.

Deposits are not normally necessary. The documents are signed before an official of the Austrian Embassy and then returned to the lawyer with a draft or cheque for the purchase price. The money is then placed in a trustee account in Germany or Austria where it remains until completion takes place. Meanwhile the new title to the property is registered at the land registry and this may take four months or more. When registration is complete the taxes and fees are paid and the purchase price released to the vendor.

Expenses total about 8–8.5 per cent of the purchase price and comprise land tax at 3.5 per cent plus a separate fee for the Land Registry Court, depending on the price of the property, but it will be around £175–£270; title registration 1 per cent; stamp duty 0.5 per cent; notary fees 3–4 per cent.

Where to live

See 'Housing' above.

Communications

Austria has excellent communications both internally and externally, including six commercial airports, well over 1000 km o motorways and 5800 km of railways, plus large stretches o navigable waterways as well as thousands of cable-based mountair lifts. Public transport in Austria is well developed.

Austria has a dense network of postal communications and new media, including fully automatic telephone, telegraph and telex as well as radio and television.

Recreation

Leisure facilities in Austria are excellent. The environment is one of stunning beauty, which encourages outdoor pursuits such as walking, camping and climbing, not to mention the ideal Alpine skiing conditions which make skiing Austria's national sport. Other popular physical pursuits include football, swimming, judo and motor racing. There is also a very strong tradition of horse riding. In general, sports facilities are excellent.

Culture and the arts also provide a rich source of interest for residents. Literature, opera, choirs and festivals combine with the fine architecture to promote Austria's cultural image. The main cities such as Vienna and Salzburg are especially fascinating.

Driving

Driving in Austria is on the right and really much the same as elsewhere in mainland Europe.

Health services

The Austrian health service is very well equipped, with an average of one doctor for every 370 patients. There are over 300 hospitals in all. Each province has its own health administration and health office. In principle, anybody is entitled to make use of the facilities in the health service as the costs are borne by the social insurance and social welfare scheme.

The influence of the Socialists in Austria has led to the development of a carefully worked-out welfare programme. An agreement does exist between the UK and Austria and details are given in DSS pamphlet SA25.

Climate

Austria belongs to the central European climatic zone, with the influence of the Atlantic felt in the west and the continental influence more strongly in the east. In general, the climatic seasonal changes are far less pronounced in the west than in the east. For the purposes of describing climate, Austria can be divided into three areas:

East–continental Pannonian climate: mean temperature for July above 19°C; annual rainfall less than 800 mm.

Central Alpine region: high precipitation with long winters and short summers.

European climatic zone: wet and temperate, July temperature 14–19°C, annual precipitation 700–2000 mm.

Cyprus

General information
Status. Independent Republic
Capital. Nicosia
Area. 9251 sq km (3570 sq miles)
Population. 650,000

Location
Latitude 30°N; longitude 32°E. The island of Cyprus, at the eastern end of the Mediterranean, is a land of contrast. In the south, where the majority of Greek Cypriots live, there is considerable prosperity; and vast sums have been invested in the construction of new roads, hotels and residential accommodation. A second airport has been opened at Paphos and the facilities at Larnaca are considerably improved.

The main business centre is Nicosia, the capital, which is partitioned by an armoured line. The towns of Larnaca, Limassol and Paphos, all on the southern coast and controlled by Greek Cypriots, have a multitude of sandy beaches which are much enjoyed by the tourist; they also benefit from considerable business activity.

In the middle of the island is a mountain range, Troodos, where it is possible to ski in the winter and then descend to sea level to enjoy a swim in the Mediterranean, all on the same day.

The northern parts of the island, including the once popular resorts of Kyrenia and Famagusta, are under the jurisdiction of Turkish Cypriots who are supported by a considerable contingent of the Turkish army. Tourism is at a low ebb compared with the rest of the island.

Political stability
Although the island is partitioned, stability seems to have been achieved but there is no apparent intercommunication.

The Greek Cypriot part of the area has one of the lowest crime rates in the world, offences such as muggings being practically non existent. The safety of individuals and property is no great problem and the risks are minimal.

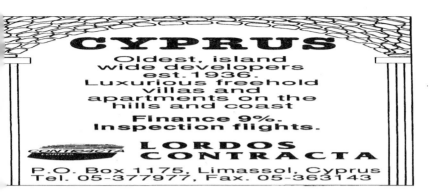
Cyprus is a non-aligned country, a member of the Common-wealth, the Council of Europe and the United Nations. Application has been made to join the EC; meanwhile an Association Agreement with the Community exists which envisages the abolition of all barriers to trade and the establishment of a Customs Union by 1998.

Economy

Cost of living. This is cheaper than in the UK. Inflation has been kept below 5 per cent in recent years, thanks to the thriving manufacturing and agricultural industries, which, together with tourism, are the main foreign currency earners. Annual growth rate has averaged 6 per cent and the unemployment rate is very low.

Local produce is reasonable, but some imported items are more expensive than in the UK because of transport costs. Because of the year-round equitable climate heavy clothes are not required.

Taxation. Income tax is charged on income remitted to Cyprus. Foreign pensions transmitted to Cyprus are taxed at about 3 per cent per annum, while income from investments suffers a tax of 5 per cent. Capital gains tax on property is charged at 20 per cent on gains over C£5000, even if the property was acquired by importation of currency and the owner is non-resident. Cyprus and the UK have a double taxation agreement.

The Off-Shore Business Centre is very successful with about 8000 off-shore companies operating from Cyprus. These companies enjoy low taxation and other benefits.

Exchange rate. Cyprus pound (C£) 0.76 = £1. Exchange control in operation.

169

Language
English is spoken by practically everybody. About 70 per cent of local TV programmes are in English and there are two English language papers. In addition, the local British Forces radio broadcasts round the clock every day.

Expatriate community
Links between the UK and Cyprus have always been strong and are illustrated in many ways, such as the similarity of property registration procedure, driving laws and the existence of a substantial Cypriot community in Britain. Links are compounded by the presence of a British military base on the island so it is not surprising that over 3000 Britons are resident in Cyprus and many more own holiday property there.

Security
The Cypriots themselves are generally open and honest and so personal property is not especially at risk. Cyprus is strategically vital to the West for monitoring the Middle East, and there also is an undercurrent of uncertainty because of the partition of the island. However, any fears should be allayed by the comforting presence of the UN peace-keeping force.

Residence permits
A permanent residence permit can be easily obtained on proof that you own a property in Cyprus, are self-supporting and no burden to the state.

Work permits
Aliens wishing to work in Cyprus require a permit from the government under the Aliens Immigration Law.

Personal effects
Personal baggage can be imported free of duty.

Housing
A wide range of recently built and new villas and apartments is available at prices from about £30,000. Also available are village houses for modernisation. Prices vary according to size and location.

Buying property
A foreign adult or family is allowed to purchase only one villa or

apartment or a building plot of about two-thirds of an acre in Cyprus.

The Cyprus legal system for property purchase is based on its English counterpart. Locally it is not considered essential to employ a solicitor to handle a property conveyance, but in the author's opinion it is better to be safe than sorry.

All property in Cyprus is registered at the local Land Registry and property purchase procedure is somewhat similar to England and Wales. The first stage is the signing of a preliminary contract, which binds both parties to the transaction on mutually agreed terms. This is subject to the purchaser being able to get a good title to the property and being able to obtain the required permits from the Cyprus government. At this stage a deposit is lodged with a notary or lawyer. Searches are then carried out at the Land Registry by the purchaser's legal adviser, to ascertain that the vendor has a good title to the property which can be transferred to the purchaser.

The application by a non-Cypriot to purchase the property, which is submitted to the Council of Ministers at this stage or earlier, is normally a routine matter and costs around £200 sterling. The final contract is only entered into when the searches have proved satisfactory and the permits approved.

Purchase expenses include a stamp duty of 0.15 per cent of the purchase price up to C£100,000 and 0.2 per cent on any purchase price in excess of this figure.

Land Registry fees are on a sliding scale of between 5 and 8 per cent, depending on the value of the property. Lawyer's fees are based on the amount of work involved and are likely to be between £200 and £500 sterling. Local authority taxes for street lighting, refuse collection, etc, generally range between C£30 and C£100 per annum, according to the size of the property. An annual immovable property tax is levied on registered properties valued over C£100,000 at 0.35 per cent on the excess value, or on the full value if unregistered.

Foreign currency must be imported into Cyprus by aliens to pay for any property purchased. On resale, repatriation of the original purchase price is allowed immediately and any profit can be exported at the rate of £5000 annually, plus interest. Foreign nationals may operate external or internal bank accounts.

Where to live

A varied choice of locations is available in the southern (Greek) sector of the island, for those seeking a villa or apartment for permanent living or for vacations. There are a number of substantial-sized towns with residential amenities, a variety of quiet villages, some attractive coastal resorts and some pretty mountain hamlets.

Nicosia. Situated almost in the centre of the island, Nicosia has an estimated population of over 150,000 citizens. It is divided into two sections, Greek and Turkish by the so-called 'Green Line' which was instituted following trouble between the Greek and the Turks which resulted in the invasion of the north of the island by Turkish armed forces, in 1974. United Nations soldiers guard the border and maintain the peace between the two factions. This situation does not, however, affect life locally and on the Greek side of the border business is brisk in the city with its wide streets, tree-lined avenues, fine shops, busy offices, hotels and government buildings. Of interest are the city walls built by the Venetians (1567–70), which are now integrated into the life of the metropolis, and the Cyprus Museum which contains the most important collection of Cypriot antiquities and art treasures.

On the Turkish side of the Green Line, business is less prosperous and life is at a slower pace.

Limassol. Population 70,000. The second largest town in Cyprus is Limassol, about 80 kms south west of Nicosia and about half way between the island's two airports at Larnaca and Paphos. It is the main port and has two fully equipped marinas. Having expanded considerably over the past decade, it now spreads for over 20 kms along the coastline where there are many new hotels on the beach and in the neighbouring hinterland. The shopping facilities are generally regarded as the best in the island. Richard the Lionheart is reputed to have married Berengaria de Navarre at Limassol Castle.

Larnaca. Population around 25,000. This is another town of importance with a large marina, where major hotels and apartment blocks have been built in profusion along the coast road and inland. Many new industries have been established in recent years, particularly in the clothing sector, and the town, the fourth largest in the island, is an important trade centre, with pleasant residential areas. Its international airport has taken the place of the one at Nicosia, which has been unavailable since the Turkish invasion in 1974.

Paphos. Situated almost at the western extremity of the island about 100 miles from Nicosia, the town was formerly outside the mainstream of island life, even though it was at one time the capital of Cyprus. Over the past two decades this region has experienced considerable growth from a fishing village to a major resort with many new hotels and other tourist accommodation. In the vicinity are some fine mosaics dating from Roman times, the Tombs of the Kings, a 13th-century church and strong associations with Aphrodite the goddess of Love.

Ayia Napa. A small fishing village at the eastern end of the south coast which has been transformed over little more than ten years into a resort of importance with numerous hotel and apartment blocks, restaurants and tourist shopping facilities.

Renting property
In order to protect the tourist industry, a regulation prevents foreigners from letting their property in Cyprus to holiday-makers. However, this rule does not seem to be imposed very vigorously.

Communications
British Airways and Cyprus Airways between them run daily services to Larnaca (flying time about $3\frac{1}{2}$ hours). On leaving, an airport tax of about £1.50 is levied. There are also scheduled flights to Paphos (4 hours). Cyprus Airways serve many European and Middle East countries.

Telecommunications are excellent, with automatic direct dialling available on a 24-hour basis to over 60 countries.

Health and welfare
Cyprus has one of the healthiest climates in the world. Medical treatment costs in government hospitals are low. Also there are plenty of specialist doctors and surgeons, and private practices for consultation.

A social security agreement exists between the UK and Cyprus, covering National Insurance and various benefits including pensions. Details are given in DSS pamphlet SA12. Pensions from UK National Insurance are index linked.

Climate

	Average daily temperature (°C)	Rainfall Average days	Sea temperature (°C)	Sunshine hours
January	9–18	12	18	169
February	9–19	8	18	197
March	10–20	7	18	255
April	11–21	4	18	285
May	15–27	4	20	355

June	18–30	1	21	379
July	21–35	0.3	26	399
August	21–35	0.4	27	358
September	18–32	1	29	321
October	17–27	3	25	277
November	11–24	6	21	231
December	8–17	11	17	175

France

General information
Status. Republic
Capital. Paris
Area. 551,000 sq km (213,000 sq miles)
Population. 55 million (approx)

Location
Latitude 42°N to 51°N; longitude 5°W to 5°E. France is surrounded by mountains and water and its natural boundaries are the Pyrénées and the Alps, the river Rhine, the Channel, the Atlantic and the Mediterranean.

Taxation. A double taxation agreement exists between France and the UK. Non-residents do not normally pay income tax if they are using a property as a holiday home for personal use only. A non-resident selling a secondary residence in France pays a tax of 33.3 per cent levied on capital gains, but quite generous allowances can reduce the actual assessment substantially. Any tax paid in France can be offset against a UK liability under the double taxation agreement. A wealth tax has been reintroduced. In 1994 assets not exceeding FF4.47 million are exempt, beyond which the rate is 0.5 per cent up to FF7.270 million and the scale increases to 1.5 per cent for amounts in excess of FF43.380 million. Married couples and common law couples are assessed jointly. Local rates and occupancy tax are calculated by the local authorities and cover such items as local schools, street lighting, road sweeping etc. Payment is assessed on 1 January annually. VAT is levied at various rates in accordance with EC regulations.

Exchange rate. French francs 8.61 = £1.

Exchange control. The purchase of real estate by non-French residents does not now require foreign exchange permission from the French authorities.

Language

French is a comparatively easy language to learn and the effort is well worth while if you live in France for any length of time.

Expatriate community

France remains defiantly popular among Britons looking to set up home overseas, despite the recession, the devaluation of sterling and the high supplementary costs of buying a French property. Lack of confidence in the economy has severely hindered property sales on both sides of the Channel, with the result that many well-intentioned buyers are unable to move simply because they cannot sell their home in the UK. There is a silver lining, however. Although devaluation has increased the price of French property to British purchasers, the recession means vendors in France are often prepared to negotiate. This, and low interest rates on sterling mortgages, offer some compensation. It is hardly surprising that the French property market has proved resilient. The appeal of the French way of life extends far beyond its own boundaries. France is internationally popular, attracting more than 40 million overseas visitors a year – almost a quarter of them from Britain. For many holiday-makers to France, buying a place of their own is simply the next, logical step. The boom years of 1988 and 1989 may be long over, but many buyers whose ambitions have been checked are merely shelving, rather than abandoning, their plans.

In the past, foreign buyers traditionally headed south – to the Riviera, inland Provence and latterly Dordogne. Now, every nook and cranny of provincial France is explored in the search for that dream home. Reaching those parts has never been simpler. Access is an important consideration in France's favour. Those apparently isolated corners of the country are, in fact, temptingly close thanks to ever-improving communications. Not only will the Channel Tunnel bring northern France within easier reach for British visitors, but rapidly developing road and rail networks throughout France are opening up the whole of the country.

The sheer variety of property available in France is another factor which guarantees the interest of overseas buyers. Although house prices in Britain have come tumbling down, real estate in France remains an attractive proposition. There are estates, country houses of great architectural value and character and restored manor houses, at prices which still compare favourably. The decline in agriculture and the migration to towns and suburbs in France since the Second World War mean thousands of redundant farm buildings and country dwellings have become available. Many of them require complete restoration and have remained on the market, unoccupied, for a number of years. Some are ruins with little or no sanitation. It is still possible to find a tumbledown cottage tucked away in the heart of the French countryside for £10,000, even less, provided you are prepared to spend more money and time making it habitable. Recouping the cost of an expensive renovation, however, could prove difficult, particularly in a buyers' market. Although the French themselves are beginning to show a greater interest in rural properties again, they do not generally share the British taste for out-of-the-way 'character' homes.

Purchasing property

Consider all the options carefully before committing yourself to buy. The importance of taking professional advice cannot be over-emphasised. Speak to lawyers, bankers, financial advisers, as well as architects and surveyors, if appropriate. Do as much homework as possible to familiarise yourself with the French system, the terms that will be used and the French professionals you will meet during the course of the transaction. Consult the 'everyday' experts, too, people who have already bought a house or business in France, and

THE GOOD RETIREMENT GUIDE 1994

Rosemary Brown

"A mine of information." Independent

Now in its eighth edition THE GOOD RETIREMENT GUIDE provides the very latest details on tax, benefits, pensions, investment vehicles, new career opportunities, holiday choices and much, much more.

This is a comprehensive guide which all your retiring staff will appreciate, whatever their age, proving to them that retirement is the beginning of a new experience.

£14.99 Paperback Ref KS098
544 pages (P & P £1.50)

Published by
KOGAN PAGE
120 Pentonville Road
London N1 9JN

who may be only too willing to pass on the benefits of their experiences

Make sure you ask *yourself* a few straightforward questions, as well. Would you be happier in a cottage that wasn't quite so isolated? Will the bargain *château* cost a small fortune in renovation and upkeep? Have you the skills, time and dedication to repair that dilapidated farmhouse and install mod cons? Be as objective as possible. Put aside the memories of carefree summer holidays in France. Visit your chosen location in the winter when its climate and character are completely different.

There is no need to be intimidated by the French system, for all its bureaucracy and paperwork, provided a number of basic rules are followed. French law provides considerable consumer protection for the home-buyer, but the procedures – legal, financial and fiscal – are as different as the customs, culture and attitudes of the French themselves and should be fully understood to avoid potential pitfalls.

The role of the *notaire* is crucial in all property transactions. The French system does not automatically provide your own personal legal representative. Unless you choose otherwise, the *notaire* will be the only legal professional involved. If you are buying a new property (off-plan), the developer will nominate the *notaire*. In theory, the purchaser has the right to choose the *notaire* when the transaction involves existing property. In practice, however, the French agent will probably suggest the *notaire* who handled the previous sale of the property.

The *notaire* is a public officer, controlled by the Ministry of Justice, who will supervise and authenticate the transfer of ownership. Whoever nominates the *notaire*, the *notaire* represents neither the purchaser nor the vendor. Instead, the *notaire's* responsibilities are to the French government: to ensure the law is properly applied and that all fees and taxes due to the state on completion of the deal are paid.

The *notaire* will make certain enquiries and searches on the property with the local authority and the Land Charges Registry, to verify that the property is the vendor's to sell and that there is no outstanding loan against it greater than the current purchase price. In the case of land or farm buildings, the *notaire* will also check that the French agricultural authorities, notably SAFER (the Société d'Aménagement Foncier et d'Etablissement Rural), will not be exercising their right to step in and buy the property instead of you. The *notaire* will not, however, make the exhaustive local searches specifically on your behalf that your solicitor in Britain would. Enquiries relate to the property itself and not to the surrounding area. So you may not be made aware of plans to build a motorway a kilometre away, right in your view of the open countryside.

It is worth carrying out your own enquiries at departmental and local level. Visit the Département de l'Urbanisme in the *mairie* (the town hall). Talk to your prospective neighbours and the patron and regulars at the local café, always an invaluable source of information. In any case, you should go along to the *mairie* to introduce yourself to the mayor. In France, the mayor is a far more influential person than the British counterpart and has greater powers – the authority and responsibility to make many decisions which could affect your property.

Although the *notaire* is not formally your legal representative, ask if you are unsure about anything. If you wish, you may appoint a second *notaire* to supervise the completion of the transaction on your behalf. You might not be popular if you do, however, because the two *notaires* would then share the same fee. Alternatively, you may decide to employ a legal representative of your own, exclusively to defend your interests and to make enquiries and searches on your behalf. In this case, of course, a separate fee for these services would be payable.

When you set out to look for your new home, contact several property agents. Those who are based in Britain will have a network of associate agents in France. Together they will arrange site visits for you, but do not expect the French office to provide detailed printed information about the properties on their books. Instead, they will tend to accompany you on your appointments. Do not be too ambitious about the number of these you can keep in a day. France is a deceptively large country, and even within a single *département* it can take longer than you anticipate to travel from one rural property to another.

Be realistic, too, about the type of property you are looking for. Decide what your priorities are, and then have a good look around. Allow sufficient time to view a number of properties within your price range to appreciate exactly what is available. Choose the dates of your visits to France carefully. Holiday times may suit you, but first make sure that the agency or *notaire*'s office will be open.

Consider carefully the precise location of your property. An idyllic quiet spot for a fortnight's vacation may not be so attractive as a permanent residence. That pleasant holiday stroll of a few kilometres to the nearest *boulangerie* could become a chore as a regular matter of necessity. Since the additional costs and fees of purchase are higher in France than in Britain, a mistake at this stage could be not only regrettable but also expensive.

Older properties in parts of south-west France are subject to infestation by wood-boring insects. The *notaire* should be able to advise you whether a property is in an affected area. In some places a survey and any necessary remedial treatment are compulsory on change of ownership.

Surveys are not common practice in French property transactions and can be expensive. Some French banks may not insist on a valuation when deciding on a mortgage application. As we shall discover, however, they will be very interested in the applicant's personal ability to service the loan.

There are professionals in France who will examine a property for you – building experts (*experts immobiliers*) and architects – and there are British surveyors who practise in France. They must have professional indemnity insurance, which should be extended to cover their work across the Channel.

If you are buying an old property or farm building in an isolated area, make sure there is a supply of tap water and electricity as well as room on your own land for the installation of a septic tank. If you wish to have the water supply analysed, contact the *mairie* or the DDASS (Direction Départementale des Affaires Sanitaires et Sociales).

You may decide that a modern apartment, in a coastal resort, perhaps, promises more carefree ownership with fewer concerns about maintenance. In this case, you will encounter the French system of *co-propriété*, under which you will own your apartment outright, rather than on leasehold. Not only will you have the freehold of the apartment itself but also a share of the freehold of the land. The size of your share is determined by the floor area of your flat, which also serves to apportion your contribution towards the general service charges. In France, the co-owners control the management of the property. Major decisions are taken by ballot at an assembly of owners, and each person's voting right is set out, with a lengthy description of the building, in the all-important document, *le règlement de copropriété*. Every apartment block should have one.

Estate agents in France are strictly regulated. They must have a professional qualification and a financial guarantee enabling them to receive your deposit. Without this guarantee, you should pay your deposit to the *notaire*. Agents in France must display details of their professional charter, the sum of their financial guarantee and the name of the organisation which covers it. Professional associations include FNAIM (Fédération Nationale des Agents Immobiliers et Mandataires) and SNPI (Syndicat National des Professionels Immobiliers).

A good agent will assist you throughout your transaction, giving advice, smoothing out any difficulties that may occur, putting you in contact with an architect or builder or helping with planning procedures. Agents must have a mandate from the vendor, authorising them to sell the property and stating the commission arrangements. Responsibility for paying the commission – whether it is the vendor or the purchaser – varies from region to region. In some parts of France the cost is shared between the two parties, although it is becoming more usual for the vendor to pay. French law protects the agent from purchasers and vendors who, having been introduced to each other, attempt to cut the agent out of the proceedings. In such circumstances, the agent would be entitled to the commission and the same amount again.

You could find your home in France through a *notaire*, because, in addition to legal responsibilities, the *notaire* is permitted to offer properties for sale. The *notaire's* commission, known as the negotiation fee, is fixed in law, but might not be included in the advertised price of a property. It is generally paid by the purchaser.

The agent's fee, on the other hand, is not fixed. It tends to be higher than the *notaire*'s and is generally included in the quoted price. Check this is the case, however, and if you negotiate a lower purchase price be clear that the new figure is still inclusive.

When you deal with a British estate agent you should not pay any more commission than if you had gone directly to the French counterpart. British and French agents working together should share the one fee. So establish the price of the property itself, the cost of any fixtures, fittings and additional land that may be included, the commission (and who pays it), the legal fees and taxes due and the monthly repayments and arrangement fee for your mortgage, if applicable.

If you require a loan to purchase the property, find out before you go to France how much you can borrow and how much the loan will cost. You might decide to remortgage your home in Britain and borrow in sterling at UK rates of interest. In this case, you simply change your pounds into francs and buy the French property outright. Alternatively, you could borrow in francs from a French lender against the security of the French home you are buying. Fixed and variable rates can be negotiated and, generally speaking, the repayment term will be 15 or 20 years. In assessing your monthly repayments you should also allow for life, health and invalidity insurance cover on the mortgage.

A French mortgage offer is subject to a compulsory ten-day cooling-off period before you can accept it. This is for your benefit, part of the consumer-protection legislation, but it does hold up the process and you should allow at least ten weeks for your French loan to come through.

Many French banks have specialist teams in Britain to help you with your mortgage application, and a number of British banks and building societies have French offices and French subsidiaries. They can often provide the paperwork for your application in English, loan terms up to 25 years and, using the *French* property as security, the option of a *sterling* mortgage (thus avoiding the necessity of monthly currency conversions for the repayments).

In processing your application, a French bank will make a cash-flow study to assess your ability to repay the loan. They will require full details of your existing financial commitments as well as your income and will not allow your new French mortgage to take your total outgoings above 30 or 35 per cent of your disposable income.

Provided you do not exceed the above restriction, a French bank will normally lend you up to 70 or 80 per cent of the basic purchase price. This means that, out of your own resources, you will have to finance not only the balance but also the legal fees, taxes and other expenses. So if these come to an additional 20 per cent, for example, and you take out a loan to cover 80 per cent of the price of the house, you will have to find the equivalent of 40 per cent yourself.

If the property needs renovation or repairs, you can apply for a second loan to help to cover the cost. The bank will require quotations with your application, and your estate agent, surveyor or French builder can advise you. Payments will be made directly to the builders on presentation of invoices. Rates could be slightly higher.

It is advisable to open a French bank account in good time. You can do this in France or Britain, in person or by correspondence (in which case your signature will have to be witnessed by a solicitor and/or confirmed by your UK bank). If you wish to open a resident's account you will have to prove that you have a job in France or means of financial support, and you will have to present some, or all, of the following: passport, proof of residence (a copy of your lease if you are renting, or a certificate of completion of purchase which you obtain from the *notaire*), a letter from your UK bank, and a copy of your *carte de séjour* or application for it.

A French bank account will simplify your payment of fuel, telephone and local tax bills as well as your mortgage commitments.

Allow plenty of time when you transfer funds into your French account. It could take longer than expected for the money to be cleared in your account, and if you go overdrawn without arrangement you could be prevented from operating a bank account in France for up to ten years.

You will not be issued with a cheque guarantee card. Cheques can be stopped only if they have been lost or stolen. The *carte bleue* is a charge card, not a credit card, with the amounts debited directly from your account by the bank. You can arrange for pensions to be paid into your bank account in France.

When you have found the property you wish to buy, you will be asked to sign a preliminary contract and to pay a deposit – usually 10 per cent on existing property and 5 per cent if it is new. Make sure you understand the differences between English and French procedures at this stage. There are various types of preliminary contract in France. Be clear about the particular document you are being offered and ensure that it contains all the conditional clauses (*conditions suspensives*) to protect your interests.

There are three main contracts in use for the sale and purchase of existing property. The *promesse de vente* is a unilateral promise by the vendor to sell the property to the purchaser at an agreed price. Normally, the purchaser has a specified period of time in which to take up the option to buy, and during this time the vendor may not withdraw from the contract or offer the property to anyone else. Although there is no obligation on the purchaser to buy, he or she could still forfeit the deposit if the purchaser decides not to proceed. With the *promesse d'achat*, on the other hand, it is the purchaser who commits him or herself to buy the property and there is no obligation on the vendor to sell at all. On the expiration of the time limit, the contract becomes null and void. Before then, however, the purchaser would lose his or her deposit if the purchaser decided not to proceed. The *compromis de vente* is a bilateral agreement, binding both parties. The purchaser may not have the right to withdraw from the transaction, even on the loss of his or her deposit, unless the contract specifically allows the purchaser to do so.

There are also three main types of contract for the sale of new (off-plan) properties – the *contrat de réservation*, the *vente en l'état futur d'achèvement* and the *vente à terme*. Each provides for the payment of a deposit and stage payments as the building work progresses. The law requires the developer or the developer's agent to produce an architect's certificate confirming that each stage of the work has been completed as specified. When you take out a loan from a French bank on a new property, the funds will be released at intervals to meet those stage payments.

If you wish to buy off-plan you could go to a developer who will sell you a building plot and who has a selection of property designs already approved by the planning authority. Alternatively, you may prefer to act independently. You will have to check that the plot you wish to buy can be developed and then apply to the *mairie* for planning permission for your house (*le permis de construire*).

Any new building in France has to be guaranteed – for ten years on the fabric of the property and two years on the internal installations. These guarantees have to be underwritten by an insurance company to protect the purchaser if the builder subsequently ceases to trade. When you take possession, you will be asked to sign a declaration confirming that everything is in order. If you observe any faults later you must point them out to the developer and claim under the guarantee.

Unless you have found your property from a *notaire*, it will probably be the estate agent who prepares the preliminary contract for you to sign. (However, the details will still have to be recorded by a *notaire*.) Resist all pressure to sign and to hand over your deposit until you understand the agreement fully and are completely happy with it. Allow yourself time to study it carefully. A translation of the document will not be enough. Take professional advice if you are unsure about anything. Consult a lawyer who is well versed in French law and taxation and who can explain all the implications of the contract – what has been omitted as well as the contents.

Whether you are buying a new or an existing property, you should make sure that your contract includes a number of *conditions suspensives*. If any one of these is not fulfilled, you can call off the deal and have your deposit returned. The most important condition, and the one that is mandatory under French consumer protection laws, will safeguard you in the event of your mortgage application being refused. If you need a loan to make the purchase, the contract must state this. If you subsequently fail in your application for finance, you may withdraw from the transaction without penalty. This condition means you can effectively secure a property before you even apply for a loan. However, the preliminary contract will set a date by which you must submit your mortgage application and failure to do so could affect your rights. If, on the other hand, you do not intend to apply for a loan, you must endorse the contract to this effect in your own handwriting. You would then forfeit the law's protection if you found that you did need a mortgage, after all.

Bearing in mind that the preliminary contract is signed before the legal searches are made, you should ensure that a number of other, optional, conditions are included. These should protect you in the event of any detrimental planning proposals or third-party rights coming to light; if the vendor has an outstanding mortgage on the property greater than the current price; if SAFER (see above) decides to exercise its rights of pre-emption on a country property; or if you want to make the transaction subject to a satisfactory structural survey. It is always possible to negotiate other conditions as well.

When the *notaire* has completed the enquiries, the *notaire* will draw up the deed of sale, *l'acte de vente*, which contains a full description of the property. Once vendor and purchaser have agreed and signed this document, witnessed by the *notaire*, ownership is transferred. The *notaire* will not hand you the original *acte de vente*, however. Instead, the details will be recorded at the Land Registry, and you must ask the *notaire* if you require a copy (*une expédition*) or a certificate stating that the transaction has been completed (*une attestation*).

The deed is signed in the *notaire*'s office, but if you are unable to travel to France, a friend or a member of the *notaire*'s staff can sign on your behalf. If you wish to arrange this power of attorney and the purchase is subject to a mortgage, you will have to sign a document before a notary public in the UK. If a loan is not required, a British solicitor can witness the document or the *notaire* may be satisfied simply with your own signature.

The additional costs involved in your transaction will vary between new and old property. Taxes and legal fees on older houses can amount to 10 or 12 per cent of the basic purchase price. To that you may have to add the commission. On new homes, the costs are less – 3 or 4 per cent – but VAT will have already been included in the purchase price.

The costs are made up of stamp duty, Land Registry charges and the *notaire*'s fee, as well as transfer duty – 0.6 per cent on new houses, 7.5 per cent on older ones. There is a higher rate of transfer duty on agricultural land and commercial buildings.

Personal finances

Local rates, which are lower than the British Council Tax, consist of an annual *taxe foncière* if the property is not let (*taxe professionnelle* if it is) and a *taxe d'habitation*, which is payable by the person occupying the property on 1 January. If you are buying a property off-plan you can apply for a two-year tax holiday before the *taxe foncière* has to be paid.

If you are resident in France for tax purposes, you are liable to

French income tax on the whole of your worldwide income. In principle, all non-residents who own a house in France are liable to income tax on three times the deemed rental value of their property. In practice, however, UK residents owning a property in France can avoid this tax under the Anglo-French double-tax treaty. Where there is no double-tax agreement with France, in the Channel Islands for example, there is no such protection.

British residents who decide to let their property in France must declare the rental income from it both to the British and the French tax authorities. This applies even if the rental is paid in Britain and the money put into a UK bank account. Under the double treaty, the tax will not have to be paid twice. The sum paid to the French Revenue will be credited against the UK tax assessment.

Wealth tax (*impôt de solidarité sur la fortune*) applies to any individual whose assets in France exceed FF4.47 million (in 1994). The tax is payable annually, at 0.5 per cent on the first band above the FF4.47 million threshold, to a maximum of 1.5 per cent on assets over FF43.38 million.

Non-residents selling secondary homes in France pay capital gains tax at 33.3 per cent. There is an allowance for inflation against the original purchase price and further reductions if the property has been owned for more than two years. British residents must also declare capital gains on the French property to the UK Inland Revenue, but the tax paid in France will again be offset under the double-tax treaty.

Non-residents of France selling property must also appoint a guarantor to the French Revenue, who will be responsible for any capital gains tax owing. The guarantor could be a bank or a resident of France. You may be able to apply for exemption from this on paying your capital gains tax.

Your property in France will be subject to French inheritance laws and taxes – whatever your nationality, wherever your permanent residence and regardless of your wishes. Many British buyers are surprised by the rigidity of these laws. Most significantly, children are given priority over the surviving spouse, male or female.

It is important to ensure that your will covers your French assets. Where there is no will, the surviving spouse receives merely a quarter of the property. For French residents this applies to the entire estate. A will can offer greater protection for the surviving spouse, but whereas English law allows you to leave your assets to whomever you please, French legislation does not. Children – including adopted or illegitimate children or those from a previous marriage – have a legally reserved share before the surviving spouse is considered. Where there is one child the legal reserve is a half-share in the property; two children receive one-third each; three or more children share three-quarters of the property equally. This is the minimum they must be left. There are particular problems where the children are very young. Legally, it could be difficult if the surviving parent wished or needed to sell the property. If there are no children or grandchildren, the legal reserve will apply to living parents of the deceased, rather than the surviving partner.

Any deliberate attempt to defeat the legal reserve could be treated as a fraud. It cannot be avoided, but its effects can be minimised or postponed by the way in which you structure your property ownership. You should take professional advice to avoid tax disadvantages.

Inheritance tax in France is paid by each individual beneficiary, rather than by the estate. The rate of tax varies according to the relationship between the beneficiary and the deceased. The closer the relationship, the lower the rate. Before any tax is due, there is an allowance, which also varies according to the degree of kinship. Attempting to avoid the reserve of children, therefore, would not only be illegal but would also waste their tax-free allowances.

One solution could be the formation of a *société civile immobilière*, a property-holding company. A husband and wife, for example, would not own the house itself, but shares in the company. These could be divided equally between the two partners, and provided the couple were resident outside France the shares would not be subject to French inheritance rules. Children could still be left a quantity of the shares, with the surviving spouse inheriting a controlling majority.

Alternatively, a husband and wife could have *la clause tontine* included in the conveyance when they buy their property. This has the effect of postponing ownership until one partner dies, when the other becomes the owner of the entire property. However, the clause cannot be added after the purchase, and while both partners are alive the property can be sold only if both agree.

Work and residence permits

EC nationals do not need a work permit in France, although certain professions are restricted and require a relevant French, or compatible, qualification. If you are planning to live in France, you no longer need a *visa de longue durée*, which was previously obtained from a French Consulate General in Britain. Instead, you apply for a *carte de séjour* from the local *préfecture* in France. Since there is freedom of movement between member states of the EC, you are entitled to receive a *carte de séjour*. In theory at least, it is not a question of submitting your application and hoping that it will be granted.

You will need to produce your passport, passport-size photographs, proof of residence in France (a copy of a lease or a title deeds certificate), a contract of employment if applicable, and possibly your birth certificate as well. So-called 'non-economically active persons', for example pensioners or students who will not be earning their living in France, may be asked to prove that they have means of financial support.

Personal effects

Under the free movement of goods, you can take your personal property and household items into France. You no longer have to declare that they have been your property for three months, nor are you restricted from selling them for a year. Televisions and video recorders in France operate off the Secam, rather than the PAL, system. A PAL video tape played on a Secam recorder will show monochrome pictures. You will need to adapt or replace your existing items, and you can buy dual-standard equipment. Satellite and cable television are readily available.

Mains services

Mains water in France is metered, with the price varying from region to region. Contact the water board to have the supply connected or if your property has no existing supply. However, the water board will not dig any channels for pipes on your property and you must arrange this work separately.

Electricity and gas are supplied by EDF (Electricité de France) and Gaz de France, although in the country you will probably need gas in bottles or a tank. Normally, there are three levels of electricity supply for domestic use – 3kW, 6kW and 9kW. The supply you choose will depend on the number and type of appliances you have in your property and are likely to use at the same time. You can request a more powerful supply.

Driving

The speed limit on French roads is 45 km/h in city centres, 50 or 60 km/h in other built-up areas, 90 km/h on ordinary roads, 110 km/h on dual carriageways and 130 km/h on motorways. There are tolls on French motorways (*péages*). You can pay by cash or credit card.

If you are stopped for speeding, you could be asked to pay an on-the-spot fine. There are random breath tests, and motorists who are over the legal drink-drive limit face a prison sentence and fine.

Health service
British nationals are entitled to the same health service as the French and should register with the local Social Security office. You can choose your GP. You pay for your treatment or prescription and the doctor or chemist will sign a form enabling you to claim back 65 per cent of the cost. However, you will not be reimbursed if the doctor is not *conventionné*, not part of the Social Security system.

If you are to receive expensive treatment, you can arrange simply to present your Social Security card to the doctor or hospital on the day, instead of having to pay.

It is possible to take out international private medical insurance to cover you in France. Some policies may cover hospital and specialist fees but not GP consultations and treatment. Repatriation can be included.

Education
Children in France go to nursery school from the age of two or three, and there are local authority crèches for babies. From primary education, State or private, there is a national curriculum. State secondary schools are either a *lycée* or a *collège*. The *collège* will take students to the age of 14 or 15, when they will go to a *lycée* and prepare for the *baccalauréat* or a vocational diploma.

Climate
France is more than twice the size of Britain and has coastlines on the Channel, the Bay of Biscay and the Mediterranean, so the climate varies from one region to another. In the south it is temperate, with warm summers and generally mild winters, but in the north there is not much difference from London.

Average daily temperatures (°C)

	Brittany	Normandy	Provence	Côte d'Azur
January	9.3	7.6	12.1	12.2
February	8.6	6.4	11.9	11.9
March	11.1	8.4	14.3	14.3
April	17.1	13.0	18.5	18.5
May	16.0	14.0	20.8	20.8
June	22.7	20.0	26.6	26.6
July	25.1	21.6	28.1	28.1
August	24.1	22.0	28.4	28.4
September	21.1	18.2	25.2	25.2
October	16.5	14.5	22.2	22.2
November	12.1	10.8	16.8	16.8
December	9.3	7.9	14.1	14.1

Conclusion

Buying a French property should not be regarded as the way to make a quick fortune. Prices are too stable and the supply of property too plentiful for that – particularly in rural areas. Resale could be difficult and there is a growing number of British owners looking to sell their homes in France.

The real investment should not be financially motivated, but one of enjoyment and lifestyle. To derive the maximum pleasure from your property in France make friends with your neighbours, take part in the life of your new community and, if you cannot do so already, learn to speak at least a little French!

Germany

General information
Status. Federal Republic
Capital. Berlin (the government is still in Bonn)
Area. 356,505 sq km (137,700 sq miles)
Population. 80.5 million (approx)

Location
Latitude 47°N to 54°N; longitude 6°E to 13°E. The Federal Republic of Germany is, in terms of population, size, geography and influence, the dominant country of central northern Europe. Although the climate is generally the same throughout most of the country (continental, influenced by the Atlantic), there are many contrasting environments, ranging from the Alpine south to the flat plains of the north and the river basins of the west. The vegetation also varies considerably, ranging from the Alpine mosses and the thick forests to the agricultural lands. The country is highly urbanised, especially in the Rhineland and the Baltic coast.

Political stability
The Federal Republic enjoyed a stable, moderate and successful government, leading the way in European unity (through the European Community). The reunification of Germany in 1990 may yet make the country ultimately the second strongest nation in the world, after the USA. Currently, however, there are numerous economic and other problems to be resolved.

Economy
Cost of living. Generally speaking, the German economy is an example to the capitalist West. Living standards, wages and

consumption are at very high levels. Inflation is nominal but unemployment is rising for the influx of East Germans has upset the balance. Goods and services are readily available and of high quality.

Taxation. Direct income tax levels range from 20 to 53 per cent in bands according to marital status and number of children. It is compulsory for workers to contribute to health and Social Security welfare insurance. VAT is 15 per cent.

Exchange rate. Deutsche Mark (DM) 2.52 = £1.

Exchange control. There are no exchange controls in operation.

Language
German. Knowledge of English is widespread.

Expatriate community
Few people move to Germany to retire. Many, however, have moved for business or career reasons.

Permits
European Community citizens are allowed to live and work in Germany without a visa; they are, however, required to register with the police and to obtain a residence permit for EC citizens and ID card issued by the local *Ordnungsamt*. This may last for one year, five years or an unlimited period and under German law the document must be carried at all times. Children aged 16 or more must have their own papers.

Personal effects
These may be imported free of duty provided they have been in possession of the owner for more than six months. A car may also be brought into Germany without paying duty provided it has been owned for at least a year and is for the personal use of the importer.

Housing
The cost of purchasing a home in Germany is often high but, if one can afford it, the best buy is generally an older property that needs a little attention. These can be quite attractive, especially if situated away from the largest cities in an aesthetically pleasant area.

Renting flats is popular among Germans and expatriates working in the larger towns and as a result these are frequently in short supply and quite expensive. Most landlords expect tenants to pay a deposit of two months' rent (returnable on leaving) and a month's rent in advance. EC citizens are permitted to put their name on the local authority housing list, like any German, but a long delay is likely before any accommodation is offered.

Buying property

There are no restrictions on the purchase of real estate by foreign nationals. All purchase contracts must be certified by a notary public and the title only passes to the purchaser on registration in the land register maintained by the district court. The fees for conveyance and certification of the land sale are between 1 and 1.5 per cent of the purchase price. The estate agent involved in the transaction generally expects a commission of 3 per cent of the price obtained from both parties to the transaction.

Where to live

Business and professional people working in Germany will probably need to reside close to one of the larger towns or cities, such as Frankfurt, Hamburg or Berlin where essential services, plus many residential amenities, are within easy reach. However, there are numerous more tranquil regions, especially in the south of the country, in, for instance, the Black Forest area, where a healthy, restful lifestyle can be enjoyed.

Communications

Communications in most parts of Germany are excellent, with plenty of autobahns, some of which have no speed limit, and good rail services. Standards are not yet so high in the former East German sector, but improvements are under way. Travel by air, for both domestic and international flights, is being improved by the formation of new and the expansion of existing carriers, plus the construction of additional terminals at major airports.

Recreation

There are plenty of opportunities for leisure activities in this large country. The Germans are very keen on sport, particularly football, athletics, tennis and motor racing. With much fine open countryside and many mountains, hiking is a popular pastime and so is camping. Facilities for sailing are available on the North and Baltic Seas.

The larger towns have a selection of cinemas, there are often clubs for English-speaking residents and the major London daily newspapers are on sale at some kiosks. Most Germans enjoy eating out and each region has its own specialities of food, wine and beer. There are also many restaurants and cafés which serve menus of other nations.

Driving

There is no requirement to take a German driving test provided that you have been in possession of a full British licence for more than one year. It is also possible to drive a British-registered car for one year before it has to be registered with the German authorities.

Third party insurance is obligatory and more expensive than in the UK. Vehicle tax will be levied, the level depending on the size of the car's engine.

Lead-free petrol is readily available where it says '*Bleifrei*'.

Speed limits are marginally higher in Germany, and on the autobahns the upper limit of 130 km/h is only 'advised'.

Health services

All foreign nationals employed in Germany are subject to the same health insurance scheme as German nationals. Contribution rates on taxable income are 10–14 per cent for health, 18 per cent for pensions and 3 per cent for unemployment benefit. Details of European Community rights are given in DSS pamphlet SA29.

Climate

Germany lies on the western edge of the European-Asiatic continent. The climate is mainly maritime in nature, but occasionally continental climatic conditions impose intense hot and cold periods. Mostly, the climate is comparable with that of the UK.

Average monthly temperatures (°C)

	Berlin	Frankfurt	Hamburg	Munich
January	–1.3	0.7	0.3	–0.6
February	0.1	2.2	1.0	0.2
March	3.4	5.3	3.5	3.8
April	7.9	9.3	7.5	7.8
May	13.2	14.3	12.3	12.9
June	16.2	17.3	15.4	15.9
July	18.0	18.7	17.1	17.8
August	16.7	17.7	16.3	17.0
September	13.5	14.4	13.6	13.5
October	8.4	9.4	8.8	8.3
November	3.5	4.7	4.3	3.1
December	0.7	1.9	1.6	0.0

Gibraltar

General information
Status. British Crown Colony
Capital. Gibraltar
Area. 5.5 sq km (2 sq miles)
Population. 30,000

Location
Latitude 36°N; longitude 5°W. The British colony of Gibraltar lies on the southern tip of Spain where the Mediterranean Sea and the Atlantic Ocean meet. It is dominated by a 430 m-high block of limestone and is itself an isthmus.

The population density is the second largest in Europe.

Political stability
Gibraltar has a large measure of internal self-government, under the Constitution enacted in 1969, which provides for a Westminster-style parliamentary system, with the Governor retaining responsibility for external affairs, defence and internal security. There are 15 elected members in the House of Assembly, plus a Speaker and two ex-officio members.

Under the provisions of the Treaty of Rome, relating to European dependent territories, Gibraltar joined the EC in 1973, but by agreement it is excluded from the administration of VAT, the Common Agricultural Policy and Customs Union.

Economy
Currency. Gibraltar pound notes and coins but UK coinage is legal tender.

Cost of living. The rocky terrain is not suitable for food production and there is little scope for primary production, so the inhabitants rely heavily on the port for their prosperity. Resourceful local entrepreneurs trade in the world markets and import goods from the most competitive sources, so prices are quite reasonable. Cheap agricultural goods, imported from Spain, keep down living costs. Cigarettes (from £5 for 200 at time of writing) and drink (£4.50 for a bottle of whisky) are also cheap.

Taxation. Income tax is levied on employees under PAYE. After certain allowances the rate is 20 per cent on the first £1500 and rises progressively until it is 50 per cent on sums over £19,500. Estate duty is levied on property in Gibraltar at the rate of 5 per cent on estates between £20,001 and £40,000, rising to 25 per cent on portions over

£100,000. Local property rates are 62p in the pound on the net annual value, payable in four equal quarterly instalments. Employees' contributions for social insurance, inclusive of group practice medical scheme, are around £12 per week. Gibraltar has no tax treaties with other countries, but a Gibraltar resident in receipt of income from the UK is entitled to a tax credit on the lower of the Gibraltar or UK tax paid.

There are no transfer taxes, surtax or capital gains tax on funds held for non-residents in Gibraltar. Exempt companies can be registered for a fee of £225 annually. Once granted, exemption is guaranteed for at least 25 years and the companies do not have to pay Gibraltar income tax.

There is a duty on all imported items, except food, amounting to 12 per cent. Under 1992 legislation, certain 'High Net Worth Individuals' qualify for allowances which restrict their total tax payable to a maximum of £17,500 and a minimum of £10,000 irrespective of income.

Gibraltar is now quite important in offshore finance with an expanding finance centre offering a variety of services.

Exchange rate. G£1 = £1.

Exchange control. There are no exchange controls.

Language
English is the official language; Spanish is widely spoken.

Expatriate community
There are 6000 British expatriates, many of whom are devoted to yachting, naval and marine pastimes.

Security
The 4 km-long isthmus, which has only one point of exit apart from the sea, means that Gibraltar is safe from many undesirables.

Residence and work permits
All visitors must have a passport on entering Gibraltar, but EC and Commonwealth nationals do not require a visa. EC citizens are entitled to live and work in Gibraltar, but non-EC nationals have to obtain a work permit. Entry is controlled by the Immigration Control Ordinance.

Personal effects
No duty is payable on personal effects.

195

Housing and development

The Gibraltar government has been encouraging private sector investment since 1988 to try to achieve economic self-sufficiency. They have been quite successful in this respect with land-reclamation projects, refurbishment of the airport, construction of finance and commercial centres and also the extension of public services. Tourism is also expanding and real economic growth is averaging around 10 per cent annually.

Although sites are scarce, some significant housing schemes have been launched including Eurotowers adjacent to the impressive Europort. The apartments offer studio, one-, two- and three-bedroom accommodation in the £55,000 to £400,000 price range. Another excellent scheme is Queensway Quay, by internationally known Taylor Woodrow. This offers one- to three-bedroom, air-conditioned apartments and three- to five-bedroom penthouses. Facilities include two swimming pools, landscaped terraces and covered parking.

Buying property

Gibraltar law and the procedure for acquiring property closely follow the practice in England. It is very desirable to employ a solicitor and there are a number of firms in Gibraltar and the UK who specialise in the conveyance of local property. Stamp duty amounts to 1.26 per cent of the purchase price, there are modest land registry and land title registration fees. Lawyers fees are according to a scale which works out at around £200 for the first £30,000 purchase price and about 0.5 per cent on the balance.

Where to live

As property on the market is very scarce, and the Rock is so small, it is difficult to give guidance on where to live.

Communications

GB Airways is the flag carrier, with daily scheduled flights from Gatwick ($2\frac{1}{2}$ hours) Heathrow and Manchester. Charter flights are offered by various operators including Britannia and GB.

A regular flight from Gibraltar by GB Airways to the city of Tangier just across the Straits provides a popular excursion in just 20 minutes. The same destination can be reached by the Bland ferry in about $2\frac{1}{2}$ hours, and in 1 hour by jet catamaran.

International direct dialling and telex make worldwide communications simple.

Recreation

Existing amenities include three beaches, two cinemas, a casino, crazy golf and scenic tours. Sights include the caves, the apes on Upper Rock, Moorish Castle, Trafalgar Cemetery and Europa Point lighthouse. A large area of the Upper Rock, including the apes' den and St Michael's cave, has been designated an official nature reserve.

For other hobbies, a trip over the border into Spain is necessary where extensive golfing, tennis and hiking opportunities exist, as well as numerous social activities.

Gibraltar Broadcasting Station operates its own radio and TV services which can also be heard or viewed along some parts of the Spanish Costa del Sol. Reception of BBC World Service is good.

Health services

A reciprocal health service agreement between the UK and Gibraltar covers emergency medical treatment required in Gibraltar. EC nationals can receive free medical treatment on production of Form E111. The International Health Clinic at Marina Bay provides comprehensive private medical facilities.

Climate

As can be seen from the table below, the climate of Gibraltar is fairly mild and sunny. Winds in the summer vary from dry westerlies to humid easterlies. The 'Levanter' is a local phenomenon caused by warm air forced up by the cliffs, which then condenses as its temperature reduces and this causes a dense blanket of cloud to form around the top of the Rock.

	Monthly rainfall (mm)	Average daily temperature (°C)	Average daily sunshine hours
January	15.4	13.6	6.05
February	64.9	13.7	6.69
March	108.7	13.8	5.35
April	12.6	16.9	5.89
May	79.8	17.1	8.98
June	6.7	20.1	9.78
July	—	24.1	10.46
August	1.7	24.3	9.25
September	0.2	23.5	9.16
October	14.7	18.9	7.12
November	15.2	16.4	4.45
December	14.4	14.5	3.94

Greece

General information
Status. Republic
Capital. Athens
Area. 131,990 sq km (51,245 sq miles)
Population. 9.7 million (approx)

Location
Latitude 31°N to 41°N; longitude 36°W to 39°W. Greece occupies the southern part of the Balkan peninsula and also has many attractive islands both large and small. The principal one is Crete, while Rhodes and Corfu are also very well known. Four-fifths of the mainland is mountainous and there are at least 20 mountains over 2000 m with a permanent snow line. Another striking characteristic is the huge areas of woodland in Greece, with 89 million hectares covering almost half of the country. Also, no part of Greece is more than 100 km away from the coast. Athens has many historic associations and is visited by millions of international tourists every year.

Political stability
As with a number of Mediterranean countries, steady democracy has only recently triumphed over its oppressors. In the case of Greece, the military junta that was running the country in an excessively brutal fashion collapsed in 1974 in a bloodless coup and was replaced by a democratic government led by Karamanlis. Greece has been a full member of the European Community since 1981.

Economy
Cost of living. Inflation is still a problem in Greece and there is considerable unemployment. Tourism remains an important sector in the economy, but the discovery of oil in the north and the Aegean Sea and natural gas in the Ionian Sea may have significant beneficial effects on prosperity in the future. Currently living standards in Greece are appreciably lower than in most other EC nations. Essentials such as food, especially from the markets, are good value for money. This, however, is not the case with luxury items.

Taxation. Personal taxation is calculated on the worldwide income of residents (usually people living more than six months of a year in Greece). A personal allowance and a wife's allowance is granted, and income tax rises from 18 to 50 per cent. When taxpayers submit returns showing their income they must also submit their expenditure for the previous year; if the authorities believe the lifestyle is too high for people on that level of declared income, the tax demand will be set at a more suitable level unless the taxpayers can prove that the expenditure emanated from funds already taxed. VAT is levied at 16 per cent with a reduced rate of 8 per cent. There is now a capital gains tax.

Exchange rate. Drachmas 367.78 = £1.

Exchange control. In operation, but relaxed for EC citizens.

Language
A basic understanding of the fundamentals of Modern Greek is advisable although a knowledge of English is often found in tourist areas.

Expatriate community
Greece has become steadily more popular during the last few years. Many people have chosen to retire there and also over 3000 people are in employment.

Security
Greece's proximity to one of the world's troubled areas results in very tight security being provided in the international airports. Internally, it is prudent to take standard precautions against theft and burglary by installing security equipment.

Residence permits
British subjects can stay in Greece for up to three months without any formalities. Thereafter a temporary residence permit is granted for six months and then a five-year permit will be issued, provided that the applicant can produce evidence of having a permanent address in Greece and an adequate income to live on.

Work permits
Under the European Community rules, work permits are no longer required.

Personal effects
No duties are payable as long as a certificate has been acquired from the Greek Embassy and a five-year residence permit has been issued in Greece. Those going to work in Greece are also allowed to import a car duty free.

Housing

Although there has been quite a lot of interest in the purchase of homes in Greece during the past two decades, there has been a dearth of specialist agencies able to offer a service to prospective purchasers. This situation has improved recently and there are now a few firms with departments handling homes on the mainland and the islands.

A mistaken impression that foreigners were not allowed to buy residential property in Greece existed for some years following restrictions, for national security reasons, on the acquisition of homes in designated border areas close to Turkey and Albania, and in some of the islands. Greece has now introduced legislation allowing EC citizens to acquire rights on properties, like the Greeks, in most of Greece. The remaining prohibited regions comprise a small strip in the north of the country adjoining the former Yugoslavia. A relaxation of the restrictions which apply to the Dodecanese Islands (these are close to Turkey) is anticipated.

Buying property

As with the acquisition of real estate in other countries, it is essential that all purchase documents are checked by a lawyer before contracts are signed, to ensure that the vendor has unencumbered and full title to the property. The purchase price is normally payable when the contract of sale is prepared and signed by both parties before a Greek notary public in Greece or before the Greek Consulate General in London or elsewhere. Power of attorney may be granted if necessary.

A property transfer tax has to be paid to the Greek Inland Revenue which amounts to 9 per cent on properties costing up to 4 million drachma and 11 per cent on sums above this figure, but an extra 2 per cent is charged for homes in major cities. In addition, a community tax is charged which comprises 3 per cent of the property transfer tax.

Notary fees are generally just under 3 per cent of the taxable purchase price and a land registry fee is likely to amount to around £60.

Prices of property vary in different regions of the country, but a reasonable apartment can be acquired for around £25,000 and a two-bedroom modern villa for a sum in the region of £45,000.

Communications

British Airways and Olympic Airways have scheduled flights from Gatwick, Heathrow and provincial airports to Athens and other destinations in Greece. The return fare midweek is around £350. Charter flights are also available to many destinations, particularly in summer from about £150.

Despite the fact that Greece is perhaps a little isolated from western Europe, road and rail links are good.

Recreation

The legacy of the past 5000 years of Greek civilisation is probably one of the greatest attractions in Greece today. Unique examples of architecture and sculpture exist in abundance, with perhaps the most impressive relic being the Parthenon which stands, together with other masterpieces, on the rock of the Acropolis in Athens, and receives about 1.5 million visitors per year. Greek culture extends into theatre, dancing and festivals.

Greek cuisine is generally very good but limited, and eating out is both popular and cheap.

Modern leisure facilities such as swimming pools and tennis courts are quite plentiful, especially in the popular resorts. Also, because of the number of islands and the large amount of coastline, water-based pursuits such as sailing, water-skiing and wind-surfing are popular.

Many of Greece's recreational facilities are very much orientated to the tourists but, because of the pleasant climate all year round, the tourist trade is not as seasonal as in some countries and so the facilities are maintained at the highest level throughout the year.

Health services

With over 550 hospitals and more than 29,000 doctors, the state-run Greek health service is adequate, but as there are often long waiting lists for treatment, private medical insurance is advisable.

Climate

The term generally associated with the Greek weather is that of an 'olive climate'. The fundamental characteristic of it is the smooth transition from one season to the next. A short spring with moderate temperatures, followed by a long, hot summer and then a pleasant autumn with average temperatures above those in spring, lead finally to a usually mild and sunny winter. There are about 3000 hours of sunshine each year, rain in summer is an unknown phenomenon and the cooling north-west winds blow. Rainfall varies throughout the country, from about 1500 mm per annum to less than a third of that in the south.

Republic of Ireland

General information
Status. Republic
Capital. Dublin
Area. 70,282 sq km (27,165 sq miles)
Population. 3,480,000

Location
Latitude 52°N to 55°N; longitude 5°W to 10°W. On the extreme
west of the European sub-continent, jutting out into the north
Atlantic, lies an island of comparatively little urbanisation or
modern agricultural land. Instead, large areas are still in their most
natural state, whether bleak moor or rocky coastline. In some areas,
only the traditional crofters make use of the unspoilt land. The Irish
Republic is dominated on the eastern side by the capital city,
Dublin, which is one of the main trade and communication arteries.
The west, however, is far more the property of nature; that is, either
the influence of the Atlantic Ocean or the river Shannon.

Political stability
The problems in the north remain largely unresolved and there is
still violence there. In the south, particularly away from the big
cities, the republic remains virtually unaffected by the 'troubles' and
life can be very pleasant in small towns and villages, where the pace
of living is much slower than in urban areas.
　　Politically, most recent governments have been rather weak and
without a substantial majority, and this has caused some uncertainty about current and future policies. Links with the UK have
improved, which must be to the ultimate benefit of both countries.

Economy
Cost of living. Apart from housing, food and clothing, living costs
are higher than in the UK, but inflation is quite low at around 3 per
cent. Petrol is about IR£2.80 per gallon and cars cost about one-
third more than in Britain. VAT is 21 per cent on most goods and
services.

Taxation. Married couples are exempt from income tax on the first
IR£4200 of income. Thereafter the rate is 27 per cent on the first
IR£6700 and 48 per cent on the remainder. A retention tax (DIRT)
of 27 per cent is deducted at source on all investment/savings

income. There are no local rates, but water charges are about IR£90 per annum and refuse collection approximately IR£40 per year.

Exchange rate. Punts (IR£) 1.04 = £1.

Exchange controls. There are no restrictions on importing money into Ireland

Language
Everybody speaks the Irish version of English, with Gaelic as a second tongue for many. Knowledge of Gaelic is essential for all top government employees, and is a qualification for many posts.

Expatriate community
Partly because of traditional links with the UK and partly because of geographical proximity, there are a large number of Britons in Ireland.

Security
Ireland does have a problem with house-breakers and petty thieves, so it is worthwhile installing burglar alarms – preferably those linked to the *Garda* (police station) or a security company. Away from border areas the 'troubles' have few practical repercussions.

Residence permits
There are no restrictions on entering Ireland for those who are citizens of European Community countries. Similarly, any person who can prove that at least one parent or grandparent was born in Ireland can enter without restriction.

Work permits
EC citizens do not require a work permit to take up employment in Ireland. Citizens of other countries require a permit from the Irish Ministry of Labour.

Personal effects
These can be imported duty free by people wanting to set up permanent residence if the items have been owned for over six months. Normally, importation should be within six months of arrival.

Housing
Like most capital cities, homes in Dublin are relatively expensive, but in country areas prices are more reasonable. In County Galway,

near Galway city, in the west of Ireland, a four-bedroom bungalow with en-suite facilities can be purchased for around £65,000. In the riverside town of Carrick on Shannon, County Leitrim, which is about 130 km north west of Dublin, pleasant modern semi-detached houses can be purchased for around £38,000, while detached versions sell for between £48,000 and £60,000. There are also smaller homes which are good value for between £20,000 and £30,000. The property market in Ireland has picked up recently and the local National Property Network, who represent estate agents in all Republic of Ireland counties, are undertaking a publicity campaign to promote the sale of Irish property to overseas owners and this includes exhibitions in London and Manchester. They report a steady appreciation in the value of Irish residential properties over the past two decades and an absence of boom-and-bust conditions.

There are numerous estate agents throughout the country, and their professional body is the Irish Auctioneers and Valuers Association.

Buying property

Property purchase procedures are somewhat similar to those in Britain. Completion normally takes place about six to eight weeks after the contract has been signed. Stamp duty is assessed on the price paid for the property. Up to IR£5000 the rate is nil; between IR£5000 and IR£10,000 – 1 per cent; IR£10,000 to IR£15,000 – 2 per cent; IR£15,000 to IR£25,000 – 3 per cent; IR£25,000 to IR£50,000 – 4 per cent; IR£50,000 to IR£60,000 – 5 per cent; over IR£60,000 – 6 per cent. The cost of registration fees depends on the nature of the title purchased. The maximum fee for registered land is IR£200. For unregistered land the fee for each deed is IR£21. Solicitors' fees tend to be higher than in Britain, as more work is required because conveyancing law in Ireland has not been updated in this century. The mortgage interest rate is 7.5 per cent.

Where to live

The most appealing locations are probably the quiet rural areas in the west of Ireland in County Kerry, County Cork and County Clare. They offer a quiet and tranquil life-style.

Communications

Air. Aer Lingus, British Airways and charter companies provide frequent flights to Dublin and Shannon throughout the year, with a journey time to Dublin of about 65 minutes.

Sea. Services from Britain are available on luxury car ferries from Liverpool, Holyhead, Swansea, Pembroke and Fishguard.

Recreation

The greatest facet of the Irish Republic is undoubtedly the countryside and this therefore provides the richest source of pleasure through recreational pursuits such as walking, climbing, camping and orienteering. The River Shannon also provides water-based activities such as boating and canoeing. Other sports facilities available in main centres such as Dublin and Cork are swimming pools and tennis courts. Golf courses are also fairly abundant. The most popular sports in Ireland are rugby, Gaelic football and hurling.

The Gaelic culture and many of the old traditional crafts, songs and dances provide a great source of pleasure.

Health services

Medical standards in Ireland are high and, subject to income limits, free medical care can be obtained in general wards of public hospitals and from certain general practitioners. Interfund agreements exist between Irish medical insurance companies and BUPA, PPP and WPA in the UK. British retirement pensions can also be paid in Ireland. Details can be obtained from the DSS.

Climate

Changeable weather is a major feature of the climate; rain falls almost every month, with the western part of the country being the wettest. Also, humidity is quite high. The months of May and June have the most sunshine, while July and August are the warmest periods. January and February are the coldest months with an average temperature of between 4° and 7°C.

Israel

General information
Status. Parliamentary democracy
Capital. Jerusalem
Area. 27,817 sq km (10,840 sq miles)
Population. 4,882,000

Location
Latitude 30°N to 33°N; longitude 35°E. Israel, the land of the Bible and historic homeland of the Jewish people, is situated in the Middle East, along the eastern coastline of the Mediterranean. The geographical diversity of Israel is quite remarkable for such a small country, as it has mountains and plains, fertile fields and barren deserts, seacoast and rocky uplands. In Galilee in the north, forested highlands merge with green valleys. Sand dunes and citrus groves mark the coastal plain bordering the Mediterranean. Deserts stretching southwards through Negev and Arava meet the tropical waters of the Gulf of Eilat on the Red Sea.

Political stability
The State of Israel was created in 1948. A system of strict proportional representation is used in the elections to the Knesset (the Israeli Parliament) and all governments have been the result of coalition agreements.

Israel's short history has been a stormy one. The country has fought five wars with its Arab neighbours. The founding of the State caused a refugee problem when 600,000 Palestinians fled to surrounding countries and 800,000 Jews fled Arab countries and were settled in Israel. The Palestinian problem is still not solved. Arabs are full citizens of the State and both Jews and Arabs have to co-exist in Israel.

The coalition government cannot rely on majority support, mainly because of the consequences of a proportional representation system that allows undue weight and influence to political extremists and religious zealots. This being the case, it means that governments progress slowly and carefully, sometimes having to fudge important yet unpopular policies.

Economy
Cost of living. Israel lacks the natural resources necessary to back up its rapid economic growth. Infrastructural growth, welfare services and massive defence expenditure have put a huge strain on the

economy. Since 1987 inflation has been approximately 16 per cent, mainly as a result of the Economic Recovery Plan introduced in 1984. Economic stability is much improved and there has been an improvement in Israel's foreign reserves. Immigrants can expect to have a high standard of living, mainly because of the strength of their home currencies. Israeli produce is of the highest standard and is reasonably priced. Petrol costs much the same as in the UK.

Taxation. Special compensations for new immigrants do exist in terms of tax regulations. All savings are tax free for the first 20 years of residence. VAT is charged on all goods and services (except in duty-free Eilat).

Exchange rate. Shekels 4.42 = £1.

Exchange control. It is possible to bring into Israel an unlimited amount of foreign currency, travellers' cheques and Israeli shekels. There are restrictions on what can be taken out, and a tax is payable on departure.

Language
The official languages are Hebrew and Arabic. English is widely spoken.

Expatriate community
Since the creation of Israel in 1948, immigration (especially by Jews) has been extensive. Eastern European, North American, Asian and African migrants have all flocked to the country. There has also been considerable migration from Britain with almost 20,000 British Jews having made the journey. Clearly, then, Israel's society is very cosmopolitan.

In 1990 the population increased by 5.7 per cent as a result of the immigration of Jews from the former Soviet Union and Ethiopia and other countries in Eastern Europe and South America. This immigration continues unabated.

Security
Fears for Israel's future, prompted by her encirclement by potentially unfriendly nations, and Palestinian terrorism, have made security a primary issue for the government. The result is that the country has one of the best equipped and most rigorously trained armies in the world. Potential adversaries realise that Israel is willing to meet force with more force.

Residence permits

All applications must be made to the Ministry of the Interior. An initial tourist visa of three months' duration may be extended by the Ministry, on consideration of the application.

Work permits

It is necessary for the potential employer to make an application for a work permit on your behalf to the Ministry of the Interior.

Personal effects

No duties are payable on household goods.

Housing

Housing in Israel varies from the Arab-style villas of simple design and the red-tile roofed houses of the early settlers, to ultra-modern seaside cottages built to exacting architectural specifications. Most Israelis, however, live in apartment blocks, ranging from one-room studios to those with four bedrooms. Many of these flats are in fact rented, as this is cheap compared with buying property. A three-bedroom apartment for rent costs about US$200 per month.

Where to live

This is very much a personal choice. Some people choose big cities, others the quieter country villages. Some move to the coast whereas others prefer to live inland.

Communications

Air. Twenty-four international airlines operate flights to Israel's Ben-Gurion international airport, which is 18 km from Tel Aviv and 50 km from Jerusalem. International charter flights also operate, as well as many internal services.

Sea. Shipping lines offer regular sailings from Europe and arrive at Haifa port.

Road. Over 1500 km of new roads have been built during the past decade and previously existing roads have also been improved.

Telecommunications. Israel is fully integrated into international communications systems by means of underwater cables and communications satellites.

Recreation

Being a warm Mediterranean nation, all kinds of outdoor activities

Israel

are popular. Facilities provided by the municipalities such as swimming pools and tennis courts are generally good, as are those in the tourist coastal regions. Spectator sports such as football and especially basketball are popular too.

Israeli cuisine is regarded as very good, although non-kosher food is a little harder to get. Therefore, those with a taste for pork or shellfish, or dairy produce with meat meals, will have to search for a private restaurant to cater for them (not hotels or large restaurants which sell only kosher food).

Israel is, of course, the Holy Land, and so is scattered with monuments and architecture celebrating that fact. Museums, theatre and cinema are also popular.

Driving
It is possible to drive in Israel on a valid UK licence. International traffic signs are used and the signposts are in English.

Insurance is quite expensive, with compulsory third party cover costing about £100 and fully comprehensive over £500. The maximum no claims bonus is only 30 per cent, which possibly reflects the quality of Israeli driving.

Seat belts are compulsory in the front seats.

Health services
The Ministry of Health is responsible for all health services in Israel. It prepares health legislation and oversees its implementation, controls medical standards and supervises the planning and construction of hospitals. In total, there are some 145 hospitals in Israel. The cost of medical treatment is quite high though, so health insurance is advisable.

A social security agreement does exist between the UK and Israel. Details are given in DSS pamphlet SA14.

Climate
Israel's climate is characterised by hot, dry summers from April through to October and wet winters from November to March. The rainfall, in general, is higher in the north and west of the country than in the south and east.

Average monthly temperatures (°C)

	Tel Aviv	Haifa	Eilat
January	9.4–18.3	7.6–17.4	9.6–21.3
February	8.7–18.8	8.5–17.8	10.8–22.8
March	10.1–20.3	8.3–21.3	13.4–26.3

April	12.4–22.3	12.6–25.5	17.1–30.7
May	17.3–25.0	14.5–24.6	20.6–34.8
June	19.3–28.3	17.7–27.6	24.1–37.1
July	21.0–30.2	20.0–29.9	25.3–39.9
August	22.1–30.1	21.2–30.0	26.0–39.9
September	20.3–31.4	19.7–29.6	23.7–36.4
October	15.0–28.8	15.0–28.8	20.4–33.3
November	12.2–24.5	12.2–24.5	16.0–28.3
December	8.8–19.0	8.8–19.0	10.6–23.3

Italy

General information
Status. Republic
Capital. Rome
Area. 301,247 sq km (116,303 sq miles)
Population. 56,336,000

Location
Latitude 36°N to 47°N; longitude 6°E to 18°E. Geographically, Italy lies in the temperate and hot temperate zone. The climate is influenced by both the Mediterranean Sea that virtually surrounds it and to a lesser extent the continent to the north. Another feature of Italy is the startling length of its coastline, and there can be little doubt that this, more than anything else, has had the most profound influence on Italy's development. The vegetation varies greatly, depending on the climatic and geological factors: in the north there are considerable areas of woodland and productive land, whereas in the south scrubland tends to predominate. The main population centres are mostly in the central northern region. A number of islands form part of the country including Sardinia, Elba and the most well known, Sicily.

Political stability
The Italian people are probably not renowned for their stability and inner calmness and, to some extent, this has been mirrored by their political system. The Republic, having fully recovered from the traumas of Fascist dictatorship, now has all the trappings of a parliamentary democracy, with the President as head of state. The one-time grip of the army, church and judiciary has been loosened, leaving sovereignty where it belongs. But for all this, Italy has been beset by political problems in recent years, caused by the inability of governments to achieve a workable majority, and scandals involving fraud in high places. The party and electoral system encourages coalition governments, and it will be interesting to see if the recent

change of leadership has any effect on future policy. Nevertheless, Italy's growing standing in world affairs is due in no small way to membership of the European Community and NATO.

Economy

Cost of living. Italy's post-war industrial development has been considerable and has brought prosperity to many people, particularly in the central and northern regions, for Italy is very much a divided nation in terms of wealth and living standards, and the south is far less affluent and successful. Prices in Italy are about the same as in the UK although some goods, especially market produce and local wine, are cheap. Top-quality goods, such as clothes, china, glassware and fine furniture, are very expensive.

Taxation. Under Italian law each individual is responsible for reporting his or her financial affairs to the local tax authorities. Personal income tax (IRPEF) is charged on income from all sources and ranges from 12 per cent on incomes up to 6 million lire, rising progressively to 62 per cent on incomes over 600 million lire. Thus it is considerably higher than in Britain, but a double taxation agreement exists between Italy and the UK.

A new Council Tax known as ICI (Imposta Comunale surgli Immobili) was introduced in 1993. This is payable by all individuals or companies (resident or non-resident) who own a property in Italy. It is paid in two instalments (June and December) at a rate of between 0.04 and 0.07 per cent of the property's statutory value, the actual rate being decided by each local council (*comune*). After the first year the tax will be administered and collected by the Comune and where it is not paid on time penalties are imposed.

Capital gains tax on properties (INVIM) will continue to be payable on gains accrued before 1 January 1993 when a property is sold, up to the year 2003.

An inheritance tax varies according to the relationship of the beneficiaries. A capital gains tax is based on the increase in value of real property when it is sold or on transfer of ownership because of death.

Exchange rate. Lira 2510 = £1.

Exchange control. Exchange control legislation has been liberalised in view of Italy's commitment to a single European market.

Language

Knowledge of Italian is very useful, as English is spoken only in the more popular tourist regions.

Expatriate community
A growing number of British people take up residence in Italy every year. There are expatriate diplomatic communities in Rome and Naples. British business executives are especially active in the northern cities.

Security
Petty crime and muggings do occur in popular resorts but this is no more a problem in Italy than elsewhere. However, one place where it is perhaps a little harder to guarantee security is Sicily, because of the Mafia.

Residence permits
British citizens, like all other EC nationals, have free entry into Italy. They must obtain a residence permit within three days of arrival, which is valid for one year and renewable annually. For full-time permanent residence, a certificate of residence is needed to make the applicant subject to Italian laws and taxes.

Work permits
These are not necessary for EC nationals.

Personal effects
They may be imported free of duty by holders of a certificate of residence.

Housing
Unlike many other Mediterranean countries, there are few developments aimed at attracting foreign nationals, and so it may be necessary to seek a place on the open market. In general, land is not cheap, but bargains are sometimes available for houses of varying size, age and quality.

When seeking a house, it is wise to show no undue interest should a property appear that meets your requirements, as keenness is often met by a price increase. It is best to leave it to the selling agent to settle matters later on. It is always advisable to deal with reputable firms. Personal contacts, say, in a bar, are less desirable, because if a deal is ever finalised, under Italian law the contact is entitled to a commission as a result of the introduction.

All Italian estate agents must have a licence to trade, issued by the local town hall, and must pass oral and written exams.

Buying a property

Before signing any document for the purchase of a property it is advisable to make enquiries both at the local Land Registry (Ufficio Tecnico Erariale) and at the Deeds Registry (Conservatoria dei Registri Immobiliari) as well as at the local municipality (*comune*) to ensure that the vendor has a registered title to the property and that the chain of title is unbroken. Make sure also that there are no mortgages or charges against the property and that planning permissions have been obtained, building regulations complied with, municipal taxes paid and, if the property includes agricultural land, that there are no pre-emptive rights of adjoining landowners.

It is helpful to employ a local surveyor (*geometra*) who will be prepared to carry out most of these searches.

The first formal legally binding step is the signature of a contract (*contratto preliminare* or *compromesso*) often drawn up by the vendor or agent and not necessarily by their lawyer. This is a legally binding contract to purchase on the terms stated, and a deposit of 10 per cent or considerably more is payable. This is forfeited if the purchaser does not conclude the deal; if the vendor reneges he or she has to compensate the proposed purchaser by the return of twice the deposit. In either circumstance it may be possible for further damages to be claimed by the disappointed party.

The final deed for the formal transfer of ownership in the property is the conveyance or transfer (*atto di compravendita*) by the vendor to the purchaser which involves the services of a notary (*notaio*) who oversees the deal and ensures that the transfer takes place according to law. This is a public official who does not act for either of the parties. The notary's duties are to draw up the deed, see to the payment of any capital gains tax and outstanding penalties for town planning irregularities and then to register the document, both for the purpose of the title being brought up to date and of the Revenue raising a tax assessment.

A certified copy, issued by the notary of this conveyance document, is evidence of title and contains the names of the two parties to the transaction, a description of the property with map references, boundaries, price, receipt for the purchase money, details of rights of way, and other easements and warranties that the vendor will be the legal owner, that the property is sold with vacant possession and that it is not subject to any charges.

To advise you personally and guide you through the transaction it is advisable to employ your own lawyer (*avvocato*) as well as the surveyor (*geometra*) referred to.

It is, of course, particularly important to remember that the documents you sign will be in Italian and that you should consult advisers who are able to explain their contents in correct and intelligible English.

There are a number of costs to be borne during and after the transaction – roughly, about 10 per cent of the purchase price should cover taxes and registration fees. Under-declaration of the purchase price in the final deed used to be common in order to reduce the vendor's capital gains tax (INVIM) and the purchaser's transfer costs, which led to haggling with the Revenue. But for some years now an official solution to this problem has been found which still permits the conveyance to contain, in many cases, a figure less than the real price paid, provided that it agrees with or exceeds the official value to be derived from the local Land Registry (*Catasto*). Such official value is based on a notional annual rent known as *rendita catastale*, which is revised upwards from time to time.

The rule does not apply when a property is registered in the rural registry. When a property is purchased from a professional builder the purchaser normally pays VAT at 9 per cent for a non-luxury building or 19 per cent for a luxury building, in addition to registration tax at the flat rate of Lira 150,000.

Of course, you must also budget for the costs and fees payable to your *avvocato*, your *geometra* and possibly your interpreters and translators as required.

Mortgages are available and both the Woolwich Building Society and Abbey National have offices in Italy.

Where to live

Over the past two decades, British buyers have generally favoured areas north of Rome as locations for their home in Italy. Umbria, known as the green heart of Italy, is still one of the most popular regions and prices have risen substantially in recent years, but it is still possible to purchase a partially restored village house for under £20,000. Homes close to the extensive Lake Trasimeno are popular and those in the Upper Tiber Valley also create interest.

The adjoining Le Marche region is less well known and, as a result, property prices tend to be lower, with a variety of old farmhouses on the market between about £15,000 and £50,000. A feature is the extensive coastline along the Adriatic where the two main towns are Pesaro and Ancona. Tuscany includes the famed towns of Florence and Siena, where prices are high, but north of Lucca there is some quite cheap property.

The areas near the northern lakes are more expensive because of their close proximity to major centres of employment and to other

European countries. Calabria in the south is now creating more interest, due to its extensive coastline and mild weather. In Sicily there are seaside holiday apartments from about £34,000.

Communications

Air. Italy has very good internal and external air services. There are some 26 airports, 15 of which are international and have services from Britain, the main ones being Rome, Milan, Bologna, Venice, Pisa and Naples. Flying time from London and Manchester is between 2 and 3 hours.

Rail. The Italian State Railway has a network of over 16,000 km of track and carries over 1 million people every day. The railways form an integral part of the commuter services.

Sea. Italy's islands are linked to the mainland by comprehensive ferry services.

Road. An autostrada network, totalling 5910 km, is the country's main artery, but tolls are charged. In general, Italian roads are good and often very spectacular.

Recreation

Italy has a great deal to offer new settlers, with a vivid history and unrivalled classical traditions and superb monuments, yet an up-to-date outlook. Italy was, of course, the birthplace of the Renaissance and consequently it is impossible even to try to list the marvellous examples of art and architecture to be found in many of the great Italian cities such as Florence, Rome and Venice. Suffice to say that anyone who appreciates fine art and beauty will appreciate Italy.

More modern arts are also very much alive and well, in the form of cinema and theatre. Equally popular is opera, which is not centralised in the main centres but performed throughout the nation in many small towns.

Sports facilities such as gymnasiums, swimming pools, golf courses and tennis courts exist in abundance. Skiing in the northern Alpine region is popular too. The most favoured spectator sport is undoubtedly football, and Italian clubs such as Juventus, Roma and Inter Milan are recognised as having some of the world's best players.

Italians enjoy eating out and plenty of good restaurants are to be found. Every region has its own speciality dish. Several different styles of eating house exist, including the *ristorante* (conventional restaurant), the *trattoria* (family-owned cheaper restaurant), the *rosticceria* (hot food) and *pizzeria* (pizzas).

Driving

It is not necessary to retake your driving test in Italy, as a British licence may be converted into an Italian one which lasts for ten years. It is also possible to drive on British number plates for the first year, after which the car must be re-registered in Italy and undergo a roadworthiness test. In Italy, road tax is based on the car's engine size. The general rules of the road are much the same as elsewhere in mainland Europe. The traffic police have a reputation for applying the law to the letter and are inclined to impose on-the-spot fines. Maintenance costs are roughly the same as in Britain.

Health services

The public health service in Italy is not highly regarded, but private hospitals, many run by the Church, are efficient. Consequently, most foreigners have private medical insurance.

Full details of social security rights can be obtained from the DSS.

Climate

The geographical aspects, such as the influence of the Alps in the north and the Mediterranean in the south, make for an interesting climatic pattern.

	Rome average		The Alps average		The Lakes average		Adriatic Coast average	
	temp (°C)	ppt (mm)	temp (°C)	ppt (mm)	temp (°C)	ppt (mm)	temp (°C)	ppt (mm)
January	7.4	74	− 2.3	51	6.0	74	6.7	11
February	8.0	87	− 1.3	447	7.0	218	9.1	43
March	11.5	79	1.8	82	9.2	91	10.3	35
April	14.4	62	5.2	138	13.3	47	13.5	42
May	18.4	57	9.1	132	16.5	105	17.7	62
June	22.9	39	13.5	128	19.7	88	21.8	66
July	25.7	6	15.8	148	23.7	12	24.3	95
August	25.5	23	15.4	117	24.3	117	23.4	69
September	22.4	66	12.7	115	18.5	35	20.0	43
October	17.7	123	7.6	119	9.8	20	10.5	132
November	13.4	121	2.8	116	8.4	79	9.8	54
December	8.9	93	− 1.6	59	7.3	70	5.7	12

temp = temperature
ppt = precipitation

Malta

General information
Status. Republic
Capital. Valletta
Area. 320 sq km (122 sq miles)
Population. 360,000

Location
Latitude 35°N; longitude 14°E. Malta, and its two sister islands, Gozo and Comino, are about half the size of the Isle of Wight. It is situated in the middle of the Mediterranean, about 36 km from Sicily and 290 km from the North African coast.

Political stability
A new, more realistic attitude is apparent under the nationalist government which is encouraging new residents who are retired.

Economy
Cost of living. In general, prices compare favourably with the UK, especially in food and essential services. Inflation is low and the economy of the island appears to be prospering. Unemployment is modest and there is a shortage of skilled labour in some of the new industries.

Impressive efforts are being made by the government to improve public services, with new water and drainage schemes, better telephones and the elimination of overhead power-lines in built-up areas. Roads are being improved and underground car parks built. A new power station has been completed and the new airport terminal is now fully operational. Many hotels are being upgraded or expanded to cope with the expansion of high-class tourism.

A Freeport has been established in the south of the island and an entry has been achieved into the offshore finance world. The Maltese currency is strong and Malta is considered to be one of the top three countries in Europe for foreign currency reserves.

Taxation. Foreigners who live in Malta for more than six months in any one calendar year using visitors' visas on a regular basis pay Maltese income tax only if the income is imported into Malta, and has not already been taxed at source in the UK. A permissible deduction is the personal allowance, which is about £3690 for a married man. The rates start at 10 per cent on the first £630 of taxable income and rise on a sliding scale to a top rate of 35 per cent on income above about £9000. A double taxation agreement exists between Britain and Malta. Death duties have been abolished. Capital gains tax is calculated on any gains made since January 1993. The provisional rate is 7 per cent.

For reduced taxation granted to permit holders, see 'Residence Qualifications' below.

Exchange rate. Maltese £0.58 = £1. Sterling sums mentioned below are based on this exchange rate.

Exchange control. Some restrictions, but Malta is to seek full membership of the EC.

Language
The national language is Maltese, but English is spoken almost universally.

Expatriate community
Evidence of the century and a half of British rule in Malta is still to be found in many shapes and forms, from red letter-boxes to a statue of Queen Victoria. The substantial British community of more than 1000, combined with a further 3000 who own property there, maintains the link with the past.

The links between the UK and Malta are still apparent and this, combined with the friendly and hospitable attitude of the Maltese, makes for a pleasant atmosphere.

Security
Standard precautions against theft and burglary are advisable.

Residence qualifications
Permit holders under the optional residence scheme for people with higher incomes (in excess of approximately £12,000 sterling per annum) are granted special taxation terms, whereby they pay a flat rate of 15 per cent on income, less personal allowances, brought into Malta.

It is also possible to apply for a permit if you have access to a proven worldwide capital of about £259,000. This does not have to be brought into Malta and can include the value of the applicant's Maltese home or any other investments on the island. There are no income requirements in this category.

Holders of permanent residence permits are allowed to repatriate any unspent income above the minimum requirements, as well as the proceeds of the sale of their property or any other investments in Malta.

Property purchased must cost in excess of approximately £34,400 for a flat or £51,600 for a house or villa.

Expatriates are not allowed to be employed or to engage in business without the authority of the Maltese government. Tourists and non-residents with entry visas do not require permits and may visit the island at any time, provided that each sojourn does not exceed three months.

Those spending less than six months in Malta, in any one year, do not pay tax on sums brought into the island.

Temporary residents staying for periods in excess of three months can apply to the immigration authorities to renew the entry visa once a year. This is a simple formality and many British people live in Malta on this basis. They are not entitled to the taxation advantages for permanent residents, but are normally subject to local tax conditions if their stay exceeds six months in one continuous period and then only on income remitted to Malta. Proof needs to be provided, however, that they have sufficient income to live in the island without becoming a financial burden to the government, and any property purchased must exceed about £26,000 in value.

Property can be used as a permanent or holiday residence by the purchaser or immediate family only, but guests can be accommodated when the owner or a member of the family is staying in the property. Funds for property purchase must originate from outside Malta.

Proceeds from the sale of a property in Malta by a foreigner may be repatriated abroad after permission has been obtained from the authorities.

Personal effects
Once a residence permit is acquired, no duties are payable on personal effects. Exemption from Customs duty is granted on household and personal effects and also on a car imported within six months of arrival in Malta. Pets can be imported from the UK with a quarantine period of only three weeks.

Housing
A wide range of modern and well-established villas and apartments is available for sale all over the island. Expatriates are limited in that they can own only one property, which must be of a value exceeding about £26,000 (if renovating an old property, this can be the total amount including building costs), in order to prevent speculation on the property market at the expense of the local residents. In general,

residential property is available at a reasonable price. However, prices are rising owing to the greater expectations of local owners and strong local demand. The popularity of Gozo is growing quite fast.

Buying property

Foreigners must apply to the Ministry of Finance, Malta, for permission to purchase; having satisfied the government of their eligibility, they may proceed to the next stage.

A notary public is employed to draw up a preliminary agreement, which contains the basic data about the transaction, and this is signed by both parties. The purchaser pays a deposit, which is normally 10 per cent. Searches are then carried out by the notary to ascertain if there are any defects in the title or liabilities which were not known when the preliminary contract was signed. If there are any problems, the purchaser can withdraw from the contract and recover the deposit paid. The searches do not cover future development plans for the area; these have to be checked at the Public Works Department.

Finally, the notary or estate agent will provide the purchaser with a full statement of account and request that the necessary foreign funds be imported, preferably by telegraphic transfer. The Central Bank of Malta requires evidence that these funds have come from outside Malta and the notary will take the bank credit note, together with the Ministry of Finance permit, to the Central Bank for endorsement. Then the final deed can be signed by both parties simultaneously and the balance of the purchase price plus fees are paid.

Deeds prepared by the notary are bound every six months and submitted to a judge or magistrate for checking. They are then taken to the notarial archives and a second set is kept at the notary's office, where it can be inspected by anyone.

Foreigners may rent property free of restrictions except where the lease is for more than 16 years, when an application to the government is necessary.

It is now possible to borrow money for house purchase at reasonable rates of interest. These are currently around 9 per cent. Normally loans of up to 80 per cent of the purchase price are granted over a maximum of 10 years. Purchasing costs break down as follows: 17 per cent for stamp duty; 1 per cent for the notary; a Ministry of Finance fee of £100; search and registration fees of between £50 and £150. There is no VAT in Malta and local authority rates are not charged.

Where to live
The capital of Malta is Valletta, a fascinating city with many fine old buildings and an excellent shopping centre. Many local families and non-islanders, however, prefer to live in nearby Sliema and its suburb of St Julians. Popular inland towns include Rabat, Mdina and Mosta and there are some attractive resorts further afield at St Pauls Bay, Marsaslokk and Mellieha. Malta is quite a small island with a good road system, so everywhere is within about half an hour's drive.

The sister island of Gozo, to the north, is less well known, but offers much peace and seclusion. It can be reached within half an hour via the ferry from Cirkewwa and is well worth a visit. Farming is an important occupation and the many green fields are a pleasure to see. To conserve the sparse soil in the valleys, many of the villages have been built on the summit of the rocky hills. The capital is Victoria.

The other island in the group is tiny Comino, which has just one hotel and facilities for water sports.

Inspection flights
Winter fares are from £128 return for a minimum three-day visit. Details from the Association of Estate Agents in Malta, c/o Frank Salt Real Estate Ltd, 2 Paceville Avenue, Paceville, Malta.

Communications
There are regular flights to Malta operated by Air Malta, and also package tours and 'flight only' offers.

Letting property
Non-Maltese owners of property with swimming pools are now allowed to let holiday homes provided that they apply for a licence, which costs about £600 per annum. Villas with these facilities command rentals of around £40–£50 per day in the high season. Licence applications must be submitted through a Maltese managing agent.

Recreation
Facilities exist for golf, football, water sports, horse racing, hockey, cycling, athletics, fishing and netball. Indoors there are opportunities for billiards, snooker, ten-pin bowling and table tennis. Non-sporting pursuits include the cinema and the theatre; there are local television and radio programmes; 700 years of historical development provide a fine heritage of remarkable architecture.

Driving

At times, standards are a little erratic. Cars drive on the left, officially. All current licences and international driving licences are accepted.

Health services

The climate is good, and the hygienic conditions help the Maltese to enjoy a high standard of health.

A health agreement between the UK and Malta is beneficial to British people living in the island. Permanent residents are exempt from hospital charges; holders of temporary residence permits pay greatly reduced hospital charges; British citizens visiting Malta as tourists are not subject to charges if treatment is required within 30 days of arrival.

Climate

The climate is warm and healthy, with mild, moist winters and hot, dry summers, as the following table shows:

	Average daily temperatures (°C)	Monthly rainfall (mm)	Sea temperature (°C)	Sunshine hours
January	9.5–15.0	88.2	14.5	5.3
February	9.4–15.4	61.4	14.5	6.3
March	10.2–16.7	44.0	14.5	7.3
April	11.8–18.7	27.5	16.1	8.3
May	14.9–23.0	9.7	18.4	10.0
June	18.6–27.4	3.4	21.1	11.2
July	21.0–32.2	0.9	24.5	12.1
August	21.8–30.6	9.3	25.6	11.3
September	20.2–27.0	44.4	25.0	8.9
October	17.1–23.7	117.9	22.2	7.3
November	13.8–19.9	75.5	19.5	6.3
December	11.1–16.7	96.0	16.7	5.2

Portugal and Madeira

General information
Status. Republic
Capital. Lisbon
Area. 92,000 sq km (32,225 sq miles)
Population. 10,299,000

Location
Latitude 37°N; longitude 6°W. Situated on the south-western tip of the European mainland, Portugal has very obvious attractions. The environment is still fairly unspoilt and there are perfect beaches.

Being on the Atlantic coast means that greenery flourishes, whereas elsewhere on equal longitudes scrub and thorn prevail. Therefore, Portugal is subjected to the warmth befitting its proximity to the equator and the cooling influence of the Atlantic, which together combine to provide ideal conditions.

Political stability

Despite many changes in government, and a bloodless revolution in 1974 which overthrew nearly 50 years of virtual dictatorship, the present régime appears to have adequate control. Portugal's stability has been enhanced by entry into the European Community.

Economy

Cost of living. Inflation is still high. Imported food tends to be expensive, but the country is beginning to enjoy some of the advantages of membership of the EC and has reaped further benefits from the abandonment of restrictions between member countries in 1993. Local produce, particularly fruit and vegetables, is of good quality and reasonably priced. Most Portuguese wine can be enjoyed far more cheaply than in Britain, and meals in restaurants compare favourably with London and other large cities.

It is considered that a couple, owning their own home in the south of Portugal, can live quite comfortably on an income of £8000 per annum.

Hambros Bank (Gibraltar) Ltd has opened a branch at Loulé, Algarve.

Taxation. A system of taxation for individuals has been introduced which provides various categories of income, such as those which come from self-employment, employment, land, commercial activities, capital gains etc. These are taxed at varying rates.

People living in Portugal for over 183 days in any one year are treated as resident and are liable to Portuguese income tax on their whole-world income. Non-residents pay tax only on any income they receive in Portugal. A double taxation agreement exists between Britain and Portugal.

Death duties are payable on transfer of a property following death or by gift. The rates charged vary from 4 per cent to 50 per cent, depending on the relationship.

The municipal tax is between 1.1 and 1.3 per cent of the value. The rate for land is lower at 0.8 per cent. This is an annual tax, but urban homes for permanent occupation, where the price is under $10 million, are exempt for ten years. VAT is 16 per cent.

Exchange rate. Escudos (written $): $261.89 = £1.

Exchange controls. Non-residents can bring unlimited foreign currency into the country, including travellers' cheques and escudos in notes or coins.

Language
Portuguese is spoken and some knowledge of it would be useful. However, English is fairly common in tourist areas, especially where there is a substantial expatriate community.

Expatriate community
The southern coastline (Algarve) attracts a variety of European citizens, particularly from the UK, Germany and Scandinavia. The business community is settled around Lisbon and Oporto. A growing number of British citizens are choosing the Estoril/Cascais area, and also the largely unspoilt coast near Oporto and the west coast close to Obidos lagoon, as the location for holiday homes.

The Association of Foreign Property Owners in Portugal was formed on the Algarve in 1987 to help expatriate property owners to understand and comply with changing legislation. This non-commercial, non-political organisation has been properly constituted under Portuguese law.

Services available to members include help and advice on purchasing residential property, guidance on the completion of official Portuguese forms, recommendations of trustworthy legal and financial consultants, and the services of a 'problems' clinic. A databank of reliable doctors and nurses has been compiled.

A newsletter is published regularly and seminars are held from time to time to discuss tax and legal problems and also health subjects.

Over 1500 members now belong to the Association. Details of subscriptions can be obtained from AFPOP, Apartado 23, Alvor, 8500 Portimao, Algarve, Portugal.

Security
It is a good idea to instal a security system to protect your property from undesirables, particularly if the house is to be closed for long periods.

Residence permits
Applications for a residence permit should be made to the Portuguese Consulate before arrival in Portugal and a residence card obtained together with a fiscal number on arrival in Portugal.

Work permits

A work permit is required by all non-EC citizens who wish to take a job. The prospective employer is responsible for obtaining one by contacting the Ministry of Labour.

Personal effects

These may be imported free of duty so long as they have been in the owner's possession for more than 12 months. Household goods need a *residencia* or *escritura* if they are to be imported duty free.

Housing

Many villa and apartment estates have been built on the Algarve in recent years and in resorts close to Lisbon. Old properties for modernisation come on the market quite frequently.

Following a directive from the EC, Portugal has prepared new planning regulations for development in the country. A regional plan for the Algarve, known as PROTAL (Plano Regional de Ordenamento do Territorio Algarve), aims to solve some of the problems created by uncontrolled development in the region over the past two decades.

Building zones, agricultural and green zones have been specified and most new building will be restricted for the next ten years. The exceptions to the new rules include new schemes on sites in excess of 50 hectares and further phases of development already approved.

Those already having planning permission to build on a single plot are advised to ensure that the building licence is still valid as these are generally only effective for one year.

Buying property

One of your first tasks should be to ascertain from the government-maintained Property Register that your chosen villa or apartment is free of all charges or liens. This is generally undertaken by the purchaser's solicitor and a certificate is obtained from the local Land Registry office.

A promissory contract (*contrato promessa de compra e venda*), giving details of the property, the price to be paid, the date of completion and the date of possession, is generally drawn up by the vendor's legal representative. This document is then signed by both parties and a deposit (usually from 10 to 30 per cent of the purchase price as agreed between the two parties) is paid. If the purchaser fails to complete the deal, the deposit is forfeited. Should the vendor renege he or she forfeits a sum equivalent to twice the deposit.

A copy of the deeds (*escritura*) is given to the purchaser after they have been signed by both parties in the presence of a notary.

The change of ownership is registered at the local Land Registry and this may take some weeks, but meanwhile the purchaser's title can be protected against third parties.

SISA (property transfer tax) changes frequently. Currently a home costing up to $8.1 million is exempt. Over this figure the scale rises from 5 to 26 per cent up to $24.2 million, after allowing significant deductions. On a $15 million property, the SISA tax is equivalent to about 3.5 per cent of the price.

Notarial and registration fees normally total between 3 and 3.5 per cent, while the charges made by the *advogado* are generally by arrangement.

VAT is levied on the supply of services, including building contracts.

Inspection flights
Cheap flights to inspect property are available via charter services throughout the year.

Communications
There are daily flights from the UK to Lisbon and Faro by British Airways and Portuguese Airlines (TAP). To Madeira, there is a twice-weekly service from Heathrow to Funchal. Internal flights (including Madeira and the Azores) are run by TAP. Lisbon airport has been modernised and its capacity increased.

Train services are available via Paris (journey time approximately 24 hours Paris–Lisbon).

Recreation
Spectator sports are a very popular form of leisure in Portugal, especially football and also the traditional bullfight (more merciful in character than the Spanish version). Golf is a popular pastime with a number of good courses within reach of Lisbon and many along the Algarve. Horse riding, water sports and camping are among other enjoyable pursuits.

Eating out is common, with restaurants plentiful and open until late. The food is possibly as good as anywhere in Europe.

As far as the arts are concerned, Portugal has its own theatre tradition, abundant museums and galleries, fine orchestras and beautiful and arresting architecture. The cinema is popular and films are often dubbed into English.

There are also many clubs and societies for expatriates' use. The Algarve region has a Lions Club and also a Lioness Club, an archaeological association, and meetings of the Rotarians and the British Legion. Bridge tournaments are held in some hotels and bingo has now been legalised. Other clubs and associations elsewhere include the Royal British Club, the Charity Bridge Association and the Royal Society of St George (or David or Andrew). The British Council in Lisbon also helps to organise exhibitions, lectures, films and concerts.

Driving

Foreign-registered cars may enter Portugal for a period of up to six months on production of the registration document. A Green Card (from your insurance company) is not required by law but is recommended.

It is advisable to carry a spare parts kit and obtain GB stickers while the car is still registered in Britain. British driving licences are valid. Carrying petrol in cans is forbidden.

Portugal uses the international road sign system. The rule of the road is to keep to the right. Traffic approaching from the right must be given priority, except when entering a public road from a private driveway or a side road with a stop sign. The speed limits are roughly the same as elsewhere on the mainland of Europe, ranging from 50 to 120 km/h.

Health services

There are many English-speaking doctors in Portugal and a British Hospital in Lisbon. Free emergency out-patient treatment is available to any Briton who produces a British passport. For permanent residents, private health insurance is advisable.

As a member of the EC, Portugal is covered by the terms of the reciprocal agreement with the Department of Social Security. For details see DSS pamphlet SA29.

Climate

Portugal is regarded by many as having one of the most pleasant climates in Europe. Throughout the year the temperature is warm without ever being sweltering. The proximity of the country to the Atlantic means that the air is freshened by the sea breezes that bring with them the moisture that allows vegetation other than scrub to flourish. The average temperatures in the two most popular areas for migration are as follows:

227

	Average temperatures (°C)	
	Algarve	*Lisbon/Estoril*
January	12	12
February	13	12
March	14	14
April	16	16
May	18	17
June	21	20
July	24	21
August	24	22
September	22	21
October	19	18
November	16	15
December	13	12

Where to live

The three regions most preferred by expatriates for permanent residence or a holiday home are the Algarve coast in the deep south of the country, the towns close to Lisbon such as Cascais and Estoril, and the Costa Verde, near Oporto.

The Algarve

The Algarve is favoured with a wide range of sandy beaches stretching from the border with Spain as far west as Cape St Vincent.

A new preservation area has been declared by the government. This covers the whole coastal area, several kilometres deep, running west from Burgau to Cape St Vincent and north to Aljezur. Local councils are not allowed to grant planning permission or even approve irrigation schemes without referring these to a control committee in Lisbon. As a result, prices of residential property on the fringe of the preservation area are rising.

The capital of the region is Faro, and the conversion of the local airstrip into an international airport speeded up the development of the whole coast as it became accessible to most northern European countries in about $2\frac{1}{2}$ hours' flying time. A new terminal, opened in 1990, has improved facilities for passengers considerably. Faro has a population of about 50,000 and is a good shopping centre. It has a small harbour and some pleasant municipal gardens, several museums and interesting churches.

To the east of the regional capital are a few places of interest including Olhao, a fishing port, and Tavira, which is surrounded by a prosperous agricultural area and some fine beaches which spread as far as Monte Gordo, a pleasant resort with an immense sandy beach, only a short distance from the border with Spain.

West of Faro the coastline becomes more indented with rocky coves, islets and sandy beaches which are reminiscent of the Cornish coastline. The town of note nearest to Faro is Almansil, a regional shopping centre, and on the coast are three major resort towns, namely Quinta do Lago, Vale do Lobo and Quarteira. Facilities include golf courses, tennis clubs, hotels and a wide range of villas and apartments used either for summer holidays or permanent living.

Further west along the coast is the well-known resort of Albufeira, originally a fishing town, with a large open-air market. The beaches are popular, with unusual rock formations; above, on the clifftop, the winding streets have a variety of well-established and recently built properties. Many retail establishments, restaurants and bars serve the local population and also the considerable number of holiday-makers who visit the town every summer. From nearly every vantage point, there are views of the sea.

The next major town on the inland road is Lagoa (not to be confused with the port of Lagos, further to the west). As the wine capital of the province, Lagoa is considered to be important as an agricultural market town.

Portimao is a large fishing port at the mouth of the river Arade, but its popular residential suburb is Praia da Rocha which has a large sandy beach, interesting cliffs and attractive rock formations. This is a family resort with a wide choice of new properties and hotels.

The last large town going westwards along the coast is Lagos, which has a variety of entertainment and shopping opportunities. At one time Lagos was the capital of the Algarve. Small resorts of interest from the residential point of view near Lagos include Praia da Luz, a true family resort, and also Burgau and Salema. This part of the coastline is memorable for the many rugged, tiny coves where the sand is regularly washed clean by the Atlantic waves.

The Lisbon area

Lisbon is a fine city located near the mouth of the river Tejo. It has many grand buildings, and the huge variety of commercial establishments makes it an ideal centre for sightseeing. This is not perhaps a place where many British people decide to spend their retirement years.

Of greater interest in this respect is Estoril, about 24 km west of Lisbon, known for most of this century as a cosmopolitan town because it provided shelter for many former administrators and even kings from bygone European states. The town has a good beach on the Atlantic and is well known for entertainment activities which include a large casino, night clubs, restaurants, exhibition halls and theatres. Modern apartment blocks vie with Victorian villas to attract those who want to live near the facilities.

Nearby Cascais is a fishing port and also the home of many well-to-do people from various nations.

A few miles inland is the ancient hill town of Sintra where Portuguese kings made their summer home from the fourteenth century. There are many fascinating buildings to be visited and sites to be seen.

Costa Verde

This is the northern sea coast of Portugal (the green coast) and lies between the frontier with Spain in the north and the mouth of the river Douro in the south.

It is not an area where many foreigners have settled for retirement, but it does attract tourists looking for somewhere different.

Oporto is the main centre of habitation and this town can be reached by domestic flights from Lisbon in a flying time of about 40 minutes. There are also rail and coach services from the capital.

As the second largest city in Portugal, it is also well known for having given its name to the famous wine – port – and British expatriates there tend to be connected with the trade.

Located at the mouth of the river Douro, this mainly working city does not necessarily impress at first sight but with time and effort many attractions can be discovered. There are numerous museums and a good selection of hotels, plus leisure amenities.

Among coastal resorts is Espinho, south of Oporto, which has a long sandy beach.

To the north of Oporto lies a large fishing port known as Póvoa da Varzim, an excellent seaside resort with good facilities for tourists; further north still lies Ofir which has a long stretch of white sand backed by pinewoods, while a few kilometres inland is Barcelos, which is well known for the large open-air market held on Thursday each week.

Another seaside resort is Viana do Castelo, 71 km from Oporto. Located near the mouth of the river Lima, the town has various hotels and good shopping.

The Anglo-Portuguese Society, Canning House, 2 Belgrave Square, London SW1X 8PJ (tel. 071-245 9738) publishes a quarterly newsletter for members and arranges events in Great

Britain to inform people about Portugal. Meetings are also held for members at the headquarters.

Madeira

This Atlantic island which belongs to Portugal lies about 1000 km south-west of Lisbon, but much closer to the African coast. It is 56 km long by 21 km wide and the terrain is very mountainous because of its volcanic origins. The coastline is largely steep cliffs so there are few beaches, but inland greenery and colourful flowers are to be seen everywhere.

About one-third of the island's population of 300,000 lives in Funchal, the capital, and the rest are scattered in towns, villages and hamlets in the countryside.

Funchal is built on a hillside overlooking the bay and harbour. The main hotels are located in or on the perimeter of the town and the central zone is packed with buildings ancient and modern containing the major shopping premises and administrative headquarters.

The choice of homes for sale to foreigners is limited and few UK firms of estate agents specialise in selling Madeira real estate, but there are a number of local firms willing to assist foreigners.

The quiet holiday island of Porto Santo has some fine sandy beaches. It lies 40 km north-east of Madeira and has a population of 3000. A local airport has regular flights to Madeira and also to Lisbon.

All procedures and taxes in the mainland of Portugal apply to Madeira.

Average temperatures range from 16°C in January to March, to 22°C in August and September.

Azores

Located in the middle of the Atlantic, about two hours' flying time west of Portugal, the Azores comprise nine islands with a total of about 2350 km. They are all of volcanic origin and each has an individual landscape, but every one enjoys lush vegetation, hills and valleys and blue seas.

Residents enjoy a temperate maritime climate, for the locality is at the centre of an anticyclone zone and bathed by a branch of the Gulf Stream. The largest island is Sao Miguel which has good facilities for visitors; services are also available on the islands of Terceira, Faial and Pico, all of which have airports.

Spain

General information
Status. Kingdom
Capital. Madrid
Area. 510,000 sq km (197,000 sq miles)
Population. 39,600,000

Location
Latitude 36°N to 43°N; longitude 8°W to 6°E. The popular image of Spain is that of Benidorm or Torremolinos, one of high-rise hotels, crowded streets and an endless nightlife. Yet there is far more to Spain than the commercialism of the popular holiday resorts. Blessed by an idyllic climate and at times breathtaking countryside, there is a different Spain which has been popular for many years among those looking for their place in the sun. Sun, of course, is one of the main attractions of the Iberian peninsula, but Spain's appeal is not limited to its climate.

Residence and work permits
Foreigners are allowed to visit Spain as tourists for up to 90 days on the production of their passport at the point of entry. Formerly the law did not limit the number of visits in any one year and as a result some foreign residents used to leave Spain for a brief period towards the end of their 90 days and then return almost immediately, have their passport stamped and so commence a further 90-day period of 'tourism'.

The authorities are now much more strict in this respect and are only prepared to give one 90-day extension, which is known as a *permanencia* and means a *temporary* stay. This is obtained at a police station and some evidence of the applicant's ability to finance the continued stay in Spain is required.

Those who are going to remain in Spain for any length of time as property owners or tenants need a residence permit. These can now be obtained immediately on arrival in Spain, whereas formerly applicants had to wait six or nine months before applying and required a visa issued by a Spanish Consulate in the applicant's home country.

Retired citizens from EC countries who wish to live permanently in Spain can now obtain a residence permit on arrival, from the local *comisaria* (police station) by presenting their passport and proof of sufficient income on which to live (pension, investments etc). Also required are proof of medical insurance through their own country's

Social Security system or private medical insurance, and four passport size photos. The completed application form requesting a residence permit has to be accompanied by the above documentation and a fee of 700 pesetas in the form of Spanish State Paper which is obtainable from official tobacco shops.

Normal residence permits are renewed after two years and after ten years an application may be made to renew the permit for a five-year period.

Along with the residence permit a tax identification number (NIE) will be issued, as anyone who resides in Spain for more than 183 days is liable to pay Spanish income tax. EC citizens working in Spain require an EC registration card, which is issued initially for one year and renewed for a period of five years.

EC citizens now have the same opportunity of employment in Spain under similar conditions to those of a Spaniard. The words 'non-discrimination' and 'equal treatment' mean that Spanish labour authorities can no longer insist that employers considering the employment of EC nationals advertise the job first at the Spanish employment office and give preference to any qualified Spanish applicant. The employer thus has a free choice who he or she employs.

Work or residence permits cannot be refused to any member of the family of any EC worker. Children under the age of 21 and spouses who are dependent on the worker have full rights to reside and obtain employment in Spain. Children of EC workers have the same rights to trade-school education and apprenticeship schemes run by the state, as Spanish nationals.

The regulations require any EC foreigner seeking work in another EC country to obtain from the State Employment Office similar treatment to its own nationals looking for work. Furthermore, when a foreigner loses a job through no fault of his or her own, unemployment pay may be claimed in the same way as a local worker. Of course, it will be necessary for EC workers to be registered by employers with the Spanish Social Security system and to have appropriate contributions and income tax deducted from pay.

Gradually, qualifications of foreign professional people, such as doctors, dentists, architects, lawyers, etc, are being recognised in Spain, enabling them to practise locally.

As from 1995, EC citizens who have held a residence permit for four years will be able to vote in municipal elections.

Personal effects

No customs duty or VAT are imposed on household goods and clothing imported for personal use, by EC citizens. Those EC citizens taking up official residence in Spain are also permitted, under certain conditions, to bring in a car free of import duty and IVA (VAT).

Housing

Spanish pueblo-style developments have been of substantial interest to overseas buyers in recent years. This is a high-density method grouping terraced houses with pedestrianised precincts. Those with larger sums to invest tend to purchase detached villas, especially if they are going to live in them for substantial periods of the year, as they offer much more privacy.

Apartments continue to be popular, especially for those seeking a holiday home, but as those overlooking the sea are now scarce and expensive, for reasonably priced apartments it may be necessary to examine the possibility of units being built a short distance inland.

Both developers and agents have improved their methods of presentation and marketing by using more sophisticated displays, models and specialised exhibitions. Inspection tours are also offered, but generally these are now of a more personalised nature and the previous practice of taking a dozen or more prospective buyers on a weekend visit to Spain, and keeping them so busy that they had time to see only the properties being offered by the agent or developer, has now gone out of fashion.

New building of homes is at a low ebb following the downturn of demand from 1990 onwards. Meanwhile there are some excellent bargains to be found among new and resale villas and apartments. Spanish business and professional families from the big cities and the north are now one of the most active groups of purchasers taking advantage of the opportunities to acquire real estate on the coast at attractive prices.

The future. A less well-known region likely to create the interest of those seeking a holiday or retirement home during the next decade is the Costa de la Luz, between Cadiz and Huelva, on the Atlantic coast. Here the terrain is varied and there are attractive beaches, mountainous regions and fertile plains close to the border with Portugal. Access is quite easy via Gibraltar Airport.

The Costa de Azahar, and also the Costa Dorada, have scope for future expansion, while the islands of La Palma, Fuerteventura and Gomera in the Canary group, which lie off the coast of Morocco in the Atlantic, could become more popular.

Political stability and economy

Following the cruel civil war between 1937 and 1939, the country was ruled by the conservative, yet repressive régime of General Franco, until 1978. Since then the stability of the administration appears to be satisfactory and undoubtedly the King, Juan Carlos, has played an effective part in maintaining calm. Filipe Gonzalez has been Prime Minister for 11 years, but in the 1993 General Election his Socialist Party lost their overall majority in the 350-member Congress. As in many other countries, Spain is still suffering from the worldwide recession and some unpopular decisions will have to be made before recovery is achieved. Unemployment continues to be a problem and inflation is higher than in many other EC countries.

Cost of living. The cost of living is now about the same as in the UK, so a move to Spain is not now so financially advantageous as in the past. However, the warmer climate in the south means that money can be saved on the purchase of heavy winter clothing and on home heating.

Taxation. Income tax is levied on everyone who lives in Spain for more than 183 days per year, be they residents or tourists. The rates may vary from year to year, but in the year 1982, payable in May and June 1983, they ranged from 20 per cent to 56 per cent, after certain deductions including payments in to the Spanish Social Security system, trade-union dues, the annual municipal real-estate tax, interest payments on house purchase mortgages (with a limit of 800,000 pesetas, or one million pesetas if a couple file their tax return jointly). Where employment requires contributions to a company pension plan, the total of these payments up to a maximum of 15 per cent of earnings, or 750,000 pesetas, whichever is less, may be deducted from income.

There is a double taxation agreement between Spain and the UK and some other countries. A 'wealth' tax or, to translate the Spanish title, 'extraordinary tax on assets' is payable annually.

Residents pay on their worldwide assets, namely everything owned, but are granted a tax-free allowance of 15 million pesetas each (ie husband and wife jointly have an allowance of 30 million pesetas). Non-residents pay on all their assets in Spain. However, the rate of tax is very low, being only 0.2 per cent on the first 25 million pesetas.

Non-resident property owners who do not let their property and only use it for a few weeks annually can be charged income tax on the estimated rental value for the period of their occupation per year. This amounts to 25 per cent of 2 per cent of the *valor catastral* (official valuation).

Plus valia is another tax. This is based on the increase in value of the land since the last sale. With apartments or pueblo-style town houses on new urbanisations, the increase is likely to be very small as only small areas of land are involved. The tax should be paid by the vendor but is often passed on to the purchaser. It is based on the 'official' value, which is always lower than the market value. The rate varies from about 10 to 40 per cent depending on location and the length of time between sales of the plot.

Property owners pay an annual real-estate tax known as *Impuesto sobre Bienes Inmuebles*. This based on the *valor catastral* of the property and varies according to the location and size of the home. The amount paid can be deducted from income tax due.

Property owners find that a very small part of the value of their property (2 per cent of the official value) is calculated as income and added to the total income of the person concerned, thus increasing their tax liability, by a small amount.

Tax on property profits. Non-residents who sell their property at a profit must pay 35 per cent tax on the difference between the original price and the new figure. To ensure that this is done anyone purchasing a property from a non-resident must pay 10 per cent of the purchase price over to the tax ministry. Where the vendor has made a loss on the transaction or the amount deposited is in excess of the computed figure, a refund is eventually made to the vendor. Residents who sell their home at a profit are allowed to re-invest the proceeds in another property without paying tax, up to the amount re-invested. Any excess is added to income for the year and taxed at the appropriate rate.

Non-residents of Spain, who own only one Spanish dwelling-place – an apartment or house – no longer need to have a fiscal representative who is living in Spain, but they do require a fiscal identification number and have to submit an income tax return each year.

General rates. These are payable to the local authority and have been modest in the past, but are being increased quite considerably. In most places no rate demand is issued, so it is necessary to check the figure due annually at the town hall. A surcharge of 20 per cent can be imposed, when payment is made after a fixed settlement date. Most authorities also make a fairly modest charge for refuse collection and sewage disposal.

The rate of VAT (IVA in Spain) is 6 per cent for basic necessities and 15 per cent for most goods and services. Purchasers of new property from a developer pay VAT at 6 per cent on the declared value. Property bought privately incurs a stamp duty of 6 per cent. VAT is not payable in the Canary Islands, but for new property there is a tax of 5 per cent.

Exchange rate. Pesetas 207 = £1.

Exchange control. Since early in 1992 foreign exchange restrictions have been virtually abandoned, so that 'convertible' and 'non-convertible' pesetas no longer exist and both Spaniards and resident foreigners are permitted to have bank accounts in any foreign currencies either in Spain or abroad. However, a somewhat complicated reporting system does enable the authorities to keep track of some larger transactions. Most of those involving foreign exchange, between residents and non-residents, with a value of over 100,000 pesetas, have to be reported to the bank on one of a series of 'B' forms.

Residents opening foreign bank accounts have to advise the authorities within 30 days of doing so and submit a form regularly to the Bank of Spain showing the transactions on the account.

Language
A knowledge of Spanish would be very useful although many Spaniards do speak English, especially in the tourist regions.

Expatriate community
There are more British people than any other expatriate nationality living in the country, but there are also substantial numbers of residents from Germany, Holland, Belgium and Scandinavia.

Security
As in most countries it is wise to be wary and to take precautions against theft by installing adequate security systems. Also, street crime and muggings in the holiday resorts are a problem.

Buying property
It is advisable, when buying property in Spain, to take all the professional help and advice available because of the presence of

less reputable property dealers, the long-winded process and the smattering of sub-standard, mostly older property.

When working through estate agents, it is sensible to ascertain their reputation and experience. In Spain the title 'estate agent' should be used only by individuals of Spanish nationality who are qualified by examination and registered. However, some licensed estate agents are little more than sleeping partners in foreign (British) firms, having few qualms about the firm's reputation. Consequently, some lapses in professional standards do occur. Although builders and developers are not required to comply with such standards, again it is advisable to check their respectability and financial soundness.

The legal process is often lengthy and it is essential to employ a solicitor. There are a considerable number of British firms of solicitors with special departments to handle overseas conveyancing, and some of these are listed under International Lawyers in Appendix 3. These firms have arrangementts with a Spanish solicitor (*abogado*) who undertakes the necessary work in Spain. It is certainly an advantage to have legal advice available in the UK to resolve any language problems and to have advice available in England whenever it is needed.

Conveyancing procedure is somewhat different from that in England. The first step, having found a suitable property, is to pay a deposit (usually 10 per cent) to the vendor's agent or legal adviser and have a private contract prepared which includes the agreed price and deposit, schedule for payment of the balance of the purchase price, intended date for completion, details of any extras agreed for purchase and any other relevant conditions or terms.

Remember that the deposit is forfeited if the transaction is halted by the buyer. If the seller does not proceed then they have to return double the deposit.

The *abogado* then conducts a title search at the land registry in the area where the property is located. This is to ensure that the vendor has a good title to pass on and that there are no charges or unpaid taxes registered against the property. Next the lawyer draws up instructions to the *notario* (notary), a public official who prepares the *escritura* (deed of conveyance) in Spanish, but does not check the title. The two parties then attend the notary's office to sign the *escritura*, but this may be undertaken by your legal adviser, if you give him or her a limited power of attorney. After it has been signed, the deed is taken by the purchaser or agent to the official property register to register the title in the buyer's anme.

After signature the *escritura* passes to the tax office and is assessed for stamp duty. It is then presented to the local land registry (*registro de la propriedad*) for inspection and recording. All the names of owners in the locality are recorded at the registry and until the new purchaser's name appears in the registry he or she is not the full owner. Only the true owner, as recorded, is capable of legally transferring full ownership.

The expenses involved are the notary fee which is according to an official fixed sale, the property transfer tax, the property register fee and the charges of your *abogado*. It is advisable to allow around 10 per cent of the purchase price to cover these items.

A *finca urbana* is a plot which is zoned for construction; building licence is usually easily obtainable from the local town hall, but there may be restrictions owing to an alteration in the town planning because the residential services for the area are insufficient. A *finca rustica* is agricultural land where normally it is possible to build for agricultural purposes only. Building permits are sometimes given by municipalities on land in this category, but they may impose density restrictions and also dictate the distance property may be built from the road, its height and distance from neighbour's property etc.

Consumer protection law

The purchase or rental of residential property is now subject to certain regulations. These require the provision of complete and precise information about the product being offered. They also require vendors to draft contracts in clear and simple terms and strengthen the principles of good faith and equal and balanced obligations in contracts of purchase and sale.

Furthermore, developers must produce on request the name and registered office of the vendor and a general plan of the property location, plus a description and plan of the public utility services, and safety measures in the event of fire. A description of the building and grounds, together with the size of the property, is required, as well as the construction and insulating materials used in the building. Other data which must be issued include land registry details, total purchase price and payment method, copies of licences and building permissions, statutes of the Community of Owners (where applicable), and information on the payment of taxes and rates levied on the property.

The total purchase price will include agent's fees and VAT unless otherwise stated; in the case of delays in construction or completion, an interest payment will have to be established in the contract.

The law also regulates the contents of sales literature, which has sometimes caused confusion in the past.

Severe fines will be imposed for contravention of the new requirements.

Mortgages

Abbey National (Gibraltar) Ltd offer mortgages on residential property in the south of Spain, the islands of Tenerife and Majorca, and also real estate along Portugal's Algarve coast.

They have extensive knowledge of legal and surveying procedures around the Iberian peninsular and provide a fast service at competitive rates of interest to those buying holiday or retirement homes in these localities. Abbey National's offices are at 237 Main Street, Gibraltar.

Property ownership through an offshore company

It is possible to form an offshore company to own your residence in Spain, which has certain advantages both fiscal and legal. When you want to dispose of the property, you transfer the shares in your company to the new owner and this is quite a simple procedure. Furthermore capital gains tax, capital transfer tax and VAT are not payable. The notary and land registry fees are also avoided.

Gibraltar is a favourite base for the registration of the offshore company, for it is easily accessible to Spain and the annual fee for the facility is quite reasonable. If properly structured no taxes will be paid in Gibraltar. Firms in Gibraltar that specialise in company formation and management include Jordan & Sons, who are also well known in London. The Spanish government imposed an annual tax on these offshore companies from 1 January 1992, amounting to 5 per cent of the rateable value.

Ley de Costas

The *Ley de Costas* (law of the coastal areas) was approved in July 1988 with the aim of protecting Spain's coastline against illegal construction and further undesirable development. It applies to Spaniards and foreigners equally.

No new construction is permitted on designated beaches and coasts, and some inland strips of land have restrictions such as maximum heights of buildings, exterior elevations and the proximity of buildings. Properties that already exist within protected areas will be allowed to remain, provided that the sites have all the required building licences, planning permission and clear titles, but the buildings cannot be extended or enlarged. Repairs and maintenance work will be permitted.

It is possible that some properties which have been constructed in public protected areas without building or planning consent may be demolished, but under the same circumstances this can also happen in Britain.

Very few British people are believed to have been affected by this law and probably most of these failed to take qualified legal advice before purchase.

Community of Owners

In Spain, the Law of Horizontal Ownership requires that in property with communal facilities such as shared gardens, swimming pools, tennis courts or public entrance halls and passages, and in blocks of apartments or peublo-style villa schemes and others, it is the owners who decide how their development is to be maintained and managed day by day. Thus the Community is run according to the decisions approved by the majority of owners, yet the rights of minorities have to be protected.

Each Community of Owners must have its own regulations which are known in Spain as the *estatutos* (statutes) and these should describe in detail the parts which are jointly owned by all the members and those that belong entirely to individual owners.

The proportionate share of the common property belonging to each owner should also be stated and so should many other matters of importance to the general well-being of all the parties concerned.

Before making any purchase in this type of scheme it is vital that every prospective owner should be fully aware of the obligations involved, so reading the appropriate documents is essential.

Every owner is required to pay his or her appropriate share of the Community expenses and, under article 9 of the Law of Horizontal Ownership, owners are required to:

1. maintain the property, fittings and installations in satisfactory repair so that no damage or danger will occur to the other owners;
2. care for all installations in the individual's property which are for the benefit of other owners; this includes water pipes, mains drainage and electrical wiring;
3. allow work to be carried out in the property as is necessary to provide new services for other owners;
4. obey Community rules and regulations contained in the statues or imposed as the result of resolutions passed at general meetings of members;
5. pay promptly the appropriate share of the general expenses.

In accordance with the law, a chairman of the Community must be elected every year. Known as the *Presidente*, this person represents all the owners and is also responsible for ensuring that the Community's affairs are conducted in accordance with the law and in the interests of everyone.

If an administrator is not appointed to handle day-to-day affairs then the *Presidente* undertakes the tasks of an administrator. The latter need not be an owner, but the *Presidente* must own a property in the development.

An administrator's duties include ensuring the affairs of the Community are run satisfactorily and that services are adequately maintained. He or she also deals with the maintenance and repairs of the buildings and other joint property belonging to the Community, prepares an annual budget for approval by the owners and, if no treasurer has been appointed, collects owners' annual contributions and also keeps adequate records of meetings.

An Annual General Meeting of the Community must be held at least once a year, and notice in writing has to be sent to every owner not less than six days before the appointed day.

A general meeting can be called by the chairman at any time of the year, or by a group of owners representing at least 25 per cent of the total of owners.

Matters to be dealt with at the AGM include election or re-election of the officers, approval of the Community's accounts for the previous year and a quotation of expected expenses for the next year, and to fix owners' contributions towards these expenses.

Voting at meetings is undertaken on a majority basis by the members or their proxy. Voting is based on the size of the property owned by the voting member, but the total of those attending a meeting must hold at least 50 per cent of community property to pass a valid resolution.

Minorities are protected by the rule that states that a group of owners who between them own at least 25 per cent can apply within one month to a judge for a decision where they consider their rights have been prejudiced by a resolution.

A resolution can be declared invalid by a judge on the application of just one owner, where it is contrary to the laws of Spain or if it is against the Community's own regulations.

Where to live

The choice of where to live is extensive. The weather is perhaps one of the most important deciding factors and, with an equitable climate for almost the whole of the year, the Costa del Sol, between

Nerja to the east of Málaga and the frontier with Gibraltar, is one of the most popular regions.

Costa del Sol. Much of the 160 km of coastline has been heavily developed with high-rise hotel and apartment buildings during the past two decades, and towns like Torremolinos, Marbella, Estepona and Fuengirola have been expanded almost beyond recognition.

The long stretches of sandy beach tend to be overcrowded in the summer with package tour holiday-makers, who patronise the many vacation attractions, such as the 30 golf courses, plus many more under construction between Málaga and Gibraltar, tennis clubs, swimming pools, nightspots, casino and an extensive range of bars and restaurants offering a worldwide choice of food. For permanent residence most expatriates prefer to seek out some of the small towns and villages largely unknown to the hordes of European tourists who descend on the coast in the peak holiday months between June and September.

Salobrina to the east of Málaga is an attractive town built on a hill. It has white painted walls and is crowned by a fine castle overlooking the sea. A town house in one of the narrow streets leading to the summit could provide a retirement home for a couple prepared to mix with local people away from the tourist traps.

Calahonda is a fishing community of interest on the road beyond Motril, a little industrial town with a port.

In the hinterland, mountain villages include Algarrobo and Competa which are deep in the Sierra Almigara, while Velez-Málaga is an inland town hardly touched by tourism – it was founded by the Phoenicians in about 600 BC.

All these locations are readily accessible to the coast, although some of the mountain roads are a little uneven.

West of Málaga, the province's capital which has a population of 400,000, the coast has been commandeered for the benefit of vacationists and there are few peaceful locations. Carvajal, near the fishing village of Los Boliches, still enjoys some serenity; Carteya, a small village with Roman ruins near San Roque, is favoured by some foreigners.

Sotogrande, a luxury urbanisation with golf courses and marina, has been developed over the past two decades. It is easily accessible from Gibraltar.

Mijas, a popular village 8 km from Fuengirola, was formerly a pretty centre of habitation but has recently been spoilt following exploitation by developers.

Mountain villages of note behind Spain's most popular coastline include Jimena de la Frontera and Casares where many old rural houses have been modernised for permanent living by foreigners. Other places to consider are Benahavís, Istán, Monda, Ojén and Coín which is now a market town serving the farming community in the neighbourhood.

Costa de la Luz. This little-known territory lies close to Gibraltar and stretches westwards beyond Cadiz to the boundary with Portugal.

Because of the distance from Málaga airport this coast has not really been discovered by the 'international set', although Spaniards from Madrid and elsewhere have enjoyed holidays here for many years. This beautiful coast, washed by the Atlantic, is expected to become more popular for permanent settlement and holidays, as it is very accessible via Gibraltar airport.

Tarifa, on the border of the Costa de la Luz, is the southernmost town in Spain. This residential resort has a population of 21,000 and enjoys excellent views to Africa, just eight miles across the water.

The major city is Cadiz and within easy reach is the nature reserve and national park of Donana, about 76,000 hectares, by the mouth of the river Guadalquivir. Inland is the city of Seville (population 600,000) with its many cultural attractions. It is Spain's only inland port and ships of 15,000 tons can still navigate the Guadalquivir for some 100 km from the estuary to the city.

Between Tarifa and Cadiz, the attractive little coastal village of Zahara de los Atunes, is worth a visit. Nearby is a discreet development of luxury villas on the hills overlooking the sea.

Costa Almería and Costa Calida. Almería is a large commercial town (population 200,000) adjacent to a stark hilly hinterland and extensive areas of open land which were formerly unproductive. Because of the warm climate it has recently been possible to produce profitable early vegetable and fruit crops, such as tomatoes, avocados and melons, under plastic sheeting. This produce is transported to England and parts of northern Europe in the winter when crops are not available from other sources.

This prosperity, together with an expanding tourist trade, has attracted investment in residential property, particularly in places such as Mojácar, Adra, Almeriamar, Aguadulce and Roquetas de Mar.

The coast of Murcia province is known as the Costa Calida. The largest town is Cartagena, which has important military and naval installations. It is also a manufacturing and shopping town.

The largest resort is La Manga, a strip of land with the

Mediterranean on one side and the Mar Menor, a shallow inland sea, on the other. Highly geared to tourism, this town is very busy in the summer but almost empty for the rest of the year. Further east along the coast are Mazarrón and Aguillas, which have many good beaches.

The town of Murcia is situated in the hills about 32 km from the sea.

Costa Blanca. The exact dimensions of the Costa Blanca are in dispute among experts. Some say the region starts at Denia and continues westwards 480 km as far as Cape Gata, beyond Cartagena. We have described Murcia and Almería under their own headings; information on the Costa Blanca is confined to the territory from Denia to east of the Mar Menor.

The capital is Alicante, a fine city and harbour with an international airport on its perimeter. It has every possible residential amenity, with a first-class shopping centre, some of Spain's best restaurants, an impressive cathedral, museums, sporting facilities, and a full range of schools; in fact, an ideal place to reside if you want to live amid the hustle and bustle of a big city.

To the east of Alicante the coast is littered with resorts, large and small, where Britons and many other Europeans have taken up residence in large numbers during the past 25 years.

There has been considerable building activity in towns such as Calpe, which has many multi-storey blocks of apartments, Moraira, a pleasant seaside town with a new marina where private villas predominate, and Jávea, where there are both luxury villas and multi-storey blocks of apartments, but practically no new hotels have been constructed, and the town is almost wholly residential.

Other small towns worth considering as the location for a permanent home include Villajoyosa, an ancient port; Altea, where the beaches are mainly pebbles and the old village is reached via 257 steps; Santa Pola, a small port where the restaurants are famed for serving some of the best seafood in the area.

Benidorm, the Blackpool of Spain's southern coast, should be avoided if you are seeking a quiet, peaceful life away from the masses, but it does have two fine sandy beaches.

Inland, Elche is renowned for its thousands of date palms which thrive throughout the city. These grow mainly in groves which are watered by a tenth-century irrigation system.

Locations away from the coast include Jijona, home of Spain's nougat manufacturing industry, Alcoy, where a variety of sweets are made, Guadalest, home of the 'eagle's nest' fortress built by the

Moors over a thousand years ago, Jalón, a centre for the wine industry, and Gata, best known for cane and basket work.

Costa del Azahar. The Costa del Azahar has 112 km of coastline stretching from Vinaroz in the north to Almena in the south where it adjoins the province of Valencia. Known as the Orange Blossom Coast, because of the extensive plantations of this delicious fruit, the landscape is quite wild in places. There are many fine sandy beaches and coves, which are particularly safe for bathers and for the enjoyment of many kinds of water-sports. This part of Spain is not well known to international tourists, yet the residential facilities are good so it is an area well worth considering for property purchase.

The main town is Castellon de la Plana, a port and the provincial capital. Other towns of note include Peniscola, Benicasim, Las Fuentes, Almazora, Nules and Chilches. There is an excellent network of roads, and some fine scenery inland.

Costa Dorada. The 'golden coast' includes the provinces of Barcelona and Tarragona. The two main cities after which the provinces were named are substantial industrial and commercial centres with large populations. Resorts include Sitges, Comarruga, Salou, Cambrils, Ampolla and San Carlos de Rapita.

Costa Brava. Just over the border with France the Costa Brava is the nearest coast for motorists from Britain. It can be reached via autoroutes all the way from Calais and is therefore popular with those who do not wish to fly to Spain.

The summer climate is not quite as warm as in the south and winters are generally cooler, but the average number of hours of sunshine in July exceeds 300.

Major resorts include Blanes, Lloret de Mar, Tossa de Mar, San Feliù, Palamos, Llafranch, Aiguablava, Estartit, La Escala, Rosas and Port Bou.

Gerona, the capital of the Costa Brava, is full of monuments to the past, for it was founded at the confluence of the rivers Ter and Onar several centuries BC. Ten bridges and an entire square cross the water and at the centre of the city is the old cathedral which dates back to the eleventh century.

Although there are a number of well-organised holiday resorts with high-rise buildings, the coastline has not been entirely spoilt by the ravages of summer visitors.

To the north of Palamos, there are pleasant small populated areas such as La Foscal, Sa Riera, Sa Tuna and Aiguablava where villas can be found in small numbers, many with sea views.

Just inland, the town of Bagur is endowed with attractive small mansions huddled amid woodland and palm trees. These are owned mainly by wealthy Spanish families from Barcelona and other large cities, who prefer to nurture their families in country surroundings or near the sea rather than burden them with the problems of city living.

Occasionally this type of property comes on the open market to be snapped up by ambitious foreigners who delight in living in an aristocratic style. Prices are high for this type of home.

Also away from the coast are Pals (not to be confused with the beach resort Playa de Pals – 6 km away) and Peratallada, once heavily fortified and where archaeologists unearthed in 1946 an entire Iberian city of the fifth to fourth centuries BC.

Northern Spain. The Cantabrian coast is far less well known to most Europeans compared to the Mediterranean Costas, but it is a region of considerable beauty. All along the coast, which is on the Bay of Biscay, there is an abundance of open green and wooded country-side, with mountains projecting into the sea. There are many fine sandy beaches which alternate with cliffs and a mixture of fishing villages, some of which have yachting harbours. Inland there are some historical villages in the valleys and tiny hamlets amid forests and meadows.

The province of Vizcaya is among the smallest in Spain, but has one of the highest per-capita incomes in the country emanating from the industrial tradition of the city of Bilbao on the left bank of the River Nervion. Surrounded by mountains, Bilbao was founded around the year 1300; it has grown into a huge industrial complex, yet still has a protected old city where the more important shops are located, also a Gothic cathedral, ancient market and some parks.

To the east of the city, other places of interest include Guernica, the seat of regional authorities and government since the Middle Ages and the fishing villages of Lekeittio and Ondarroa, both of whch have fine sandy beaches.

The adjoining province of Guipuzcoa, also to the east, stretches up to the border with France. Its most important town is San Sebastian, a resort of about 170,000 inhabitants, which is very popular with Spanish city dwellers for summer holidays. The modern town has wide boulevards and elegant tree-lined avenues, while the picturesque old quarter is grouped close to the fishing port and River Uremea. Much of the town is near the superb sandy beach of La Concha, which curves elegantly around the bay. San Sebastian is certainly well worth considering as a place of residence for those requiring a home in the north of Spain and there is a good selection of modern and well-established homes for sale.

The Balearic Islands

Majorca. The largest island in this group is Majorca (in Spanish, Mallorca) with an area of 3640 sq km (1405 sq miles), about the size of Cornwall. Located in the Mediterranean over 150 km off the Valencia mainland, this island is heavily involved in mass tourism and attracts around 3 million visitors each year.

The majority of facilities and hotels for holiday-makers are located around the bay of Palma in places such as Magaluf, El Arenal, Illetas, Ca'n Pastilla, Palma Nova and Cala Mayor. Many high-rise apartments have been built overlooking the sea between Santa Ponsa and Paguera, while on the east coast much development has taken place at Cala Figuera, Cala d'Or, Porto Cristo, Cala Millor and Cala Bona.

Close to the north-west is a range of hills. The town of Soller is surrounded by citrus fruit groves and almond trees, and Valldemosa is the home of a former Carthusian monastery.

The centre of the island is flat and fertile, with two main towns: Inca, where there is a leather factory, and Manacor, centre of the island's artificial pearl industry.

Pollensa, Alcúdia and Ca'n Picafort in the north are favourite residential districts for foreigners who want to live well away from the centres of intense activity.

Minorca. The second largest island in the group is Minorca, which measures about 50 by 20 km and has a permanent population of 50,000. It is about 40 km from Majorca and is quite different in character. Occupied for long periods by the British in the eighteenth century, the island has many souvenirs of the former garrison including Georgian architecture and sash windows.

Far less dependent on tourists to earn a living, the islanders manufacture a wide range of leather goods (particularly shoes), distil gin to English recipes and produce fashion goods.

Mahón, the capital, is a tidy town with a main square, several principal streets and a host of narrow lanes. It adjoins a 6 km-long natural harbour, claimed to be the finest deep-water anchorage in the world after Pearl Harbour.

Many new estates have been built in recent years for local people and new residents from Britain and elsewhere. These are mainly located on the south and east coasts at Santo Tomas, Son Bou, Calan Porter, Binibeca, Villa Carlos and El Grao. On the north coast there are settlements at Fornells and Cala Morell.

The main town on the west coast is Ciudadela, the former capital. It has a picturesque harbour. Very little development has taken place in this region and deserted beaches are frequently discovered.

Minorca enjoys a temperate summer climate, but does suffer from cool winds at times during the winter.

Ibiza. The third largest of the Balearic Islands, with an area of 570 sq km, is located about 40 km west of Majorca. It is nearer to the coast of North Africa than to the Catalan city of Barcelona.

A relatively mild climate is enjoyed throughout the year with an average of 300 sunshine days per annum. In the peak summer month of August temperatures reach 26°C, and in the winter the average temperature is 12°C.

Ibiza town, the capital, has a permanent population of 23,000 people. There is a modern town with shops near the harbour, but the fascinating part is Dalt Vila – the old town whose narrow cobbled thoroughfares climb steeply to the summit, where the cathedral and fortress have superb views over the town and across the sea.

The other principal towns are quite small, with populations of around 10,000 people. These comprise San Antonio Abad and Santa Eulalia del Rio. They have both surrendered to tourism and are not ideal for residential purposes. Small resorts which attract prospective home owners include Cala Longa and Roca Lisa.

The Canary Islands
Tenerife. The largest island is Tenerife which is almost in the centre of this group of seven inhabited islands. A long-time favourite with northern Europeans keen to escape from the winter rigours of their homeland, Tenerife has the highest mountain (Teide) in Spain, a long coastline with sandy beaches in parts and a climate described by some as 'eternal spring'. Average air temperatures range from 16°C in February to 24°C in August. Most of the rain falls between November and February, but cloud can accumulate over Teide occasionally to hide the sun from towns in the north.

The capital is Santa Cruz, a busy commercial and industrial town, also a port, but not much favoured for property ownership by foreigners.

Puerto de la Cruz on the opposite side of the island has all the facilities desired by vacationists. The lower part of the town adjoins the sea. Sandy beaches are rare but a huge lido has been built on the promenade to accommodate sun and sea enthusiasts. In the higher part of Puerto are some of the best hotels, also apartment blocks, a casino and the Botanical Gardens.

The expatriate community resides mainly on the outskirts and in the nearby Orotava valley where a considerable number of villas have been built among banana plantations and on hillsides.

Several years ago a new international airport was built in the south of the island and to make it accessible a fine new road was constructed.

The improved communications have been largely responsible for an entirely new holiday community built at Playa de las Americas and for the expansion of Los Cristianos village. Huge new hotels and apartment blocks, some villas and a yacht marina have been completed.

The climate in this corner of Tenerife is warmer than elsewhere and the average number of sunshine hours is greater; hence the popularity with the international community.

Further north-west, on the coast, Los Gigantes and Puerto de Santiago are also expanding.

Gran Canaria. Gran Canaria is well known worldwide because of its capital, Las Palmas, but it is in fact only the third largest of the islands.

Popular with British people in the first third of this century as a place for rest or retirement, the island has not maintained its attractions in post-war years compared with Tenerife. Although a number of holiday packages are offered by tour operators, there is a lack of organisations in Britain selling residential property in Gran Canaria.

With a population totalling over a quarter of a million people, Las Palmas is the largest city in the Canaries. It is a major commercial centre, a seaport and a cosmopolitan resort all at the same time. Major attractions include Santa Catalina Park, described as a huge outdoor café, Las Canteras, a 3 km-long beach of fine sand, the Canary Village featuring local folklore, and the Garden City with palatial residences and more modest houses all set in gardens with colourful blooms all year round.

Like Tenerife, Gran Canaria has some new resorts in the south, such as Playa de San Agustín and Playa del Ingles which are connected with the north by a good road. Tall hotels, blocks of flats, squat villas, pools and self-service food parlours are there in abundance.

A little further west beyond Maspalomas, some more modest urbanisations have been built around Puerto Rico.

Fuerteventura. The second largest island has an area of 2000 sq km. It is claimed that Fuerteventura has more beaches than hotels, but this may remain true for only a few more years.

Of the total population, which is around 20,000 people, over 7000 reside in the capital, Puerto del Rosario, a modest place with a harbour.

The nearest beach is Playa Blanca which is close to the airport. On the north coast Corraliejo was a small fishing port, but is growing in popularity because the bleached sand and the azure sea are so inviting for holiday-makers.

The southern strip of the island is known as Jandia. Along both sides of the peninsula are many more virgin beaches.

Property development is slowly taking place.

Lanzarote. This island (800 sq km) has enjoyed boom conditions over the past decade, with many new developments both private and commercial.

The capital, Arrecife, has only modest attractions but the shopping facilities are adequate and the international airport is nearby.

On the north-west coast, the Fire Mountains are spectacular and reminiscent of a lunar landscape. More than 300 extinct volcanic cones still exist and in parts volcanic fires glow a few feet below the surface.

In the north, the land is sufficiently fertile to grow crops such as onions, tomatoes and vines with the aid of volcanic ash piled around the plants. This absorbs moisture from the night air and supplies water to the plants.

Costa Teguise, a few kilometres north-east of Arrecife, is a large urbanisation owned by an international company which installed all the necessary services and roads some years ago and the land is now being developed gradually, by a number of contractors, with apartments and villas. A nine-hole golf course is in operation and this is irrigated daily with part of the output from a desalination plant.

Some residential schemes have been completed at Puerto del Carmen and Playa Blanca in the south.

The other islands. In order of size the remaining inhabited islands in the Canaries are as follows:

La Palma (725 sq km). A green island with a mountain peak nearly 8000 feet above sea level. Volcanic activity on the southern tip of the island occurred as recently as 1971. The capital and port, Santa Cruz de la Palma, is an attractive, clean place with new offices and flats blending quite well with traditional architecture.

A small colony of foreigners have made La Palma their home, happy to be well divorced from the materialism of the late twentieth century.

Gomera (378 sq km). Located offshore from Los Cristianos, the port in the south of Tenerife, Gomera has a peak nearly 5000 feet above sea level in the centre of the island. The capital, San Sebastian, was the place where Christopher Colombus left the known world in September 1492 on his voyage of discovery to America.

Gomera's whistling language was used in former years for hilltop to hilltop communications. Now it attracts the attention of the day tourists who come on the car ferry from Tenerife, which takes about $1\frac{1}{2}$ to 2 hours.

Occupation of residential property by foreigners is gradually taking place.

El Hierro (277 sq km). A wild island rarely visited by tourists because of the lack of hotels and facilities. The landscape varies from volcanic to verdant soil. The capital is Valverde which was built on a mountainside to counter attacks from pirates.

Inspection flights
Some firms dealing in property in Spain have inspection flights on a regular basis. Specific details will be given by individual companies.

Recreation
Spain has been Europe's sunshine playground for many years and so it is hardly surprising that there is a vast range of leisure activities.

Sport is popular in Spain. As well as the traditional bullfight, football and cycling attract a large and enthusiastic following. For many, one of Spain's main attractions is golf; the many courses in such a perfect setting are hugely popular. Also, other facilities such as tennis courts and swimming pools are plentiful. Contrary to many people's image of Spain, there is still a great deal of stunning countryside left, and this encourages many to take up walking and camping.

In contrast, the main resorts and cities provide a large array of entertainment, varying from cinemas, theatres and nightclubs to shops. In many parts of the country, the traditional culture is very strong and can be observed in the form of crafts and dancers. Food is also taken very seriously and restaurants are plentiful and very good in value.

The size and nature of the British expatriate community has encouraged the growth of clubs specifically for them. These include the British Society, the Rotary Club, the British Legion, the International Music Society, theatre groups, clubs for bridge, dancing, gardening and flower arranging, the Malaga Cricket Association, and bowling and numerous golf clubs.

Communications

Air. Excellent selection of scheduled flights via Iberia, British Airways and other European airlines, plus a wide range of charter flights at competitive prices.

Rail. The nation is well served by an efficient rail service, and regular trains to and from France make for an adequate international service.

Road. Good trans-Pyrenean road communications have vastly improved the journey by road (via the cross-Channel ferries or Channel Tunnel) from the UK. Now motorways have been constructed in the north and south of the country.

Commuter services in Spain are frequent, if a little crowded.

Driving

There are some good roads in tourist areas and around the large cities, but some of the country and mountain roads are rather primitive. Traffic drives on the right-hand side of the road and passes on the left. All traffic approaching from the right has right of way. The wearing of seat belts is compulsory and those who do not comply will be fined heavily. Third party insurance is compulsory and a Spanish bail bond is advisable, as, if you injure a pedestrian or damage another vehicle, you can be gaoled while the accident is being investigated. You must always carry your driving licence. An international driving licence is recommended, but is not compulsory.

Health services

In general, public hospitals and medical practices are good although perhaps not quite UK standard. Private health insurance may be worthwhile, to cover such things as post-operative or geriatric care. An agreement with BUPA exists also. Details of other welfare rights can be gained from the DSS.

Private medical facilities for the elderly are gradually expanding. For instance, Interpares is a sheltered housing scheme near Malaga, where the residents are mostly over 65 years of age and come from many different countries, yet live together in a friendly community. It has functioned successfully for the past 19 years. There are 73 apartments designed for the needs of older people, set in extensive attractive grounds with a swimming pool. The facilities include a restaurant, small shop, reception, guest rooms, post and bank service and cleaning service. The apartments vary in size from 62 square metres and prices start at about £42,500. Service charges are from about £230 per month and include nursing service, if needed, for up to six weeks per illness per year. Owners are guaranteed lifetime residency if they wish, regardless of physical health.

Climate
Spain's climate varies from the temperate in the north to hot and dry in the south and inland. Those who can, desert Madrid in the hottest months.

	Madrid		Barcelona		Palma	
	Temperature (°C)	Rainfall (mm)	Temperature (°C)	Rainfall (mm)	Temperature (°C)	Rainfall (mm)
January	− 4–14	39	6–13	31	2–18	39
February	− 3–17	34	7–14	39	2–19	34
March	0–22	43	9–16	48	3–21	51
April	2–25	48	11–18	43	6–23	32
May	4–29	47	14–21	54	9–27	29
June	9–23	27	14–25	47	13–31	17
July	12–36	11	21–28	27	16–33	3
August	12–35	15	21–28	49	16–33	25
September	8–31	32	19–25	76	14–31	55
October	3–24	53	15–21	86	9–27	77
November	0–18	47	11–16	52	6–22	47
December	− 2–14	48	8–13	45	3–19	40

Switzerland

General information
Status. Confederation
Capital. Berne
Area. 41,288 sq km (15,945 sq miles)
Population. 6,437,300

Location
Latitude 46°N to 47.5°N; longitude 6°E to 10.5°E. Switzerland is situated in the central Alpine region of Europe and borders Italy to the south, Austria and Liechtenstein to the east, Germany to the north and France to the west. The south of the country is dominated by the Alps, which reach an altitude of more than 4000 m, and the north-west by the Jura range. In between this spectacular yet unproductive land lies the hilly 'middle land' where the majority of the towns and villages are situated.

Political stability

There can be little doubt that Switzerland is the most politically stable nation in Europe, if not the world. It is a federal state made up of 26 cantons, which in turn are split into some 3000 communes. This is the basis of a unique political structure in which direct democracy is paramount. In terms of international relations, Switzerland has remained neutral since the Congress of Vienna in 1815. In economic matters changes may be on the way during the next decade, for the country is currently outside the EC but in EFTA and there is talk of an EFTA-EC link-up. If this happens the Swiss might have to drop certain restrictions they currently impose on foreigners. Under the Treaty of Rome, Switzerland may have to change over 60 laws in order to qualify and this could produce insurmountable difficulties.

Economy

Cost of living. The Swiss economy is undoubtedly in a very buoyant state and consequently living standards are high. The prosperity is also reflected in wage levels; when this is combined with the strength of the Swiss franc against other currencies, a move to Switzerland would appear to be a costly one. Necessities such as food and clothing are especially expensive when compared with elsewhere. The Swiss are renowned for the production of certain luxury items such as music boxes, lace, chocolates, ladies' fashions and, of course, watches, and while these are very expensive, as are most things in Switzerland, they are of the highest quality.

Taxation. Tax sovereignty is vested in the Swiss Confederation and in the 26 cantons, all of which grant taxing powers to their communes as well. This means that there are 26 different cantonal tax laws as well as federal tax legislation, and that taxes are levied by three separate authorities: federal, cantonal and communal.

There are no standard rates of income tax or capital tax, as these are normally levied at progressive rates. Federal withholding tax (*impôt anticipé*) and federal stamp duties are levied at flat rates. Taxes from 0.5 per cent per annum of the value of any property owned are payable to the commune, canton and Swiss government. In the Swiss tax system, the accent is on cantonal and communal taxes which form the bulk of the total tax revenue.

Exchange rate. Swiss francs 2.13 = £1.

Exchange control. There are no restrictions on the import and export of currency.

Language

There are four national languages in Switzerland: German, spoken by 65 per cent of the population in northern, eastern and central areas; French, spoken by about 18 per cent mainly in the west; Italian, spoken by about 10 per cent of the population in the southern Alps; Rhaeto-Romanic, spoken by less than 6 per cent in certain villages in the canton of Grisons. Knowledge of English is widespread, especially in the tourist areas.

Expatriate community

A cosmopolitan population is one of the hallmarks of Switzerland. About 15 per cent of the total population is made up of foreigners, and the country has been favoured by British expatriates for many years.

Security

All Swiss males are conscripted into the army for military training and so the country has a powerful militia, well able to defend the interests of the federation, should the need arise.

Residence permits

Tourists are not allowed to stay in Switzerland for more than six months in any one year. Residence rights are not granted automatically to those who own property in the country. Applications are considered from those who have adequate finances to support themselves and are of retirement age, having ceased all business activity, or suffer from poor health (needing mountain air). Those who have a job or own their own business in Switzerland are also considered.

Work permits

Before an alien can acquire a work permit, a valid passport, an assurance of a residence permit and an employment contract are required.

Personal effects

No duties are payable.

Housing

At first glance, it may appear that Swiss property prices are very much higher than in comparable countries, but one must not forget that, to the Swiss, it is unthinkable that anything should be built that is not up to the highest standards of quality and craftsmanship. This standard can be recognised in the new chalets and apartments which all have interior finishes, fitted kitchens, sanitary-ware, double glazing, and joinery work of the best quality.

It is attention to detail that leaves nothing to chance. Usually separate laundry rooms and ski stores will be included in the price. Apartment buildings may also contain a sauna or a swimming pool and will usually be managed by a highly efficient concierge.

Without taking into account the strength of the Swiss franc against other international currencies, property prices in the past have risen by 3–5 per cent per annum on average.

Government policy still tends to restrict the number of properties purchased by non-Swiss nationals. Each canton has its own rules or restrictions which are frequently altered at short notice. Certain of the most elegant resorts are entirely closed to foreign purchasers.

Size for size, new apartments are more expensive than those offered for resale. In the latter category fully-furnished studios can be purchased from about £32,000, one-bedroom apartments cost around £60,000, while chalets start at about £130,000.

Government figures disclose that in one recent year, of a total of 953 properties sold to foreigners, 340 were acquired by Germans, 131 by British and 75 by French nationals; 184 went to other Europeans, 44 to Americans and the rest to various categories. Thus, despite the unfavourable rate of exchange, the British were the second most numerous buyers.

In order to prevent property speculation, foreigners are restricted to ownership of just one property per family. Non-dependent children over 20 may also purchase a single property. A foreign owner or member of the family is expected to spend at least three weeks per year in the property.

Buying property

The legal formalities are handled by a public official known as a notary, who acts for both buyer and seller. The notary registers the change of ownership at the Central Land Registry at Berne which normally approves the transaction within three months on average. The two parties sign a purchase contract and, if a mortgage is required from a bank, provision is made for the contract to be rescinded if the finance is not forthcoming, in which event the purchaser has to pay only half the legal fees incurred.

The legal fees, taxes and registration fees payable by the purchaser normally total between 2.8 per cent and 5 per cent of the purchase price.

A notary can be granted power of attorney to sign all documents on behalf of the purchaser.

Mortgages are very difficult to obtain in Switzerland, at 7.5 per cent.

Selling property
Foreigners are allowed to sell their property in Switzerland after they have owned it for ten years. (A five-year restriction appears to apply to villas and apartments in the canton of Fribourg.) There is no price restriction, but there is a capital gains tax on the profit, after allowing for any improvements and sales expenses.

Foreign owners are permitted to transfer the property to their heirs, and English law normally applies. Death duties are payable in Switzerland, but if the home is registered in the name of the children over the age of 20, the tax is only 7 per cent of the property's fiscal value, which is usually 80 per cent of the actual value. If registered in the name of more than one person, the tax is paid on each individual's share.

Where to live
See 'Housing' above.

Inspection flights
Scheduled flights only, not specifically for property inspection.

Communications
Air. Excellent services from Heathrow, Gatwick and Manchester to Basle, Berne, Geneva and Zürich international airports, via Swissair and British Airways. Flying time is between 1½ and 2 hours.

Rail. The Swiss Federal Railway network is about 5000 km in all, having over 1800 stations and being fully electrified. The rail service is integrated closely with other modes of transport to provide a close-knit and efficient facility, which includes direct links to international airports, a wide range of postal, coach and boat services, and mountain railways and cable cars. All this means that the internal communications network in Switzerland is of the highest standard.

Road. The network is about 69,000 km long, with the national motorways stretching to about 1800 km.

Recreation
The Swiss environment is ideally suited to the pursuit of a number

of outdoor activities. Obviously, the Alpine regions have some of the finest winter sports facilities in the world, including skiing, skating and curling. The mountainous environment provides wonderful climbing, and hiking and camping are also very popular. The Swiss life-style necessitates quality facilities and so tennis courts, swimming pools and golf courses exist in abundance. The Swiss lakes provide plenty of opportunity for water sports and fishing.

Some of the most popular areas of Switzerland are the health resorts and spas. The clean air and pleasant climate make spas a blessing both for the sick and for those merely seeking relaxation.

Nor is the cultural side of Swiss life lacking in any way. Music and theatre are thriving, the successes ranging from traditional yodelling to modern jazz concerts. Also, throughout the year, many festivals and celebrations occur based primarily on old folk traditions. All this, combined with fine examples of art and architecture in the larger towns, makes Switzerland an enjoyable and fulfilling place.

There is no lack of good restaurants offering exemplary cuisine of many different types. Traditional Swiss food is not of any distinct type, but eating houses do specialise in the local delicacy.

Driving

The rules of the road differ little in Switzerland from elsewhere in mainland Europe. The minimum age for driving is 18 years. Drivers and front seat passengers must wear seat belts and children under 12 must travel in the rear of the car. Vehicle lights in heavy rain must be switched on, and dipped headlights are compulsory in road tunnels. All laws concerning speed, lights and seat belts are strictly enforced by the police, who are authorised to collect fines on the spot.

Health services

Health insurance is not compulsory, but as there is no national health scheme it is advisable, as treatment may be expensive. Such insurance is necessary for all members of the family and not just the breadwinner or head of the house.

A social security agreement does exist between the DSS and the Swiss authorities and details are given in DSS pamphlet SA6.

Climate

The climatic conditions of Switzerland vary considerably and perhaps no country in Europe combines within so small an area such marked climatic contrasts. In the northern plateau, surrounded by mountains, the climate is mild and refreshing. South of the Alps the climate is warmer, coming as it does under the influence of Mediterranean weather. The Valais area is noted for its dryness. Summer brings warm weather but at high altitudes it is often quite cold at night.

	Average temp (°C)	Geneva Average ppt (mm)	Sun (hours)	Average temp (°C)	Zürich Average ppt (mm)	Sun (hours)
January	3	60	54	2	66	46
February	4	57	98	4	60	79
March	8	66	149	8	69	149
April	12	63	206	12	90	173
May	17	69	243	18	114	207
June	21	87	269	21	150	220
July	22	72	297	22	150	238
August	22	105	266	22	141	219
September	18	99	198	18	165	166
October	13	87	131	13	81	108
November	6	93	61	6	72	51
December	4	81	44	2	72	37

temp = temperature
ppt = precipitation

Turkey

General information
Status. Republic
Capital. Ankara
Area. 780,000 sq km (296,380 sq miles)
Population. 60 million

Location
Latitude 36°N to 42°N; longitude 26°E to 44°E. Turkey stands both in Europe and Asia, so it has two cultures. To the west of the Bosphorus, which connects the Black Sea and the Aegean, is the European part; to the east, Asian Turkey comprises much high table land and mountains. Ankara is in the centre of the Anatolian peninsula in Asia, while Istanbul, the largest city, is in Europe and has suburbs in Asia.

Political stability
Surrounded by Russia, Iran, Iraq, Syria and Greece and having annexed the northern part of Cyprus following an invasion, Turkey is an important bridge between east and west. Increasing links with the west through membership of NATO, OECD, the Council o

Europe and associate membership of the EC, combined with expanding tourism and greater internal security, will help to increase stability, although the perceived close proximity of the Gulf War caused a temporary setback despite Turkey's clear Western Stance.

Economy
Cost of living. It compares favourably with the West, especially in the goods that can be purchased in the markets (food and produce, crafts).

Taxation. There is a double taxation agreement with the UK. Income tax ranges between 25 and 55 per cent. VAT is 12 per cent, but higher on luxury items.

Exchange rate. Turkish lira 36,134 = £1.

Exchange control. In operation in a limited way.

Language
The Turkish language belongs to the Ural-Altaic group and is spoken by about 150 million people in the world. It is written in Latin characters. More and more Turks, especially among the young generation, are studying foreign languages. Turks who have daily contact with foreigners (in shops, hotels, hospitals etc) know at least one of the major European languages.

Expatriate community
The expatriate community is gradually expanding and a growing number of British citizens now own holiday or retirement homes.

Residence permits
Application for residence permits for stays exceeding three months should be made to the Turkish Foreign Office or the local area police station, where each case is studied on its individual merits. Personal income is a factor.

Work permits
The potential employee should apply to the Turkish Consulate-General for a work permit or obtain one through his or her potential employer.

Personal effects
No duties are payable on personal effects imported by permanent residents but may be charged on electronic goods.

Housing
There are some estate agents in the UK who market homes in Turkey. Information is best gained from the Turkish Tourist Office or from a personal visit to Turkey.

Buying property
Ill-informed statements have frequently been made in recent years that foreigners are not allowed to buy homes in Turkey, or that they must purchase jointly with a Turkish national. In fact, foreigners residing outside Turkey are permitted to buy residential real estate if it is situated within a municipality (towns or villages with at least 2000 inhabitants) and it is advisable that funds for the purchase should be in foreign currency from abroad which has been exchanged in Turkey for the local currency (lira).

Having selected a suitable freehold property a lawyer with experience in Turkish property transactions (names of appropriate firms can be obtained from the Law Society in London or the vendors agent) is appointed, a deposit is paid and a purchase contract is signed. It is often convenient to grant a power of attorney to the solicitor to deal with the legal procedures. A fully notarised contract is completed between the vendor and the purchaser or holder of the power of attorney, the balance of the purchase price is paid and the *tapu* (title deed) is issued in due course. Permission has to be obtained from the authorities to ensure the property being purchased is not in a militarily sensitive area.

Notary fees and taxes for the purchase of property are somewhat complex, but are likely to total around 9 per cent of the purchase price, including stamp duty of 4 per cent.

The acquisition of leasehold property outside a municipal area can be achieved through the Yapi Kredi Bank (the third largest in the country) from whom the buyer leases the property in perpetuity, at a charge of 8 per cent of the original purchase price. The lease can be transferred to a new buyer simply and at a reasonable cost.

There is no capital gains tax provided the property has been owned for at least three years. On resale the original purchase price plus a reasonable profit can be exported, through the normal banking channels.

With the Turkish lira substantially depreciated, property prices for UK buyers are reasonable and it is possible to purchase a new two-bedroom villa near Bodrum, close to the sea, for around £28,000 from the British-managed local agents Pozcu & Collard or a spacious three-bedroom house grouped around a garden near the bus station at Bodrum for £44,500. Quality of new construction is generally improving. On a 'best value for money and quality' site at Torba, several sales of villas for retirement to British citizens have been made at £57,500.

Where to live

Although Turkey has a wide variety of environments and cultures, Europeans seem to prefer to live in resorts on the Aegean and Mediterranean coasts. Among the most popular towns with British people are Antalaya, Bodrum and Izmir.

Antalya is located on what is known as the Turquoise Coast, so named because of the alleged colour of the sea in this area, where swimming is possible almost all the year. The coastline has many attractive beaches, yet in places the mountains tumble straight into the sea. Wet winters and hot summers encourage the growth of a wide variety of Mediterranean plants. Banana plantations, citrus groves and ornamental palms are also found in abundance.

Antalya, which enjoys spectacular views over the Bey Mountains, is an ancient town with a history which goes back to the 2nd century BC. It has many historic buildings, but now most of the 200,000 inhabitants live in modern apartment blocks. However, the old town has been successfully restored, and there is a yacht marina for boating enthusiasts.

About 290 km further west, opposite the Greek island of Kos, lies the expanding resort of Bodrum, which is quite well known to British tourists. Again the town's origins date back thousands of years and there are some impressive monuments to the past including a fine amphitheatre and a castle. Today this is a prosperous town with a yacht marina, extensive shopping facilities and some pleasant beaches. The town centre is well built up, but there are numerous villages along the coast of the peninsula where there are new developments of homes and other residential amenities.

Izmir is Turkey's third largest town, with over 2 million inhabitants, the second port after Istanbul and headquarters of the south-east sector of NATO, so it is a place of importance. Much of the town centre is relatively modern, for a horrific fire destroyed the heart of Izmir in 1922 and there is little of historic interest in the central area. Modern buildings and large new apartment blocks abound and there is a good shopping area, some excellent hotels and a wide range of restaurants.

Inspection flights

These are arranged individually by selling agents.

Recreation

There is a wide variety of pursuits available in Turkey including yachting, hunting and fishing, skiing and mountaineering, as well as sampling the different cultures. The traditions (both religious and folk) and a rich heritage of monuments and museums are of interest. Shopping in the markets and bazaars is also very popular, where traditional crafts such as carpets, ceramics, copper and brassware can be purchased.

Communications

Air. Regular flights to Istanbul and Ankara by Turkish Airlines and British Airways, which take about 4 hours.

Sea. Passenger services from Italy, Greece and Cyprus.

Road. From London, Istanbul is about 3000 km. The journey can be made either all the way by road or part way by car ferry from Italy.

Telephone, postal and broadcasting facilities are adequate and western newspapers are available daily.

Driving

Vehicles can be brought into Turkey for up to three months by registering them on the owner's passport.

Speed limits are enforced at 50 km/h in built-up areas and 90 km/h elsewhere.

Health services

Many Turkish doctors and dentists have received training abroad and do command a foreign language. There are also some foreign-operated hospitals in Istanbul.

A social security agreement between the UK and Turkey exists to protect entitlement to benefits.

Climate

	Temperature (°C)			
	January	*April*	*July*	*October*
Marmara region	7	16	28	19
Aegean region	9	20	30	21
Mediterranean	11	22	32	23
Black Sea region	8	16	27	18
Central Anatolia	4	15	30	18
Eastern Anatolia	− 9	6	20	12

Chapter 23
Countries Across the Oceans

Australia

General information
Status. Independent state
Capital. Canberra
Area. 7,686,884 sq km (2,967,909 sq miles)
Population. Approximately 16,200,000

Location
Latitude 10°S to 43°S; longitude 113°E to 153°E. Australia is the only continent entirely occupied by one nation with one central government. It is the world's smallest continent in both population and size (except Antarctica) although it is 25 times larger than Great Britain. It is also the most remote continent, which has meant that the flora and fauna have developed in a unique way.

Political stability
The method of government is based on the British parliamentary system. There are three tiers of administration: Commonwealth, state and local government. Voting for those of age is compulsory for both federal and state elections.

Important factors of Australian heritage are a democratic government, a free press, respect for individuals and an independent judiciary.

A moderate Labour government has been in office since 1984. Close constitutional links are maintained with Britain and allegiance is given to Queen Elizabeth II, who is formally the Queen of Australia, but it is likely that Australia will be declared a republic within the next decade.

Economy
Cost of living. Locally-grown food and meals in restaurants are comparable with the UK or cheaper away from the big cities. Clothes, shoes and larger items of household equipment tend to be more expensive. Inflation has been a problem for some time.

Unemployment is also high at around 11 per cent. Now that Sydney has been awarded the Olympic Games in the year 2000, economic prospects look rosier. The aim is to keep inflation at around 3.5 per cent.

Taxation. Taxes are levied at federal, state and local government levels. All areas of taxation, except Customs and Excise duties, are available to state and federal governments. Income tax is collected at national level through a PAYE system. The basic rate of income tax starts at 20 per cent on incomes over approximately £2450 and rises to 47 per cent on incomes over about £22,720. Rebates can be claimed for dependent spouse and children. Interest payments on home loans are not an allowable deduction from taxable income. There is a double taxation agreement with Britain.

There is a sales tax on some goods and a fringe benefits tax at 48.25 per cent on the taxable value of benefits provided by an employer, such as low interest loans and cars used for private purposes.

There is a capital gains tax, but it is not chargeable on the sale of the taxpayer's principal residence or motor vehicle.

Every resident requires a personal tax file number.

Exchange rate. Australian dollars (A$) 209 = £1.

Exchange control. There are no restrictions on currency imports.

Language
English is spoken everywhere with some local variations on pronunciation and phrases.

Expatriate community
Since the Second World War, over 4 million migrants from over 120 countries have settled in Australia. Britain remains the largest source of immigrants (mainly because of the Commonwealth connection) but there are substantial communities from Malta, Cyprus, America and the Far East.

Security
In international relations, Australia's geographical position helps to make it one of the most secure of nations. Nevertheless, a powerful military force is ready to repel any potential aggressors. Internally, Australia faces problems typical of an advanced capitalist nation, with one especially worrying aspect being the increasing menace of drugs.

Residence permits

An active immigration programme encourages new residents, although there has been a slight reduction in approvals recently, to avoid the entry of people who may have difficulty in obtaining employment, during a period of recession.

A points system is operated for deciding if a person or family is eligible for emigration and it is necessary to pass health and character checks. The main aim is to recruit those who have skills and other attributes that will enable them to enter the Australian workforce quickly, to support themselves and their families without relying on the government. Those with close relatives in Australia can be sponsored by them under the Concessional Family Migration category.

Rules under the business skills category have recently been changed to encourage those likely to be employers of labour and may be able to bring capital into the country. A temporary residents programme is also available in addition to the normal migration programme. Working holiday-makers are allowed to stay for up to one year and can undertake casual or temporary employment. Those with specialist skills are also welcome, but must not be recruited for a job which could be filled by an Australian resident. Other categories for temporary residents include entertainment and sport, media and film staff, religious workers, lecturers and visiting academics, educational and medical practitioners. There are some restrictions for most of these categories.

Extended temporary stay for people who want to retire to Australia is also available. About 80,000 people entered Australia under these arrangements in the past 12 months. Applications for entry to Australia, including tourists, must be made to the nearest Australian Consulate.

Work permits

On applying to the Australian Consulate, details of work skills and professional experience are required so that it may be decided whether the immigrant's skill is of use to Australia.

Personal effects

Personal effects and household goods owned for at least one year may be imported free of duty.

Housing

About 75 per cent of all homes in Australia are owner-occupied. The average design is often single-storey with three bedrooms.

Construction is generally brick, weatherboard, fibre cement or brick veneer. The last-mentioned is most popular and has an inner frame structure of timber lined with plasterboard. This is ideal for the Australian climate and costs less than a full brick home. Prices vary substantially in different parts of the country, but are well below similar homes in Britain.

Three bedrooms, lounge/dining room, kitchen, bathroom, toilet and laundry room is an average house in Australia. The term 'home units' is commonly used to describe flats, where the purchaser can obtain the equivalent of a freehold title. They are found mainly in the inner-city areas, where sites are scarce and expensive.

House prices vary considerably in different parts of the country, but are generally well below those of similar homes in Britain. For example, Sydney is heavily developed, so most new homes are being built in the outer metropolitan areas, where three-bedroom brick-veneer houses cost around £44,000 and four-bedroom two-storey homes from about £68,000. In Melbourne, three-bedroom brick-veneer houses range from £25,000. In Brisbane, from £43,200 is the price range for a four-bedroom lowset brick-veneer unit with concrete tile roof and car port. In a prestigious suburb of Adelaide, £111,000 is required for a three-bedroom brick house with double garage, but at a beachside suburb a three-bedroom medium-quality home can be purchased for around £34,000. In Perth an average standard-finish three-bedroom home costs under £25,000 and a four-bedroom unit can be acquired for £31,000. Finally, at Canberra the average cost of a new three-bedroom house is £40,000.

The Financial & Migrant Information Service of the Commonwealth Bank of Australia, 1 Kingsway, London WC2, produces an excellent cost of living and housing survey twice every year.

Savings banks, building societies and government housing authorities provide the bulk of housing finance. Purchasers are expected to have a deposit of about 20 per cent of the purchase price. Total repayments are normally limited to about 30 per cent of the applicant's combined annual gross basic income, excluding overtime. Interest rates are approximately 9.5 per cent and the maximum term is 30 years.

Stamp duty varies between states. First-time buyers purchasing a property costing over £75,000 pay 2.5 per cent in Sydney, 3.5 per cent in Melbourne and about 2.3 per cent in Perth. Legal fees also vary from one part of the country to another, but are generally around 1 to 2 per cent.

Education

Except at private establishments, tuition fees are not charged at primary or high schools, but parents are expected to pay for certain items including uniforms, fares, textbooks and writing materials, arts and crafts materials, library and sports facilities and excursions.

Where to live

In such an enormous continent, the choice of residential zones is vast. The suburbs of Sydney, New South Wales, are an excellent base for permanent residents, for the comprehensive facilities of the cosmopolitan city are close at hand. Brisbane's Gold Coast in Queensland is popular for retirement and holidays, while Melbourne, Victoria, has its devotees who seek a more traditional way of life. The coastal cities in the south are popular with expatriates from Europe.

Inspection flights

None, but charter flights from the UK can now be purchased for less than £600 return.

Communications

Transport and communications present enormous challenges for Australia because of the vastness of the country and the sparse population in most inland areas.

Air. Twenty-seven international airlines including Qantas, the national airline, operate to and from Australia. Domestic airlines carry about 10.4 million passengers a year. Following deregulation, internal air fares are being reduced.

Rail. The railways are mainly government owned and operated. Much of the 39,000 km of track is used by freight, but over 300 million passenger journeys are also made, mostly on the frequent and cheap commuter lines.

Road. There are over 822,000 km of road in Australia, used by more than 3.6 million motor vehicles. The trans-continental routes are used especially by the trucking industry but most towns and cities have excellent networks that are heavily used by commuters each morning and evening.

Telecommunications. The long-established postal, telephone and telex systems make use of the most modern equipment and are generally very good for such a large country so isolated from the rest of the world.

Recreation

About 6 million Australians take part in sport, which includes tennis, cricket, surfing, the various forms of football and swimming, and a wide range of newer sports which are rapidly increasing in popularity. Recent Australian successes, especially in sailing, golf, squash and cricket, have prompted a surge in the popularity of these sports.

The climate lends itself to the pursuit of many outdoor activities including bushwalking, fishing and boating. The fine beaches, wondrous underwater scenery and ideal coastal waters are also a rich source of pleasure.

Club life, run by sporting or social organisations, forms the main source of nightlife. Membership entitles one to use the sports facilities, too. Bars are usually male preserves, with heavy drinking taking precedence.

Entertainment and cultural pastimes are strengthening. The theatre and especially the cinema have gained international reputations. Television includes home produced 'soaps', many of which are seen in the UK, and also British 'serials' including *Coronation Street*. Sydney Opera House and Australian opera singers are world famous.

Driving

Short-term visitors may drive on a British licence or international driving permit, but long-term or new residents must take another test soon after arrival. Regulations for the driving test vary slightly from state to state as do the regulations on vehicle safety and speed limits. Details are obtainable from the Agent General's Office.

Health services

Since 1984 a universal contributory health scheme (Medicare) has been in existence. This guarantees to all Australians 85 per cent of their medical costs, and access without charge of any nature to public hospital in-patient and out-patient treatment. Short-term visitors will have to pay the full cost of treatment and so require private cover. Medicare is financed by a 1.40 per cent levy on taxable income.

Climate

Australia's climate ranges from tropical in the north to temperate in the south. The surrounding oceans moderate the extremes of climate, giving the coastal areas a very pleasant weather pattern. It is important to remember that summer lasts from December to February and winter from June to August.

	Average daily sunshine (hrs)	Annual ppt (mm)	Average temp for hottest month (°C)	Average temp for coolest month (°C)
Adelaide	6.9	531	23.0	11.1
Brisbane	7.5	1,157	25.0	14.9
Canberra	7.2	639	20.3	5.4
Darwin	8.5	1,536	29.6	25.1
Hobart	5.9	633	16.7	7.9
Melbourne	5.7	661	19.9	9.5
Perth	7.9	879	23.7	13.2
Sydney	6.7	1,215	22.0	11.8

temp = temperature
ppt = precipitation

Canada

General information
Status. Commonwealth nation
Capital. Ottawa
Area. 10,010,000 sq km (3,850,000 sq miles)
Population. 25,354,064

Location
Latitude 48°N to 70°N; longitude 60°W to 140°W. Canada is about the same size as the whole of Europe and is the second largest country in the world. In this vast area are some of the world's largest lakes, huge prairies, massive mountain ranges and broad expanses of tundra. The north of the country is very cold as it stretches right up to and beyond the Arctic Circle. The majority of the population live within 500 km of the border with the United States.

Political stability
Canada is regarded by many observers as being the epitome of a stable and strong democracy. Internal conflict is rare and the party system, though well developed, is regarded as being more consensual than divisive. The country plays a leading role in foreign affairs and is a well-respected member of the Western Alliance.

Economy
Cost of living. Canada is considered to be one of the most financially

stable countries in the world. High standards of living are enjoyed by most sectors of the population, because of the low level of inflation and high wages. The recession caused unemployment to rise to nearly 12 per cent but it is now decreasing. Generally, the cost of living in all sectors of the economy is now lower than in the UK. Heavy winter fuel bills are to be expected. The long-term future for the economy looks bright, as Canada is blessed with an incredibly large reservoir of natural resources.

Taxation. Under the Canadian taxation system individuals are taxed on a calendar year with returns due by 30 April in the following year.

Residents are taxed on their world-wide income, non-residents on income from Canadian sources. There is a double tax agreement between Canada and the UK.

For those in employment, a 'tax deduction at source' system operates for income tax and employers issue a T4 form by the end of February each year indicating the previous year's tax deductions, pension contributions and unemployment insurance. Tax rates vary from one province to another.

Non-residents who sell a property in Canada will be subject to a withholding tax of 33 per cent, unless a tax return is filed in Canada, reporting any taxable gain.

Exchange rate. Canadian dollars (C$) 2.02 = £1.

Exchange control. There are no restrictions on the export or import of currency from or into Canada.

Language
The existence of two major linguistic groups is one of the features that helps to give Canada its unique character. English and French are both official languages and enjoy equal status, and the latest statistics show that nationally over 16 per cent of the population are fluent in both languages. Owing to the increased number of Asian immigrants, Chinese is the country's third most popular language.

Expatriate community
The population consists of people from a variety of cultures and traditions but many Canadians trace their origins back to French and Anglo-Saxon ancestors. Integration is encouraged but cultural traditions are still strong.

Security
Canada is rightly regarded as being free of any major internal

problems that threaten security. In any case, the military and the police force are well trained and equipped. Therefore, apart from such common 20th-century problems as are experienced through-out the Western world, Canada can be said to be secure.

Residence permits

Canada is one of the few countries worldwide with a permanent programme for immigration. During 1993, the government expected to accept more settlers in proportion to its total population than any other country, with a target of 250,000 newcomers.

However, a selective policy is operated and a major objective is to favour independent category applicants with job skills likely to contribute to the country's economy. A new Immigration Act came into force in February 1993, and greater emphasis is being placed on language skills. A points system is operated, which will make it more difficult for an applicant with poor English or French and limited education to be accepted as a migrant. A list is issued regularly showing the occupations most in demand and the number of points allocated for each job, and there are bonus points for the applicant's age, vocational training, applicants who already have a close relative in Canada, and migrants with sufficient funds to establish or run a business in Canada. The retirement category has now been abolished and retired people can now only emigrate to Canada if sponsored by a son or daughter in the family class.

Initially, all applications must be submitted for consideration by the Office of the Canadian High Commission in the home country. Visitors who decide they want to live permanently in Canada cannot apply from within Canada.

Work permits

People who wish to work in Canada must obtain authorisation from a Canadian immigration office.

Personal effects

Provided they are kept for a minimum of one year after arrival, most personal effects may be imported into Canada without incurring any duty.

Housing

Generally, migrants rent houses or flats on arrival and fortunately there is a reasonable to good availability of properties in this category. This is due to more established families moving out and buying homes following a recent federal housing programme which allowed 5 per cent down payments and other attractions. Condominiums (apartments or houses in a row) are popular for renting, but community charges have to be paid each month. Many houses have below-ground basements for storage and are generally two storeys high.

The Roy LePage Annual Property Market Survey of 11 Canadian cities disclosed that house prices in British Columbia rose by 15 per cent in 1992, but in much of the rest of the country house purchase became steadily more affordable. They forecast that property prices will rise by about 3 per cent over the next 12 months. Average house prices in selected cities include:

Vancouver, British Columbia	£134,500
Toronto, Ontario	£113,500
Ottawa, Ontario	£74,600
Edmonton, Alberta	£67,900
Montreal, Quebec	£59,500
Halifax, Nova Scotia	£56,000
Winnipeg, Manitoba	£43,500
Regina, Saskatchewan	£37,300

At the time of going to press the interest rate for mortgages had dropped considerably and was around 6.5 per cent. The home-loan interest rate is usually fixed for periods of 6 months to 5 years. Apart from a special government scheme, 90 per cent loans are generally the maximum and these require an insurance premium of up to 2.5 per cent of the amount borrowed, which is added to the loan. Advances of 75 per cent or less do not require payment of the premium.

Fees for house purchase generally amount to between 2 and 3 per cent of the purchase price to cover legal charges, title registration, appraisals, survey and compliance certificates.

Newcomers who take up residence in Canada are not restricted from buying residential property.

Education

There is no single national system as each province is responsible for its own arrangements. The main difference between the UK and Canadian system is that each student accumulates credits in a grading system which remains with them throughout their school career. Basic education is mainly co-educational, is compulsory from ages 6 to 116 years and free in public elementary and secondary schools. Some pre-school facilities are available for 4- and 5-year-olds.

Buying property

Legal fees charged by lawyers range from 0.75 to 1 per cent of the purchase price, but some lawyers who specialise in house conveyancing charge a flat fee of around £150, plus disbursements for title searches and other expenses.

A local transfer tax is assessed in most provinces when a property changes hands. This is usually less than 1 per cent of the purchase price.

Mortgages are generally arranged through banks, trust or insurance companies and credit unions. They normally require an up-to-date survey report on the property, to be submitted with applications for home loans.

Where to live

The British will probably prefer the milder coastal climates. The bitterly cold winters in the middle of the country make first-floor access to houses essential because of the deep snow. Therefore Vancouver is very popular in the east, together with Montreal and Toronto in the west.

Communications

Air. In such a vast country, effective air communications are vital. Therefore, the 61 airports in Canada are kept very busy by international flights, internal passenger flights and other varied services such as crop dusting, forest fire patrol, pipeline inspection and aerial surveying. Over 8 million people travel every year on international air services and over 20 million on domestic flights.

Rail. The railways have played an important role in the development of Canada. Today, two continent-wide lines, Canadian National and Canadian Pacific, span the country. They are used especially for the transportation of large quantities of goods. Smaller railway operations run on a provincial basis.

Road. About 14 million vehicles use Canada's excellent road network.

Water. As Canada has some of the world's largest lakes and is dominated in the east by the St Lawrence Seaway, communications on the water form an integral part of Canada's transport network.

Telecommunications. The Canadian telecommunications network is vast and is regarded as being one of the most efficient in the world.

Recreation

Canadians spend about 20 per cent of their income on leisure activities, so recreation obviously forms an important part of their life.

With four distinct seasons, the choice of outdoor activity is wide. In winter, there are opportunities for ice hockey, skating, tobogganing and skiing. The summer months can be occupied by playing tennis, swimming, golf, cycling and jogging. Spectator sports include hockey, ice hockey and baseball.

Canada's major cities have theatres, cinemas and concert halls. Smaller communities participate in amateur theatricals, annual fairs, folk music and handicraft exhibitions. In terms of history Canada does not have many monuments to a glorious past, but the Indian cultures and 'gold rush' memorabilia provide a source of great interest.

The greatest single asset in Canada is the stunning environment. The vast countryside provides an idyllic setting for pursuits such as walking, cycling, hunting, fishing and camping.

Driving
Driving is on the right.

Health service
Responsibility for health and welfare is distributed between federal and provincial governments, who administer the services, which are paid for by National Insurance contributions. The cost of medical and hospital treatment is high, but a government-sponsored insurance plan is available (details vary from province to province). However, dental and drug prescriptions are not normally covered by the schemes. Private health insurance is an option and is tax deductible.

A wide range of social services and benefits is available (family allowance and pensions) and details of rights as an immigrant can be obtained from the DSS (pamphlet SA20).

Climate
Being such a vast country it is impossible to categorise the climate; it varies greatly, from tundra to cool temperate, from snow-covered peaks to windy dry prairies, from climates that vary little during the year to those susceptible to great extremes without warning. Between November and April the temperature can fall as low as minus 30°C.

Average mid-summer temperatures (°C)

Quebec City (Quebec)	18.1–25.8
Ottawa (Ontario)	12.6–25.3
Vancouver (BC)	20.9–22.5
Montreal (Quebec)	20.9–26.4
Toronto (Ontario)	23.6–28.1
Calgary (Alberta)	19.8–25.8

The United States of America (Florida)

General information (USA)
Status. Federal Republic
Capital. Washington DC
Area. 9,399,300 sq km (3,615,125 sq miles)
Population. 250 million (approx)

General information (Florida)
Status. State
Capital. Tallahassee
Area. 151,670 sq km (58,560 sq miles)
Population. 13,000,000

Political stability
The USA is the richest and most powerful country in the world. US politics tend not to reflect the huge divide between rich and poor and recent years have seen growing stability and success. The country is also regarded as the leader of the Western Alliance. Since the US is a federation, Florida is run with a certain degree of autonomy with regard to local issues. At national level, Florida is represented in both the House of Representatives and the Senate.

Economy
Cost of living. The cost of living is higher in the US than in the UK, but this is compensated for by much higher wages. Thus, when all factors are taken into account, living costs in real terms are reasonable.

Exchange rate. US dollars (US$) 1.48 = £1.

Location
Latitude 24°N; longitude 80°W.
   The Sunshine State of Florida forms the south-east peninsula of mainland USA, separating the Atlantic Ocean from the Gulf of Mexico, Florida is on the same latitude as the Sahara. Winters are

mild and generally dry, summers are hot and humid – with average temperatures above 80°F – and subject to short, sharp torrential storms. There is also a risk of hurricanes in the late summer and early autumn, but their paths are watched closely and there is a well-practised alert system.

Florida is one of the world's fastest-growing tourist destinations, and the resident population of 13 million is boosted each year by more than 40 million visitors, about a million of whom are from Britain.

Communications are excellent – flights from the UK are frequent and competitive, with a good choice of first-class, economy, excursion and discount fares.

The state is also developing quickly as a desirable area for international property purchase. The standard of living is high and housing represents good value for money. Land and property may be expensive near the fashionable coastal resorts and central-state attractions, but prices remain very attractive in less-developed areas.

In the 1960s, the Florida authorities granted permission for the Disney corporation to develop a 27,000 acre site near Orlando – 42 square miles, twice the size of Manhattan. Since the construction of Disney World, there has been an explosion of tourist attractions and theme parks unmatched anywhere else. Today there are more than 50 entertainments in addition to the Disney complexes themselves, which also include EPCOT Centre and Disney-MGM.

Like Orlando, southern Florida and the central Gulf coast have shared in the tourism and development boom. These areas, too, are expanding fast, particularly around Miami, the affluent cities of Palm Beach and Fort Lauderdale and the popular destinations of St Petersburg and Clearwater with their magnificent sands. Tampa is one of the largest ports in the USA and developers have been laying claim to the coastal strip north from this metropolitan bay to New Port Richey and south to Fort Myers and Naples.

Celebrated beaches and extravagant man-made amusements are by no means the only reasons for Florida's popularity. Nature has been kind here. There is extensive forest, as well as concrete jungle. Vegetation is lush and there are thousands of lakes, mangrove swamps and marshes. South and west of Miami are the fabulous Everglades, a national park of almost one-and-a-half million acres.

The Everglades are not a swamp, but a vast, shallow river, only inches deep, which rises and falls during the rainy and dry seasons and flows from Lake Okeechobee to the sea. There are hundreds of species of birds, mammals and fish and varieties of tropical and temperate plants and grasses. The ecological balance of the

Everglades has been upset by the construction of canals and dikes, which have impeded the natural flow and water levels of the so-called 'River of Grass'. Conservationists fear that the delicate environment which took millions of years to evolve could soon cease to exist unless the balance is restored.

The coral and limestone islands of the Florida Keys derive their name from the Spanish word *cayo*. They stretch for 320 km into the Gulf of Mexico, many of them linked by the 42 bridges of the overseas highway. Diving is a popular activity, and conditions are superb, particularly off Key Largo, where there is a prolific coral reef.

Florida's natural beauty has become even more important in the campaign to repair an international reputation seriously damaged by attacks on tourists. Several overseas visitors have been murdered, and in a single year there were more than 12,000 crimes against tourists in greater Miami, mostly thefts from cars and muggings. The Governor of Florida appealed to President Clinton for $4 million extra funding to fight street crime, and the British Foreign Office has issued guidelines highlighting potential dangers to visitors in Florida.

The vast majority of people encounter no difficulties, but Foreign Office advice includes:

- Don't collect a hire car from the airport at night. Take a taxi to your accommodation and collect the car the following day, preferably from town.
- Buy good maps to help you with unfamiliar routes, and pay close attention to directions from the rental company.
- Keep to main highways. Use well-lit car-parks.
- Don't stop if your car is bumped from behind. Drive on to the nearest public area, hotel or busy shopping precinct and try to get police assistance.
- Be vigilant at all times and be on the look-out for suspicious people when returning to your car or hotel, especially at night. Seek help as soon as you feel threatened. Always err on the side of caution.
- Use proper, organised accommodation. Don't sleep in your car, particularly in rest areas on highways or in isolated places.
- Carry the minimum of cash. Leave valuables at the hotel.
- Do not resist theft.

The Florida authorities provide advice on routes to take and the locations of guarded rest areas – freephone 1 800 342 7768. The

Foreign Office travel information service can be contacted on 071-270 4129.

Buying a property

Property transactions in Florida, and the professionals involved in them, are subject to state laws and the code of practice of the Florida Real Estate Commission. Procedures are very different from those in the UK and careful planning is required to ensure a satisfactory purchase.

Basic rules

The following principles should be rigorously applied. Building standards are high in Florida and most builders, developers and agents are thoroughly reputable, but check their credentials and make sure they are licensed.

Do not buy a property unseen. Visit the house or development personally. When building work is finished, make sure all is in order and to specification.

Refuse to sign a contract before you and your legal and financial advisers have studied it carefully. Do not rush your decision. Once signed, the contract is binding on both parties, so ensure it contains all the protection you need.

Do not hand over any money directly to a vendor, builder or developer. Instead, pay your deposit into a secure escrow (third-party) account. Shop around for finance. Interest rates and deposits required can vary from lender to lender.

Identify the total cost, including the fees and taxes payable on completion. Negotiate which of these 'closing costs' will be paid by the vendor and which will be your responsibility. Confirm what is included in the price – furniture and fittings, swimming pool, for example.

If you intend to rent out your Florida property – and strict immigration laws could limit the time you spend there yourself – check existing and imminent regulations on short-term lets, which are prohibited or severely restricted in many parts of the state.

If you are buying a business in conjunction with a visa application, make sure before you commit yourself that the enterprise fulfils immigration requirements.

The real estate broker

Real estate brokers in Florida must be licensed by the state and can lose their licence if they contravene the regulations. The Florida Real Estate Commission administers a compensation fund for buyers who suffer losses from unprofessionalism by licensed brokers. If you agree to do without a broker in return for a discount on the purchase price, you will be forfeiting this protection.

Although brokers are legally obliged to act fairly to all parties, remember they generally act for the vendor, who is paying their commission and who will expect the highest price possible. You could hire a separate buyer's broker to look after your interests. In this case you will pay his or her commission.

Insist that the broker or agent shows you a selection of houses and developments. There is a wide choice in Florida, with no shortage of new property. Compare prices and quality and check what other development plans exist in the neighbourhood.

The broker should assist you throughout the transaction, keeping an eye on the progress of building work, inspecting the property when it is finished, attending the closing meeting with you or on your behalf, and helping with your mortgage, insurance, taxation, visas and even the connection of electricity and water supplies.

The contract
The contract sets out the details and conditions of the purchase. Have it checked by a lawyer who is experienced in Florida property transactions and make sure you understand it fully before you sign. It will state the purchase price, terms for payment, known restrictions and easements affecting the use and enjoyment of the property and the closing date when deeds and money will be exchanged.

The contract will also state how the closing costs are to be divided between the buyer and seller. This is subject to negotiation and there are no fixed rules. For example, you can negotiate that the vendor will pay for the title search. Other financial matters to be agreed include an adjustment for annual bills, such as property tax and insurance.

It is important that the contract contains all the conditions and clauses to guarantee your full protection. In particular, you should make sure you will have clear title to the property and the right to a refund of your deposit if your mortgage application – or the mortgage terms you require – are refused. These details, therefore, must all be included in the contract.

You should be similarly protected if the vendor fails to fulfil any condition of the contract or if further restrictions become known (regarding short-term lets, for example). The contract should clearly state what land, buildings, fittings and furniture are included and whether the purchase depends on other matters, such as the successful sale of another property or the structural soundness of the house and its freedom from termite infestation.

Finance

Banks in Florida are becoming increasingly cautious, particularly about loans to non-resident aliens, and often require deposits of 30 per cent or more. You will have to make an initial down payment, known as earnest money, when you sign the contract and pay the balance of the deposit when the purchase is completed.

In deciding how much you can afford to pay for your property, also allow for your closing costs, including legal and mortgage fees, and your regular expenses – monthly mortgage repayments, property taxes, insurance, management fees and maintenance costs. Repayments on property loans (including any in the UK) should not exceed 28 per cent of your gross monthly income.

The bank will employ an agency to check your credit worthiness. Enquiries will be exhaustive. You will need to prove your financial status by showing evidence of your current and last two years' salaries, or balance sheets and tax returns if self-employed, and your prospects of future employment. The bank will want to see recent credit card and UK bank statements and will require evidence that you have fulfilled your mortgage and other loan commitments in Britain and can meet the costs of purchase.

Shop around to compare the loans, interest rates and loan terms on offer. There are variable and fixed rates, and a mortgage broker will advise you on your particular requirements and circumstances.

You can choose to pay 'loan discount points' – a point being equal to 1 per cent of the sum you are borrowing. This one-off payment will serve to bring down the overall rate of interest and you need to calculate the long-term saving it affords.

Lenders vary in the fees they charge and the services they require in making the loan, services for which you will have to pay. Lenders will want mortgage insurance against payment default, life and disability insurance and hazard insurance against events such as fire and storms.

US law entitles property buyers to receive a 'good faith estimate when they apply for a loan. It lists the likely costs of obtaining a mortgage and closing the transaction. These expenses (some of which may be met by the vendor) will include:

- administration and legal fees;
- brokers' commission;
- lender's fees;

- loan discount points;
- fee for your credit report;
- mortgage and hazard insurance;
- property valuation (not a structural survey);
- termite inspection;
- survey of boundaries;
- title examination and insurance;
- the closing fee;
- fees for recording the deed and mortgage;
- local, county and state taxes;
- balance of the deposit;
- initial mortgage repayment.

The lender must make it clear if he or she requires a particular attorney, title company, title insurance company or other closing agency.

Before deciding on your loan, therefore, shop around not only for the mortgage itself but also for the most competitive closing services and costs. Since you must pay these fees on the day of closing, negotiate well in advance with the vendor, the lender and other agencies involved.

Bank accounts

You should open a US bank account and deposit enough money to meet the closing costs. Allow plenty of time for the transfer of the funds. The closing costs will also include a sum to be deposited in an escrow account to cover property taxes and insurance. From then on, you will pay in a monthly amount for these with your mortgage repayments.

To protect your credit rating, make sure your mortgage and other bills are paid on time and keep enough in the account to meet unforseen expenses. Your homeowner's insurance should cover the building and outbuildings, contents and third-party liability and should provide cover even when the property is unoccupied.

Some bills already paid by the vendor will overlap into the period when he or she is no longer the owner. Similarly, some of the bills you are going to receive will apply to the time before you took possession. The amount you owe each other will be worked out proportionately and settled at completion.

Property taxes, for example, are usually paid annually. Statements are sent out on 1 November, based on the value of the property the previous January. There is a small discount for prompt payment.

Condominiums

The condominium is a special legal concept, similar to the French system of *co-propriété*. The development is divided into individual apartments or houses. Buyers own their unit outright as well as a share of the buildings and land, and receive a recordable deed as proof of ownership.

The construction and management of condominiums and the conditions for their use and enjoyment are strictly controlled. They are managed by an association of owners, with an elected board, and each owner contributes towards the annual maintenance budget.

This method of purchase has a number of advantages. If you are unable to occupy your Florida property permanently there are obvious benefits in terms of security and maintenance, and you may be able to let your unit. The development could have its own leisure facilities, such as a swimming pool and tennis courts. On the other hand, you will not have complete control over the running of the property; the board of management may reach decisions with which you disagree; and there could be restrictions on your use and enjoyment of the property.

New property

When a new house has been finished, you or your representative will be required to make a thorough examination of it to check the work has been carried out exactly as you wished. You should note everything you would like the builder to make good.

Make sure all the building costs have been paid, and that the contract relating to your individual construction and purchase has been approved by your lawyer. When you are satisfied that everything is in order, completion can take place.

Title

Title search in Florida is done by a title company or an attorney, who will examine the public records or the 'abstract' (legal documents relating to the property) to confirm that the seller is the legal owner and there are no title defects, restrictions or easements.

Your lender will insist you buy title insurance as protection against any future claim on the title from a third party. This insurance will protect only the lender, however, and you should also take out an *owner's* title insurance policy.

Closing

The completion of the transaction – known as closing or settlement – will be co-ordinated by the title company, the lending institution, your mortgage broker, real estate broker and lawyer. When clear title has been established, you can assume ownership of the property and pay the closing costs. If you cannot attend the closing meeting in person, you may be represented by your lawyer or broker. In this case, you will be sent the documents to study, sign and return, and you should consult a lawyer with specialist knowledge and experience.

In addition to the earlier good-faith estimate, you are entitled, one day before closing, to see the settlement statement, which lists the services you are receiving, their costs and the money to be exchanged between buyer and seller.

The statement is explained at the closing meeting and your deed and mortgage will be recorded at the county courthouse. The documents can then be handed over to you and the vendor and other parties involved can receive the money and fees they are due. The deal is complete.

Rental

If you wish to let your property, especially on a short-term basis, make sure before you sign the initial purchase contract that you will be allowed to do so. Many local authorities in Florida limit or prohibit property rentals for periods of less than one or even three months.

You must have a licence and a licence number, and you must charge your guests a sales tax on every short-term rental. This has to be paid monthly to the state and, in some areas, to the county as well. It applies even if the rental is paid overseas. If you fail to charge and pay the tax you could face harsh penalties.

Tax

British nationals who spend 183 days or more in a calendar year in Florida are deemed resident in the USA for tax purposes. Other-wise, they are classed as non-resident aliens and will be taxed on income arising in the USA, including income from the rental of property. There is also a personal property tax, which is based on the value of furniture and household goods in rental properties.

The US tax year is from 1 January to 31 December. Annual income must be declared by 15 June of the following year. You may apply annually for a reduction in tax payable by offsetting various expenses against your rental income. These include mortgage interest, the costs of maintenance and repairs, management fees, property taxes, insurance and an allowance for depreciation. If your allowances and deductions are greater than your income, you can carry forward the difference to offset future income.

A husband and wife must complete separate tax returns, entering on each form 50 per cent of the rental income from a jointly owned property and 50 per cent of the appropriate allowances.

A double tax treaty exists between the UK and the USA. Tax paid by non-resident aliens on US property rentals may be credited against their British tax liability.

Non-resident aliens selling property in Florida will be taxed on their profit. The buyer must withhold 10 per cent of the purchase price and pay it to the US Revenue. If the gain being made is less than 10 per cent, application can be made for a smaller sum to be withheld.

Gift and inheritance tax. If you buy your Florida property in joint ownership, you should take specialist legal advice on the gift and inheritance tax consequences. Tax on the gifting of property is charged at gradual rates after an exemption allowance and inheritance taxes are also liable on property owned by non-resident aliens in the USA.

Visas and residence

The USA has strict immigration laws and you should ensure you are eligible for the visa you require before committing yourself to buying a property or business in Florida. Immigration experts such as Ira Levy, a former US consular officer and now a visa consultant based in London, can help you to select and apply for the most appropriate visa.

In particular, you must confirm that the business you are buying fulfils immigration requirements.

Permanent residence

Permanent residence (the 'green card' or immigration visa) can be obtained through the sponsorship of a close family member who is a US citizen or permanent resident. However, in many cases there are long waiting periods.

It is also possible to secure the green card through an offer of employment. The US employer must file a petition with the immigration authorities and will normally need a 'Labor Certification' indicating that no American worker was available to fill the position.

Professionals with a further degree or exceptional ability in the arts, science or business are eligible, and the 'Labor Certification' and job offer requirements may be waived in the national interest.

The 'Labor Certification' is not required for certain priority workers – individuals with 'extraordinary ability' in science, the arts, education, business or athletics, 'outstanding' professors and researchers and executives and managers of international companies. Various other professional, skilled and non-skilled workers might also qualify for employment-based permanent residence.

The green card may be acquired through an investment of at least $1 million in a new business ($500,000 in a rural or high unemployment area). The enterprise must provide at least 10 full-time jobs for American workers. It can be newly created, or can involve the reorganisation or expansion of an existing business or the rescue of an ailing enterprise.

Temporary residence
British visitors wishing to spend up to 90 days in the USA do not need a visa. The *B-2 visa* (B-1 for business trips) will permit stays of up to six months at a time. Holders must have enough money to fund their visit, and their permanent residence must remain outside the USA. This can be a relative's or a friend's house and not necessarily one they own themselves. The B-2 visa is for pleasure only, and the holder is not allowed to work in the USA.

The B-2 visa should not be used for regular visits of six months with only a brief absence from the USA in between. Unless there is a substantial interval between visits, immigration officials could refuse admission or extension of the visa on the grounds that the holder has abandoned overseas residence.

There are, however, a number of temporary (non-immigrant) work visas which permit extended stays in the USA.

E-1 (Treaty Trader) and E-2 (Treaty Investor) Visas. These visas require the establishment or purchase of a business in the USA and are available to citizens of countries which have a trade or investment treaty with the USA. These citizens can be the owners of the business, or executives, managers or other essentially skilled employees.

The E-1 and E-2 visas are often appropriate for small- and medium-sized enterprises. With extensions, there is no maximum limit on the overall stay in the USA.

In the case of the E-1 visa, 'substantial and frequent trade' in goods or services must exist between the US company and the applicant's own country before the visa application is made.

The E-2 visa requires an investment in a new or existing business in the USA, creating jobs for Americans. No minimum investment is specified, although in practice most are of $100,000 or more. The investor should own at least 50 per cent of the business and be involved in its development and direction – even if there is a partner or manager. On this basis, visas can be renewed as long as the business continues.

In Britain, the visa application should be made at the American Embassy in London. Money must already be made available for the investment.

L-1 (Intracompany Transferee) and H-1B (Temporary Worker) Visas. The L-1 and H-1B visas require a job offer, and the Immigration and Naturalisation Service must approve a petition filed by the US employer. Unlike the E-visas, the L-1 and H-1B do not depend on the nationality of the applicant.

The L-1 visa is available to executives, managers or employees with 'specialised knowledge', who are employed by foreign companies with a parent, subsidiary, branch or affiliate in the USA. The applicant must have been employed by the company outside the USA for one of the previous three years.

The L-1 visa permits a maximum stay of seven years for executives and managers and five years for employees with 'specialised knowledge'. The H-1B visa is for university graduates and other professionally qualified employees being posted to a job in the USA. The one-year previous employment rule does not apply. The maximum stay for an H-1B visa is six years.

Part 5
Appendices

1. Telephoning Home

Subscriber trunk dialling is now available in many countries, and the codes for dialling the UK are given below, together with the time differences. The 0 which prefixes all UK numbers is omitted.

On new developments, in busy towns and in many rural locations it may take several months to have a telephone installed and the cost can be high. In some new apartment complexes enlightened builders arrange for the initial wiring to be installed prior to occupation by owners, so connections to individual flats are quite simple.

Do not delay in the payment of telephone accounts when they are rendered or you may find your line cut off and it may take weeks to have it reconnected. If you occupy your accommodation for only part of the year, it is a wise precaution to arrange for accounts to be sent to your local bank and for you to instruct them to pay the accounts on presentation.

British Telecom have introduced an International Credit Card which enables holders to ring UK numbers from 120 overseas countries and charge the cost to the holder's UK number or an agreed business account. Calls can be initiated from overseas public or private rented payphones and an itemised bill showing time, duration, date, destination and cost of each call is sent with the quarterly account. It is possible to dial direct to a British Telecom international operator, thus avoiding any language difficulties, or to use the services of a local international operator. Each cardholder has an individual PIN number for added security. Further information can be obtained free by dialling 0800 272 172.

	Code for UK	Code from UK*	Time difference Hours +/ – GMT
Andorra	00 44	010 33628	+ 1
Australia	001 144	010 61	+ 8 to 10
Austria	00 44	010 43	+ 1
Canada	011 44	010 1	– 3½ to –9
Cyprus	00 44	010 357	+ 2
France	19 44	010 33	+ 1
Germany	00 44	010 49	+ 1
Gibraltar	00 44	010 350	+ 2

Greece	00	44	010	30	+ 2
Israel	00	44	010	972	+ 2
Italy	00	44	010	39	+ 1
Malta	0	44	010	356	+ 1
Portugal	00	44	010	351	Nil
Spain	07	44	010	34	+ 1
Switzerland	00	44	010	41	+ 1
Turkey	00	44	010	90	+ 3
USA	011	44	010	1	– 5 to –11

* The international dialling access code will change from 010 to 00 on 16 April 1995.

United Kingdom telephone numbers are due to change on 16 April 1995. After that date, please check any numbers in this book that you plan to use.

2. Radio and Television

For many years the BBC World Service has been a valued and much appreciated source of reliable information about world affairs for British expatriates in almost every corner of the world. It still broadcasts for 24 hours a day throughout the year with news bulletins on the hour every hour, plus many informative and entertaining programmes in between.

London Calling is a monthly magazine which contains much information about programmes on the BBC World Service. It can often be studied at British Consulates, or an annual postal subscription can be ordered from *London Calling*, BBC, Bush House, Strand, London WC2B 4PH.

Forces' broadcasting in English is heard in Europe, from either British or American networks.

Another source of English language radio programmes is Voice of America. This powerful station can be received on a number of frequencies and it broadcasts news and feature items with an American bias. Frequency charts and programmes can be obtained from Voice of America, 300 C Street SW, Washington DC 20847, USA.

Modern technology is having a considerable effect on radio and television transmissions and with the aid of satellites British TV programmes can be received over a wide area of the globe. BBC programmes are often available in western Europe; in south-west Spain, for instance, it is possible to receive British transmissions from Gibraltar TV.

Watching foreign television can be a considerable aid to learning the local language. Constant repetition of certain words in the advertisements finally lodges vocabulary in the memory of even the worst linguist. Watching the numerous British or American films with sub-titles can also help.

BBC World Service Television is a new venture, beaming news and entertainment programmes across Europe and throughout Asia. No advertising is transmitted and viewers have to pay for a decoder, an annual subscription, and need a satellite dish.

3. International Lawyers

There are a number of lawyers with experience in handling the sale of overseas properties who have offices in London and other cities. They can help to ensure that a proper, unencumbered title is obtained to villas and apartments purchased overseas, and help with foreign legal matters generally.

Their fees tend to be higher than for similar transactions in the UK, because of the technical work involved, but are normally a worthwhile expenditure.

A selection of these firms is given below:

Amhurst Brown Colombotti, 2 Duke Street,
St James's, London SW1Y 6BJ; 071-930 2366.
(Specialists in Spain and Italy)

Bennett & Co, 39 London Road, Alderley Edge, Cheshire SK9 7JY;
0625 586937
(Specialists in Spain, France, Portugal, Greece, Cyprus and Florida)

Cornish & Co, 1–7 Hainault Street, Leford, Essex IG1 4EL; 081-478 3300
(Specialists in Spain, Portugal and Gibraltar)

de Fortuny, 16 Berners Street,
London W1P 3DD; 071-436 4353.
(Specialists in Spain)

Neville de Rougemont, Suite C4, City Cloisters, 188–196 Old Street, London EC1V 8BP; 071-490 4656.
(Specialists in Portugal)

Griffinhoofe, 5 Coldbath Square, Rosebery Avenue,
London EC1R 5HL; 071-713 7887.
(Specialists in Italy)

Hedleys, 15 St Helen's Place, Bishopsgate,
London EC3A 6DJ; 071-638 1001.
(Specialists in Portugal, Spain, Scandinavia, Germany and France)

John Howell & Co, 427–431 London Road,
Sheffield S2 4HJ; 0742 501000.
(Specialists in Spain, France, Portugal, Cyprus and the USA)
and:
6–11 Bolton Street, London W1Y 8AU; 071-495 2361
(Specialists in Spain)

Leathes Prior,
74, The Close, Norwich NR1 4DR;
0603 610911.
(Specialists in France, Holland, Portugal, Spain and Germany; also
timeshare)

Sean O'Connor & Co, 4 River Walk,
Tonbridge, Kent TN9 1DT; 0732 365378.

William S Oddy, Rua 5 de Outubro 174, 8135 Almancil, Portugal;
351 89 395556
(Specialists in Portugal)

Osbornes Solicitors, 93 Parkway, London NW1 7PP; 071-485 8811.
(Specialist in Switzerland)

Pannone and Partners, 14 New Street, London EC2M 4TR; 071-972
9720; and at 41 Spring Gardens, Manchester M2 2BB; 061-832 3000.
(Specialists in France, Germany, Italy and Spain)

Penningtons, Dashwood House, 69 Old Broad Street, London
EC2M 1TE;
071-457 3000.
(Specialist connections in Italy, France, Denmark, Holland and
Germany)

Russell-Cooke Potter & Chapman, 11 Old Square,
Lincolns Inn, London WC2A 3TS; 071-405 6566.
(Associate offices in France and Spain)

Michael Soul Associates, 21 Gough Square,
London EC4A 3DE; 071-353 3358.
(Specialists in Spain)

Sparrow & Sparrow, 2 The Fairway, Aldwick Bay Estate,
Bognor Regis, West Sussex PO21 1EL;
0243 268161.
(Timeshare solicitors)

Turkish Law Office, 93 Westway,
London W12 0PU; 081-740 5581.

John Venn & Sons, Imperial House, 15–19 Kingsway,
London WC2B 6UU; 071-836 9522.
(Specialists in Spain, Portugal, Italy, France, Florida and Colorado,
USA)

Taylors Solicitors, The Red Brick House, 28–32 Trippet Lane,
Sheffield S1 4EL; 0742 349084.
(Specialists in France)

4. Further Reading

A good selection of specialised books and magazines is now available through the retail trade and some can be consulted at public reference libraries. A few of these publications are listed below:

General

Retiring Abroad, Financial Times Business Information, 7th floor, 50–64 Broadway, London SW1H 0DB.

Sun, Sand and Cement by Cheryl Taylor. Rosters, 60 Welbeck Street, London W1M 7HB.

Villa Guide, published by Private Villas, 52 High Street, Henley-in-Arden, Solihull, West Midlands.

Working Abroad, the Daily Telegraph Guide to Working and Living Overseas by Godfrey Golzen. Annual. Kogan Page, London.

Australia

Long Stays in Australia by Maggie Driver. 1990. David & Charles, Newton Abbot.

France

Buying a Home in France by Vivienne Menkes-Ivry. 1993, revised edition. International Book Distributors, Hemel Hempstead.

Buying and Renovating Property in France, Flowerpoll Ltd, Linton, Cambridge.

Buying and Selling Your Home in France by Henry Dyson. 1991. Allied Dunbar-Longman, London.

Buying a Property in France, the Daily Telegraph ed. Philip Jones, 4th edition 1993, Kogan Page, London.

French Housing Laws and Taxes by Frank Rutherford, Sprucehurst Ltd, c/o Rutherfords, 25 Vanston Place, London SW6 1AZ.
A handbook full of useful information for those planning to buy a home in France.

French Real Property and Succession Law by Henry Dyson. 1991. Robert Hale, London.

Living in France by Philip Holland, New edition 1993. Robert Hale, London.

Setting Up in France by L de Warren and C Nollet. New edition 1990. Merehurst Ltd, London.

Taxation in France by C Parkinson. Wisefile Ltd, London SW20 0LR.

Germany

Long Stays in Germany by J A S Abecasis-Phillips. 1990. David & Charles, Newton Abbot.

Italy

Buying a Property in Italy by Steve Emmett. 1991. Brian A French & Associates, Knaresborough, North Yorkshire.

Living in Italy by Y M Menzies. 1991. Robert Hale, London.

Your Home in Italy by Flavia Maxwell. 1989. Longman, Harlow, Essex.

Malta

Malta Fact File. Price £5 from Cassar & Cooper (Real Estate) Ltd, PO Box 36, Tigne Sea Front, Sliema, Malta.

Portugal

Buying Property in Portugal, published by the Portuguese Chamber of Commerce, London.

Living in Portugal by Susan Thackery. 3rd edition 1990. Robert Hale, London.

Your Home in Portugal by Rosemary de Rougemont. An Allied Dunbar Money Guide 1989. Longman, London.

Spain

Living in Spain by John Reay Smith. 1990. Robert Hale, London.

Spanish Property Owners' Community Handbook by David Searl. Lookout Publications, Pueblo Lucia, 29640 Fuengirola, Málaga, Spain.

You and the Law in Spain by David Searl. 1993. Published by *Lookout* Magazine, Lookout Publications. Address above.

Your Home in Spain by Per Svensson. An Allied Dunbar Money Guide. 3rd edition 1991. Longman, London.

Switzerland

Living and Working in Switzerland by David Hampshire. 1990. Robert Hale, London.

United States of America

Living and Working in the USA by David Hampshire. 1992. Survival Books.

Timesharing

Timesharing – All You Need to Know. 1988. Robert Hale, London.

Periodicals

Algarve Gazette, published monthly. A general interest magazine, with a property section. Annual subscription £17 from *Algarve Gazette*, Rua Pé da Cruz 8, 8500 Portimao, Algarve, Portugal.

The American, a newspaper published in Britain for Americans living in the UK. Fortnightly, price 20p; subscription £8.50 per year from *The American*, 114–115 West Street, Farnham, Surrey.

Belle Cose, a quarterly magazine for Italian property. Brian A French Associates, 12 High Street, Knaresborough, Yorkshire HG5 0GQ.

Costa Blanca News, a weekly newspaper in English; Apartado 95, Benidorm, Alicante, Spain.

Cyprus Daily and *Cyprus Weekly*, English language newspapers. PO Box 1992, Nicosia, Cyprus.

Cyprus Magazine, published alternate months, on property and tourism. Subscription £12 per year from PO Box 45Y, London W1 45Y.

Entertainer, the English language weekly in three editions for the coast of Spain. Plaza de la Constitucion No 15, Atico, Fuengirola, Málaga, Spain.

The European, a newspaper with a regular property section. 5 New Fetter Lane, London EC1A 1AP.

Florida Real Estate News, published monthly. E W Publicity Ltd, 15 King Street West, Stockport, Cheshire SK3 0DT.

France, a quarterly magazine for Francophiles. Dormer House, Stow-on-the-Wold, Gloucestershire GL54 1BN.

French Property News, monthly, 2A, Lambton Road, London SW20 0LR.

Iberian Daily Sun, an English language daily newspaper; San Felia 25, Palma, Majorca, Spain.

International Herald Tribune, an English language edition is produced in Paris and is available in many European countries, mainly at airports or railway bookshops. It tends to relate an American version of world news.

International Property Magazine, published quarterly. European and British property for sale. £1.80. Station House, 2A Station Road, Gidea Park, Romford, Essex RM2 6DA.

Living France, a guide to France and French property. Alternate months. 9 High Street South, Olney, Buckinghamshire MK46 4AA.

London Calling, the monthly journal of the BBC World Radio Service, published from Bush House, Strand, London WC2B 4PH.

Lookout, a general interest English language monthly magazine with regular features on property and procedures for living in Spain. Publisher's address: Pueblo Lucia, 29640 Fuengirola, Málaga, Spain.

Mallorca Daily Bulletin, address as for *Iberian Daily Sun*.

Malta Property News, local information and details of property available for sale in Malta and Gozo. Published by Frank Salt Ltd, 2 Paceville Avenue, Paceville, Malta.

Marbella Times, monthly social magazine in English. Address: Alonso de Ojeda 2.1°, Km. 188, Carretera de Cadiz, Marbella, Málaga, Spain.

The News-France, a monthly English language newspaper, price 50p. Postal subscription £11 per year. *The News*, 24500 Eymet, France.

Nexus Expatriate Magazine, published monthly, to link employers of expatriates and expatriates seeking work. Postal subscription £45 per year from Expat Network Ltd, Carolyn House, Dingwall Road, Croydon, Surrey CR0 9XF.

Overseas Property – Buying or Selling. Published quarterly with classified property advertisements by Overseas Property Match, 54 Wandle Bank, London SW19 1DW.

Portugal Post and *Algarve News*, English language newspapers published fortnightly. Algarve office: PO Box 13, 8400 Lagoa, Portugal. Annual subscription £35 including postage.

The Riviera Reporter, published alternate months. 35 Avenue Howarth, 06110 Le Cannet, France.

The Sunday Sun, the only Sunday newspaper in English on Spain's Costa del Sol. Centro Commercial el Zoco, Mijas Costa, Malága, Spain.

Villa Guide, published six times per year. Lists privately owned self-catering villas and apartments to rent in many European countries and Florida. Address 52 High Street, Henley-in-Arden, Solihull B95 5AN.

Weekly Telegraph, a newspaper for expatriates which summarises news and features from the *Daily* and *Sunday Telegraph*. Subscription Services, PO Box 14, Romford RM3 8EQ.

5. Useful Addresses

American Embassy
Grosvenor Square, London W1A 2JB; 071-499 3443
Andorran Delegation
63 Westover Road, London SW18 2RF; 081-874 4806
Association of Malta Estate Agents
7 Whispers, Ross Street, Paceville, Malta; (010 356) 337 373
Australian High Commission
Australia House, Strand, London WC2B 4LA; 071-379 4334
Austrian Embassy and Consular Section
18 Belgrave Mews West, London SW1X 8HU; 071-235 3731
Bank of England
Threadneedle Street, London EC2R 8AH
Blackstone Franks
Barbican House, 26–34 Old Street, London EC1V 9HL; 071-250 3300
British Association of Removers & Federation of International Furniture Removers
3 Churchill Court, 58 Station Road, North Harrow HA2 7SA;
081-861 3331
British Embassy in France
35 Rue du Faubourg St Honoré, 75383 Paris
British Embassy in Portugal
Rua S Domingos à Lapa 35–37, Lisbon, Portugal.
British Embassy in Spain
Fernando El Santo 16, Madrid 4, Spain
BUPA International
Equity & Law House, 102 Queens Road, Brighton BN1 3XT
Canada Immigration & Visa Enquiries
38 Grosvenor Street, London W1X 0AA; 071-409 2071
Channel Islands
Guernsey States Office, St Peter Port, Guernsey; Jersey States Office, Royal Square, St Helier, Jersey
Cyprus High Commission
93 Park Street, London W1Y 4ET; 071-499 8272
Department of Social Security
Overseas Branch, Benton Park Road,
Newcastle upon Tyne NE98 1YX; 091-213 5000

Department of Social Security
Information Division, Leaflets Unit, Block 4 Government Building,
Honeypot Lane, Stanmore HA7 1AY
Europea – IMG Ltd
Provender Mill, Mill Bay Lane, Horsham, West Sussex RH12 1SS, 0403
51884
Exeter Friendly Society
Beach Hill House, Walnut Gardens, Exeter EX4 4DE
**Federation of Overseas Property Developers, Agents and Consultants
(FOPDAC)**
PO Box 3534, London NW5 1DQ
French Embassy
56 Knightsbridge, London SW1X 7JT; 071-235 8080
German Embassy
23 Belgrave Square, London SW1X 8PZ; 071-235 5033
Gibraltar Tourist Office
4 Arundel Great Court, 179 Strand, London WC2R 1EH;
071-836 0777
Greek Consulate General
1a Holland Park, London W11 3TP; 071-727 8040
Inland Revenue
For payments of pensions or dividends overseas: Inspector of Foreign
Dividends, Inland Revenue, Lynwood Road, Thames Ditton, Surrey
KT7 0DP; 081-398 4242
Inland Revenue
For booklets: Public Enquiry Room, Inland Revenue, West Wing,
Somerset House, London WC2R 1LB
Interval International
Leaguestar House, 4 Citadel Place, London SE11; 071-955 9550
Irish Embassy
17 Grosvenor Place, London SW1X 7HR; 071-235 2171
Isle of Man Government
Government House, Bucks Road, Douglas, Isle of Man
Israel, Embassy of
2 Palace Green, London W8 4QB; 071-937 8050
Italian Consulate
38 Eaton Place, London SW1X 1AN; 071-235 9371
Law Society
113 Chancery Lane, London WC2A 1PZ; 071-242 1222
Ira H. Levy, U.S. Visa Consultants
27 York Street, London W1H 1PY; 071-224 3629
Malta High Commission
16 Kensington Square, London W8 5HH; 071-938 1712
McCarthy & Stone Overseas Ltd
26–32 Oxford Road, Bournemouth BH8 8EZ
New Zealand High Commission
New Zealand House, Haymarket, London SW1Y 4TQ; 071-930 8422

Norwich Union Healthcare
Yelverton Business Park, Devon PL20 7LG; 0822 855452
Portuguese Consulate General
62 Brompton Road, London SW3 1BJ; 071-581 8722
Private Patients Plan
PPP House, Upperton Road, Eastbourne BN21 1LH
Property Owners Club
Brittany Ferries, Plymouth; 0752 227941
Resort Condominiums Europe Ltd
Kettering Parkway, Kettering, Northamptonshire NN15 6EY; 0536 310101
Royal Institution of Chartered Surveyors
12 Great George Street, London SW1P 3AD; 071-222 7000
Spanish Consulate General
20 Draycott Place, London SW3 2RZ; 071-581 5921
Spanish National Tourist Office
57 St James's Street, London SW1A 1LD; 071-499 0901
Swiss Embassy
16–18 Montagu Place, London W1H 2BQ; 071-723 0701
Timeshare Council
23 Buckingham Gate, London SW1E 6LB; 071-821 8845
Timeshare Trustees (International) Ltd
Bourne Concourse, Peel Street, Ramsey, Isle of Man; 0624 814555
Turkish Consulate General
Rutland Lodge, Rutland Gardens, London SW7 1BW; 071-589 0949
Turkish Embassy
43 Belgrave Square, London SW1X 8PA; 071-235 5252
Villa Owners Club Ltd
HPB House, Old Station Road, Newmarket CB8 8EH
Women's Corona Society
Commonwealth House, 35, Belgrave Square, London SW1X 8QB; 071-235 1230. Runs one-day courses for emigrants; has overseas branches in many countries and provides a welcome link for newcomers.
WPA Health Insurance
Rivergate House, Blackbrook Park, Taunton, Somerset TA1 2PE; 0823 623330

List of Advertisers

Index